PROBLEMS IN MODERN GEOGRAPHY

Rural
Communities

PROBLEMS IN MODERN GEOGRAPHY

| Series Editor | Richard Lawton *Professor of Geography, University of Liverpool* |

Andrew W. Gilg	*Countryside Planning: The First Three Decades 1945–76*
Patrick Lavery (editor)	*Recreational Geography*
Andrew Learmonth	*Patterns of Disease and Hunger*
J. Allan Patmore	*Land and Leisure*
V. R. Prescott	*Political Geography of the Oceans*
John R. Tarrant	*Agricultural Geography*
Kenneth L. Wallwork	*Derelict Land: Origins and Prospects of a Land-use Problem*
Kenneth Warren	*Mineral Resources*
Kenneth Warren	*World Steel*

Associated Volume to the Series

| Gerald Bloomfield | *World Automotive Industry* |

PROBLEMS IN MODERN GEOGRAPHY

G. J. LEWIS

Rural Communities

David & Charles: London
Newton Abbot   North Pomfret (VT)

5401

British Library Cataloguing in Publication Data

Lewis, G J
  Rural communities. – (Problems in modern
  geography).
  1. Sociology, Rural
  I. Title II. Series
  301.35   HT421

ISBN 0–7153–7768–X

Library of Congress Catalog Card Number: 78–74090

Photoset and printed in Great Britain
by Redwood Burn Limited,
Trowbridge and Esher
for David & Charles (Publishers) Limited
Brunel House Newton Abbot Devon

Published in the United States of America
by David & Charles Inc
North Pomfret Vermont 05053 USA

Read pgs. 21-45

Contents

List of Figures

List of Tables

To Vivien

Preface

In the rapid growth of social geography as a systematic branch of geography during the past decade the rural community has been largely overlooked, a development which is a little surprising in view of the fact that the majority of human beings still live in rural communities. Even the widespread industrialisation and urbanisation in Western Europe and North America has not destroyed completely a distinctive rural way of life. By focusing exclusively on the rural community this volume presents an attempt to redress the urban bias within social geography. As for readership it is hoped that this book may be useful for courses in environmental studies as well as social and rural geography in a variety of educational institutions: colleges, polytechnics and universities.

In the writing of this book I am indebted to the assistance of a number of people: Emeritus Professor E. G. Bowen and Professor W. Kirk, who initially guided my interest in social geography and matters rural; Professor N. Pye, who provided me with the opportunities and facilities to develop my interest in social geography; Mr D. J. Maund, who commented on an early draft of the manuscript; Miss Ruth Rowell, who drew the maps and diagrams so expertly; Mr T. Garfield, who supervised the cartographic and reprographic procedures; and Miss Jean Smith, Mrs Pat Herbert and Mrs Elaine Humphries, who speedily and cheerfully typed the manuscript. Special mention must be made of Professor R. Lawton, who encouraged me to write this book and spent considerable time editing the manuscript. Lastly, thanks go to my parents for their consistent support, and to my wife, Vivien, whose interest and encouragement allowed the idea to become a reality.

Introduction

Considering that the majority of the world's population is still overwhelmingly rural it is surprising that more interest has been shown by social scientists in towns and town dwellers. A number of factors have probably combined to bring this about, not least that research in the social sciences has evolved principally in Western Europe and North America where widespread industrialisation and urbanisation have virtually destroyed a distinctive rural way of life. In these areas modern communication and the mass media now bind the rural to the urban to such an extent that what happens in the city has significant repercussions for the countryside. Even with greater attention being paid recently by social scientists to the developing world, research is still biased in favour of the 'exploding city'.[1] As a consequence little is known in detail about either the structure and functioning of the 'new' rural society of the developed countries or the effect of modernisation upon the rural population of the developing world;[2] Halpern's plea for a greater depth and rigour in the investigation of rural society seems, in general, to be ignored.[3]

Despite the importance of studies in urban geography[4] during the post-war era there is still a strong and long-established tradition of rural studies within geography.[5] Many of the concepts of early regional geographers were conceived in a rural context,[6] and a good deal of systematic attention has been paid to such themes as the origins of rural settlements,[7] the location of agricultural activity,[8] the diffusion of agricultural innovations,[9] and the migration of people from the countryside to the towns.[10] Moreover, the human geographer has tended to ignore the 'social' aspects of the geography of

15

both town and country. Only with the shift in geographical methodology from a place- to a process-oriented approach during the last two decades has a distinctive social geography begun to emerge.[11]

Social geography of communities

The slow development of social geography is most easily explained by a widely held viewpoint that all geography 'starts from soil, not from society'.[12] This approach, with its deterministic overtones, is now largely discredited, and with a shift of interest within human geography to locational analysis[13] the consideration of social as well as economic factors has become essential. The recent flowering of social geography should not be over-emphasised since the seeds of its success preceded the Second World War. First, in the United States the distinctive spatial perspective of the city developed by the Chicago group of human ecologists had as its basic premise that 'there are forces at work within the limits of the urban community – within the limits of any natural area of human habitation, in fact – which tend to bring about an orderly and typical grouping of its population and institutions'.[14] Secondly, a parallel development in the University of Wales under the leadership 'of three such remarkable professors of geography as H. J. Fleure, Daryll Forde and E. G. Bowen'[15] focused on the social geography of rural communities.[16] A whole series of studies, beginning with Rees's study of Llanfihangel yng Nghwynfa in north-east Montgomeryshire,[17] was initiated in different parts of Wales.[18] Many of the ideas and methodologies in these studies were derived from the then widely acclaimed functional school of anthropology.[19] However, despite the obvious geographical nature of the concepts introduced by both the American and British schools of human ecology, their full recognition by, and incorporation into human geography has, surprisingly, only taken place during the last two decades.[20]

With the emergence of human geography during the fifties and sixties as a social science concerned with the identification and explanation of the spatial organisation of society, social geography developed as a significant and meaningful branch of the discipline.[21] A further impetus to its recognition has been given by a revival of interest in communities as 'local groups possessing some cohesiveness and some common institutions'.[22] This revival has been fostered by a feeling that communities can provide a framework within which many of the ills of modern society may be alleviated.[23] However, it is interesting to note that this recent emergence of social geography as the study of 'the processes and patterns involved in an understanding of socially defined populations in their spatial setting'[24] appears once again to have flowered more profusely within an urban as opposed to a rural context.[25] Building upon the ideas of the early urban ecologists geographers have introduced more behavioural modes of explanation[26] as well as more sophisticated techniques of measurement.[27] Although these exciting new developments appear to be in the forefront of socio-geographical research there is, as a consequence, a tendency to overlook the smaller, but fast-growing literature on rural communities.

Social geography and the rural community

Any study of the contemporary rural community, no matter how it is defined, must inevitably be concerned with social change. Urban growth involves the encroachment of the city upon the countryside as well as an increasing dependence of the rural upon the urban for a whole range of its social and economic needs. The spread of modern communication and the mass media have accelerated the role of the city as a source of innovation and increased the level of social interaction among individuals over a wider area. Such themes are not the preserve of the geographer, but social geographers are particularly concerned with the processes involved in the location of people and their social institutions as well as with the flows and linkages which bind them together. This book, by emphasising the rural community, at once places a limit upon the material and content to be discussed and brings the geographer close to the approach of anthropology and sociology.[28] Although the problems and their context are the same, the geographer has developed his own distinctive perspective.[29]

Individuals and the communities they create exist in a spatial milieu, a dimension which is often considered by geographers as both a dependent and an independent variable. The prime concern with space as a dependent variable is the way in which people adapt and adjust to it. Throughout history man has increased his ability to modify and manipulate space, and obviously the degree of adjustment will depend upon the cultural heritage and level of technology of the people involved. This approach to space has traditionally been the *raison d'être* of geographical analysis, but with the increasing concern with process during the last two decades there has been a marked shift of emphasis towards considering space as an independent variable. This spatial viewpoint can assist in explaining the persistence and universality of communities as well as their location and growth. The influence of resources and accessibility upon the growth potential of communities has developed an extensive theoretical and empirical literature but the continued significance of the 'locality' in explaining patterns of social life has, surprisingly, engendered little interest among geographers. With modern communication individual mobility has increased markedly, yet the majority of man's needs are still met locally, reflecting not only a failure to transcend space completely but also the social and psychological satisfaction provided by propinquity. Kingsley Davis has claimed that 'it is no accident that people cluster together. Nearness facilitates contact, furnishes protection, and makes easier the organization and integration of the group.'[30]

Both of these approaches have been adopted in this book. An examination of the theories of community is followed by a discussion of the main agents involved in social change – the diffusion of ideas and the migration of people. This process-oriented approach provides a basis for a detailed consideration of the changing rural community from four

19

different perspectives: as a settlement; as a locality; as an ecological system; and as a social system. Although the emphasis
will be on concepts and methods of analysis, a variety of
case-studies will be introduced to illustrate the world-wide applica-
bility of these ideas. Lines of further enquiry and more meaningful methods of analysis, rather than definitive answers, will
be suggested. As a backcloth to the main theme of the book the
next chapter will consider the problems of defining the term
'rural' within the context of a changing rural society.

CHAPTER ONE

The Urbanisation of the Countryside

During the past century rural dwellers have experienced widespread changes in their working and living habits and the distinction between rural and urban communities has become increasingly blurred. In Western Europe and North America this process has accelerated to such an extent that it is questionable 'whether there are now any significant differences between rural and urban people in the life they live, in their hopes and aspirations, and in their attitudes and mores'.[1] Previous bases of distinction between town and country, for example population density, settlement size, and agricultural employment, are of little relevance today, hence the necessity to adopt a more pragmatic definition to the term 'rural'.[2]

Defining 'rural'

To the layman the definition of terms 'rural' and 'urban' appears simple and straightforward, yet it is fraught with pitfalls and uncertainties. These difficulties are exacerbated by a failure to agree upon standard criteria of definition. Although the majority of countries employ size and density of population there is little agreement as to the significant cut-off figures; for example, in Canada a population of 1,000 constitutes a town but in Japan the figure is as high as 30,000 people.[3] Some countries, like the United Kingdom, attempt to overcome this weakness by adopting an administrative urban definition, but anomalies again occur since settlements of comparatively few inhabitants can have urban status while others with much larger populations are defined as rural. Despite inconsistencies both urban geographers and planners have consistently utilised official designations of urban and rural, and even the most recent advanced urban geography textbooks do not attempt a precise definition of their field of study.[4] In contrast, a number of writers on rural areas have sought alternative means of distinction. For example, Wibberley has claimed that the word rural 'describes those parts of a country which show unmistakable signs of being dominated by extensive uses of land . . . this allows us to look at settlements which to the eye still appear to be rural but which, in practise, are mainly an extension of the city resulting from the development of the commuter train and the private car.'[5] Best and Rogers have taken this approach a stage further by specifying that 'in a land-use context, rural land encompasses areas which are under agriculture, forest and woodland, as well as wild, unutilised tracts in a natural or semi-natural state. Urban land comprises not only the sites of cities and towns . . . but also includes villages, hamlets and even individual or isolated dwellings which perform a similar function whether located in town or countryside.'[6] Therefore, the prime concern of the rural social geographer would be those forms of settlement ranging from isolated farmsteads to the market towns serving a tributary area. Despite alternative approaches to the definition of the term rural there is still need for an agreed quantitative distinction. A number of useful suggestions have been made. In the context of the developing world Halpern regarded rural places as those which range 'from nomadic tribes of fifty members up to densely settled villages of several thousand inhabitants'[7] whilst according to Morrill the village in North America contains 'from 500 to 2,500 persons (mean population about 1,000) and serves an area that may include up to 1,000 persons.'[8] The United Nations has adopted the size criterion of 20,000 people[9] to determine the upper limit to rural places and, in Britain, the Department of the Environment takes a population of 10,000. In order to provide a workable definition, the latter figure has been adopted within this text since it distinguishes those places which have been simply termed 'small settlements'[10] by Best and Rogers and which, according to Haggett, form the 'lower limb of the urban hierarchy'.[11]

The process of urbanisation

The blurring of the distinction between rural and urban had its roots in the Industrial Revolution. The slow, yet irresistible, spread of industrialisation has taken several forms which had at least three significant effects on the countryside: firstly, the emergence of an urban-located factory system based upon a largely rural-born labour force; secondly, the transformation of agriculture from a way of life into a capital-intensive business; and thirdly, a greater interdependence between town and country. All three in their own way have contributed to urbanisation, and throw considerable light on the nature of social change within the countryside. A brief review of each will give some insight into the nature of the process.

1. *Urban growth* Of the three dominant interpretations of urbanisation the first is probably the best known. In Britain rapid urban growth began some two hundred years ago when over three-quarters of the population lived in rural areas. By the middle of the nineteenth century about half of the population was rural and by the turn of the century this proportion had fallen to one-quarter (Fig. 1A). This involved large-scale migration from rural areas.[12] In more recent decades, however, the rural population has become more stable as a result of widespread residential developments. In continental Europe and North America where large-scale urbanisation came later, the change was even more rapid, but similar to that of England and Wales (Fig. 1B).

In the developing countries, on the other hand, since the overwhelming majority of their populations still live in rural areas, the growth of cities is paralleled, as a result of high birth-

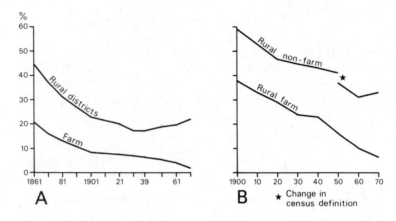

Figure 1. Rural population change in England and Wales (A) and the United States of America (B)

rates, by similar increases in rural communities, although rural-to-urban migration is accelerating. According to Halpern, in the developing world today 'there may be from three to five million rural communities . . . such groups comprise up to eighty per cent of the people of the so-called economically less-developed countries'.[13] Moreover, marked variations exist in the ratio of urban to rural population in different parts of the world (Fig. 2).

The explosion of city populations in the developing countries fails to absorb the migrants into regular employment whereas in the developed countries the growth of cities was generally more closely related to the needs of economic development. Indeed in the majority of the countries of the third world urban growth is taking place with little reference to industrialisation. Clearly the majority of the developing countries are suffering from what Galeski has described as 'involuntary or implosive urbanization',[14] rather than economic development.

2. *Transformation of agriculture* The second interpretation of the urbanisation process involves the spread of new technology into the countryside, in particular that specifically related to agriculture. Before the nineteenth century agricultural change depended upon the inventiveness and initiative of a few

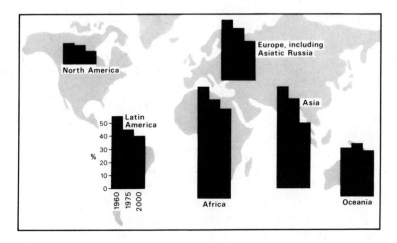

Figure 2.   Estimated and projected rural population by continents, 1960, 1975 and 2000. (Source: Hoyt, H., *World Urbanization: Expanding Population in a Shrinking World*, Urban Land Institute Technical Bulletin No 43, Table 15)

farmers and rural craftsmen, but with the demands of the rapidly growing industrial populations more systematic research was initiated which led to improvements in machinery, crop varieties, animal foodstuffs, and artificial fertilisers. According to Bertrand, the application of new technology in agriculture not only changes productivity and efficiency but also initiates new ideas, new modes of living, and new patterns of interaction that influence man's relationship to the land.[15] In Western Europe and North America technological change in agriculture has led to a decrease in the number of farms, an increase in productivity, and a decline in the numbers employed in agriculture (Fig. 1). Above all the typical farm has become progressively more analogous to a large commercial enterprise.[16] This situation is very different from that in the countries of the developing world where the peasant farmer still predominates.[17] Even in parts of Western Europe agricultural innovation has been so limited that a form of peasantry still persists; however, its survival has been aided by a growing tendency for the farmers to take up urban employment and to work their holdings on a part-time basis.[18]

3. *Rural–urban linkages* A third approach to the urbanisation process is that which focuses upon the interdependence between town and country. Although the two have to a certain extent always been interdependent, industrialisation has led to an overwhelming dependence by the city on the countryside for food, raw materials and people, whilst conversely the countryside has looked to the city for a whole range of economic and social needs. This interdependence has been facilitated by the availability of new forms of transport and mass communication. The coming of the railway and, later, the motor car, enabled the rural dweller to expand his sphere of activity, while the wider circulation of newspapers and magazines and the diffusion of radio and television throughout the countryside has brought the world into his living room. According to Fuguitt this change was initiated in the Mid-West of the United States around 1920. Prior to that date informal visiting and work took place within the country neighbourhood. 'Beyond the country neighbourhood was the nearby city or village, which often was the only centre to which the rural person turned for other goods and services and to market his farm products.'[19] Even in the developing countries the sharp distinction between town and country of a generation or so ago is being weakened by the linkages provided by the temporary urban migrant and the development of a rudimentary market economy. However, this interdependence must not be overemphasised, a caution which is well illustrated by Mehta's claim that among Indian daily newspapers of nation-wide circulation 'weeks often go by without the appearance of a single story originating in the 600,000 villages in which most of the people live'.[20]

Urbanisation has been a mixed blessing, creating a whole series of social and economic problems within both the city and the countryside.[21] However, there has been a tendency for the townsman to overlook the problems of the countryside, often viewing it in idyllic terms, possibly as an antidote to the stresses and strains of the city.[22] Nowhere is this better illustrated than in Ronald Blythe's account of life in Akenfield, a small Suffolk village: 'it is patently the real country, untouched and genuine . . . Its very sounds are formal, hieratic; larks, clocks, bees, tractor hummings. Rarely the sound of the human voice. So powerful is this traditional view that many people are able to live in the centre of it for years and see nothing more.'[23] In fact, as Nan Fairbrother has claimed, 'it is natural for urban people to idealise the country life; indeed it is a measure of our distance from country reality'.[24] Despite this romanticising there has been, since the Second World War, a growing awareness particularly among planners[25] and academics[26] of the difficulties of the countryside, though the nature and form of these difficulties differ quite markedly between the countries of the developed and developing world.

Although urban influences have significantly altered rural life it must, however, be said that much that is traditional to the countryside, even in Western Europe and North America, will remain for decades to come.[27] However, the social and economic problems of all rural communities, whatever their present and future degree of urbanisation, will remain a matter of national importance, since they cannot be isolated from the society in which they are located: their analysis and solution, on the other hand, must stem from an appreciation of their specifically rural character.[28] Although the main focus of this book is not on rural problems the viewpoint adopted is similar to that suggested by Dickinson in a discussion of the relationship between urban geography and planning: 'it is concerned with aspects of the internal or geographical structure of society upon which planning is based and it insists that a knowledge of the anatomy of society precede a treatment of its defects'.[29] Of course, this does not mean that geography can remedy all the defects of rural society, but, like every other social science, it has a role to play, the significance of which can only be assessed after adequate understanding of the spatial structure of society has been achieved.

CHAPTER TWO

Aspects of Community Theory

It is generally agreed among social scientists that a necessary preliminary to any systematic study of society is the construction of a conceptual framework within which reality may be analysed. A model-building approach within human geography has been developed essentially during the last two decades,[1] and the experience of using both normative and stochastic models has led geographers to question the deterministic nature and low explanatory powers of such models and to turn to more suitable alternatives.[2] Behavioural approaches, attempting to incorporate decision-making into explanation, reflect this increasing dissatisfaction with purely stochastic approaches to human geography.[3]

Although in any study of community change the focus must be upon the concepts of 'community' and 'social change', neither has received much attention from geographers. Too often communities have been conceived as places rather than homes of individuals and social groups, whilst overemphasis of a cause-and-effect paradigm has hindered the conceptualisation of social change as a process.[4] It would appear, therefore, that there is a need, as Harvey has claimed, to introduce a greater sociological imagination into the geographical analysis of communities.[5]

The concept of community

There is still considerable confusion over the meaning of the term 'community', which has been used in so many different ways that it has been described by Hillery as an 'omnibus term'.[6] Some interpretations encompass almost any form of social grouping—for example, the family, professions, prisoners, etc.[7]—whilst others have restricted it to 'a locality group which contains the major social institutions'.[8] To several scholars a community has a more humanistic manifestation since 'it expresses our vague yearnings for a community of desire, a communion with those around us, an extension of the bonds of kin and friends to all those who share a common fate with us'[9] and, therefore, provides 'the co-operative fullness of action, the sense of belonging, the face-to-face association with people well known'.[10]

Of the numerous attempts to unravel the term community, probably the most penetrating and comprehensive was that of Hillery in 1963.[11] Using nineteen traits, he concluded that the social organisations defined by earlier social scientists as communities formed two specific types, the communal and the formal: the latter contains one or more specific goals which it seeks to attain; the former 'refers to a system of institutions formed by people who live together'.[12] This communal definition views a community as an ecological or social organisation arising from the fact that people share a common area for a large number of their activities. In other words, 'a community arises through sharing a limited territorial space for residence and for sustenance and functions to meet common needs generated in sharing this space by establishing characteristic forms of social action'.[13]

Within the field of social geography there are two major approaches to the concept of a community. First, the well-established approach of an ecological system in which community structure manifests itself in a spatial and temporal sense:[14] it 'includes the area, the population of which, however widely distributed, regularly turn to a common centre for the satisfaction of all or a major part of its needs',[15] and 'differs from other systems in that locality is a datum in the integration of the system'.[16] According to R. E. Park the purpose of human ecology is 'to investigate the process by which the biotic balance and the social equilibrium are maintained once they are achieved and the process by which, when the biotic balance and the social equilibrium are disturbed, the transition is made from one relatively stable order to another'.[17] Obviously such an approach contains two distinct forms of explanation of community life: first, a biotic, or sub-social, based upon processes such as competition, invasion, and succession; and, secondly, a socio-cultural, based upon co-operation and commensalistic relations. However, pioneer social ecologists believed that only the first of these could be analysed by means of ecological methods. Such restriction produced a widespread criticism of human ecology and hindered its development until it widened its horizons during the 1950s. A number of neo-ecologists now insist that it should not be limited to the sub-social since 'you cannot throw away what is most distinctly human—communication with symbols, custom and the artificial or cultural transformations man makes in his environment—and treat the residue as the ecology of the species'.[18] This change of attitude has led to a revival of interest in human ecology within the social sciences,[19] and to its emergence as a focal point within social geography.[20] Despite the growth during the last two decades of a considerable body of ecological literature on communities, criticism has continued unabated. It has been argued that, as a result of increasing wealth and enhanced aspirations, man's spatial horizons now extend beyond the locality and, therefore, the ecological explanation of behaviour is insignificant. For example, R. E. Pahl believes that 'any attempt to tie the patterns of social relationships to specific geographical milieux is a singularly fruitless exercise'[21] and the *avant-garde* planner, Melvin Webber,[22] envisages the emergence of an aspatial society in the not-too-distant future. Another form of criticism has emerged from those who argue that, despite the broadening of its perspective, human ecology still remains essentially deterministic, and therefore any consideration of process is still precluded.[23] Within geography this approach manifests itself in three types of study: the community as a settlement, as a locality, and as a social ecological system; in this book these form the basis of chapters five, six and seven.

The second socio-geographical approach to community views it as a social system; that is, the smallest spatial system which encompasses the major features of society. According to Reiss there appear to be two, albeit relatively similar, ways of analysing social systems.[24] The first, the collective-action approach, views the community as a place where there is a common cultural or psychological bond among its members which manifests itself in the recognition of 'local' goals and the creation of a common motivation towards these goals, whether of co-operation or conflict. According to Sanders the major determinants of such feelings are tradition and local values,[25] although others, such as Warren,[26] argue in favour of a sense of security provided by the identification with a locality. Both ideas are encompassed in the more generalised concept of community sentiment, or 'an awareness of sharing a way of life as well as the common earth'.[27] In the majority of modern communities these common ties have been broken down and, therefore, the use of this approach to identify community variables has been weakened. However, interest in this approach continues, in particular among those who believe that much of the alienation, frustration and loneliness experienced by individuals could be overcome with the restoration of the common bonds.[28]

A different emphasis to the view of the community as a social system has been provided by those who adopt a social-group approach. Briefly, a community is a place where individuals interact with each other and receive the greater part of their physiological, psychological and social needs. This most recent approach to community analysis is primarily concerned with the identification of those forms of interaction which integrate individuals into a community and the stages through

which they evolve.[29] Obviously, one of the problems involved
with this approach is the fact that not all interaction within a
single territorial area derives solely from a community. However, Margaret Stacey has attempted to overcome these weaknesses by conceptualising the community as a local social
system.[30] In this book the social-systems approach to community study forms the main theme of chapters eight and nine.

Rural–urban continuum

The position of the rural community within the total framework of community types is traditionally identified by adopting a polar typological approach. Basically, this is a simplified
model of the social and cultural system under examination,
which emphasises the degree of similarity between two or more
communities. The best known of the typologies used to differ-
entiate rural from urban communities is the rural–urban continuum. In its original form this typology merely distinguished
the extremes, but more recent interpretations have emphasised
the transformation which occurs from one pole to the other. In
other words, this typology is also a theory of social change
which can be used to identify the nature and direction of the
social processes involved. In a review of this typology Reissman has identified at least seven terms which have been used to
describe the two poles;[31] of these the most influential in social
geography is the folk–urban concept of Redfield.[32] Considerable support for the existence of a rural–urban dicho-
tomy/continuum has come from several quarters, in
particular Louis Wirth's influential paper 'Urbanism as a
Way of Life'. According to Wirth 'the bonds of kinship, of
neighbourliness, and the sentiments arising out of living together for generations under a common folk tradition are
likely to be absent, or at best, relatively weak in an aggregate,
the members of which have such diverse origins and back-
grounds. Under such circumstances competition and formal
control mechanisms furnish the substitutes for the bonds of
solidarity that are relied upon to hold a folk society together.'[33]

Thus, an urban society is characterised by a predominance of secondary over primary contacts, a high division of labour, high rates of vertical mobility, a formal mechanism of social control, and communication via the mass media.

In recent years a good deal of criticism has been levelled at this typology both as a means of locating communities relative to each other and as a conceptualisation of social change.[34] Probably the most crucial is its failure to recognise the possibility of a co-existence of different societal elements within the same community. So widespread is the empirical evidence in support of this that Gans has concluded that 'if ways of life do not coincide with settlement type and if these ways are functions of class and life cycle rather than the ecological attributes of the settlement a sociological definition of the city cannot be formulated'.[35] Similarly, objections to the continuum have been raised over its western ethnocentrism and particular ideological stance as a result of the realisation that the transformation of social values is not a universal process but solely one related to a particular cultural context. Pahl has even argued that the use and interpretation of the continuum has been too simplistic, leading to sweeping and often inaccurate generalisations.[36] However, despite these widespread criticisms the defenders of the concept of the rural–urban continuum have claimed that it still has much of value in it.[37] There exist at least three contexts in which this defence has taken place:

1. *Theoretical* A number of the supporters of the continuum have pointed out that many criticisms of it are based on a misinterpretation of the role of ideal constructed-types in social scientific investigations.[38] Too often these were interpreted as generalisations which, according to Hauser, 'without the benefit of adequate research, well illustrates the dangers of catchy neologisms which often get confused with knowledge'.[39] In an analysis of Tönnies's ideas Loomis argued that 'no social system could persist if relations were either completely *Gemeinschaft*-like[40] or completely *Gesellschaft*-like.[41] This fact does not prevent the human mind from conceiving of such

"ideal-types" and using them for comparative and ordering purposes. In fact, this is their chief value.'[42]

2. *Multi-dimensional* Duncan's assertion that 'it is highly doubtful that the uni-dimensional continuum, in any rigorous mathematical sense, is a sufficiently realistic model for research on inter-community variation'[43] led a number of researchers to claim that there exists a series of non-overlapping continua. Such a multi-dimensional continuum is composed of a series of continua, for example social demographic, cultural, political and economic, which need not all be present in every situation and which do not necessarily change along its continuum in a similar fashion. This realisation of the complexity of socio-cultural variation within communities has

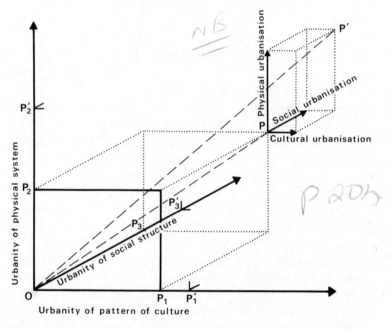

Figure 3. The process of urbanisation of an imaginary community (P) represented in three-dimensional space. (Source: Burie, J. B., 'Prolegomena to a Theoretical Model of Intercommunity Variation', *Sociologia Ruralis*, 7, 1967, pp 347–64)

generated a growing literature in recent years. After a review of community life in town and country in his book *Communities in Britain*, Frankenberg develops 'a theory of social change, a progressive and historical development from rural to urban, mediated by industrialization, division of labour and role of differentiation',[44] and then aligns the communities along what he calls a 'morphological continuum'. An alternative, yet similar, approach is that adopted by Burie in his model of inter-community variation, which conceives change as multi-dimensional and dispenses with terms like 'city', 'countryside', 'rural' and 'urban'.[45] Each community varies on a physical, cultural and structural dimension and, therefore, any group of communities can be placed with regard to one another in a three-dimensional space (Fig. 3). Despite Burie's promising attempt to operationalise his ideas empirical studies along these lines are scarce.

3. *Core institutions* Another significant criticism of the rural–urban continuum is its failure to reveal how one type of community changes into another, and to suggest some means of measuring change. An interesting perspective on this weakness has recently been given by Lockwood, who suggested that a community can be viewed as changed if the 'core' or 'dominant' institutional orders change.[46] Although these may vary from one society to another they are capable of cumulative change. Such an approach can aid an understanding of the co-existence of traditional and modern elements of social structure and values but attempts to operationalise it are bedevilled by the complexity of the dimensions involved.

The rural–urban continuum, as originally conceived, is an inadequate framework to analyse the changing rural community since even its defenders have broadened its conceptual base. As research has progressed it has been realised that the 'manifold threads of inter-relationships make the community a very complex system',[47] and this has resulted in a questioning of the model's underlying assumptions. This does not mean that total attacks on the continuum are fully justified.

Schnore's comment that ''on demographic and settlement criteria, rural–urban differences while clearly diminishing are still crucial',[48] offers the view that the continuum is a simple starting-off point to the analysis of change.

Concept of social change

The increasing attention being paid by geographers to the concept of social change is due largely to the argument of the Swedish geographer, Torsten Hägerstrand, that there is a prime necessity to consider the processes involved in spatial behaviour.[49] In contrast, sociology and anthropology have always considered social change to be a major focus of interest, although they have tended to view rural society as static and unchanging in comparison with urban society. A much truer picture is the contention that social change is a 'theme that runs like a red thread through the fabric of rural society'.[50]

The concept of social change can be interpreted in different ways and at different scales. At an individual level it can be defined as 'the process by which individuals change from a traditional way of life to a more complex, technologically advanced and rapidly changing life style'.[51] This type of definition is often described as 'modernisation' and is analogous to development at a societal level. According to Rogers and Burdge, development is 'a type of social change in which new ideas are introduced into a social system in order to produce higher *per capita* incomes and levels of living through modern production methods and improved social organisation'.[52] The transition from one type of society to another as a result of these processes is closely interwoven with changes in their demographic structure. Changes in the birth- and death-rates result partly from rising socio-economic expectations consequent upon economic development and partly from the spread of information about new medical and family planning techniques. At the same time economic development both causes and results in population movements. Zelinsky has, in fact, gone as far as to claim that 'there are definite, patterned regularities in the growth of personal mobility through space–time during recent history, and these regularities comprise an essential component of the modernization process'.[53] His five-stage model links the mobility and vital transitions 'as a kind of outward diffusion of successively more advanced forms of human activity'[54] (Fig. 4). However, this type of interpretation of social change has been severely criticised for its western or European overtones and value judgements, and its failure to consider other forms of change.

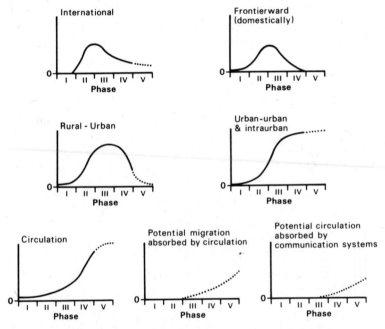

Figure 4. Comparative time profiles of spatial mobility. (Source: Zelinsky, W., 'The Hypothesis of the Mobility Transition', *Geographical Review*, 61, 1971, pp 219–49)

Probably a more effective way of considering social change is to define it simply as the process by which alteration occurs in the function and structure of a community. Even when viewed in this manner, social change is still made up of a series of sequential stages; for example, the creation of new ideas, the communication of these ideas and the changes which result from their adoption or rejection. The sources of these changes may emanate from within or from without the community, and empirical evidence would suggest that the latter is by far the most dominant among rural communities. An increasingly significant source of change, in particular among rural communities in the developing world, comes from outside organisations, for example through sponsored development projects with specifically defined goals. Once again these changes often result in the migration of individuals which in turn initiates further community change. It is well established that individuals favour change to varying degrees, and therefore communities can be conceived in terms of their susceptibility to change. Some twenty years ago Mitchell, from a detailed study

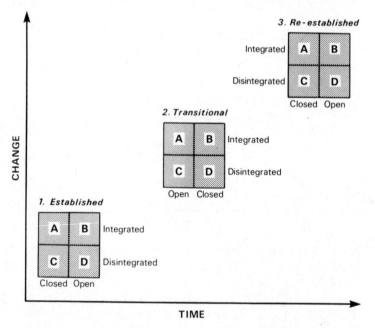

Figure 5. A social typology of villages. (Source: Thorns, D. C., 'The Changing System of Rural Stratification', *Sociologia Ruralis*, 8, 1968, pp 161–78)

of a number of Devon villages, differentiated rural communities on the basis of their attitude to change and degree of
integration.[55] The twofold distinction between open and
closed communities and integrated and disintegrated has since
been interpreted by Thorns within a time perspective[56] (Fig. 5).
Such a conceptualisation of rural social change has been extended by Rogers and Burdge with their identification of the
factors controlling the differential levels of favourable orientation towards change.[57] Table 1 is a summary of this distinction.

TABLE 1   Traditional and modern norms

Modern community	*Traditional community*
Positive attitude to change	Lack of a favourable attitude to change
Technologically developed	Simpler technology
High levels of education and science	Low levels of literacy, education and science
Cosmopolite; high levels of inter-action with outsiders	Little communication with outsiders
Empathic; ability to see oneself in others' roles	Lack of ability to empathise

After: Rogers, E. M. and Burdge, R. J., *Social Change in Rural Societies*, Prentice-Hall, 1972, p 15

   The rate at which social change takes place is of crucial significance for the functioning and structure of a community. A
failure by a community to adjust fully to change can cause considerable problems of conflict and adjustment for the individuals involved. In systems language there are three basic
states in which a community may find itself in attempting to
adjust to change.[58] A stable equilibrium occurs when there is
almost no change in the structure or functioning of a system.
In rural societies this type of situation is most likely to be
found among an isolated and peasant community. A typical
case in point is the anthropologist Firth's classic study of the
Tikopia, a small island community in the British Solomon

Island Protectorate.[59] Apart from limited occasions no innovation has entered the community. As a result its economic
and social structure are in an interrelated balance and it functions as a harmonious whole. A community may be in state of
disequilibrium if the rate of change is too rapid to allow it to
adjust. The features of such a community are clearly exemplified by the changes recently experienced by the Chimbu
peoples of the New Guinea Highlands.[60] The introduction of
commercial coffee growing has disrupted its previously
smooth social relationships since conflict has developed between the coffee growers and the established peasant farmers.
The community is split into the pro-change and anti-change
cliques. A community may be in a state of dynamic equilibrium if its ability to cope with change is equal to the rate of
social change. A typical example of such a community has
been revealed by Williams in his study of Ashworthy, a small
Devon parish.[61] Although man–land relationships have under-
gone considerable change during the past hundred or so years
it has not been sufficient to disrupt the community's social relationships.[62]

Social change and the rural community

Too often social change as experienced by communities located in the countryside has been viewed within the rural–
urban continuum. As a result of the continuum's failure to
explain adequately the nature of rural social change Lewis and
Maund[63] have, in their attempt to unravel the processes
involved, presented an alternative framework (Fig. 6). Following the lead of Pahl[64] and Burie[65] they have conceived social
change as a process of diffusion of new ideas and attitudes
which involves the whole of society irrespective of geographical location. The diffusion path is socially and spatially
selective and consequently produces differential aspirations
and codes of behaviour based upon social class and life-cycle
differences. Such communities experience considerable
change in structure and values the consequence of which is a

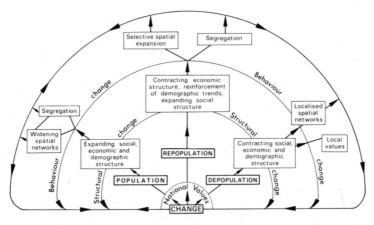

Figure 6. The components of an urbanisation system. (Source: Lewis, G. J. and Maund, D. J., 'The Urbanization of the Countryside: a Framework for Analysis', *Geografiska Annaler*, 58B, 1976, pp 17–27)

change in behaviour patterns of the population in both their intra- and inter-community relations.

Social change in these terms is associated with the process of industrialisation which established a number of long-term trends of considerable significance for the countryside. Industrialisation, defined in simple terms as the process whereby a subsistence economy gives way to a market-oriented one, leads to the systematic and scientific advance of technology and the development of a means of exchange based upon a monetary system. A major consequence of such a change is an increase of economic opportunity, with the growth of tertiary employment and a reduction in the primary. An expanding and diversifying tertiary sector offers an increase in employment opportunities and creates new aspirations for more people. Since such opportunities tend to be located in specific places then migration results. This is assisted in the countryside by the pull force of tertiary employment and the push force of a contrasting primary sector. Even change in agriculture 'is accompanied by a set of changes which affects the rural population itself but also human society as a whole. The technological and economic changes have an influence on culture and social structure'.[66]

In post-industrial societies these processes are well established. Since they affect the young and socially ambitious first they can be examined through the concepts of social class, life-cycle and mobility patterns. In the countryside a series of population movements have been effected. First, *depopulation* as a result, primarily, of net outward migration. At a later stage, the nature of the community may be changed by a growth in *population*[67] as a consequence of a net in-migration of adventitious population at an early stage of the life-cycle. Thirdly, there is *repopulation*, which refers to the retirement to the countryside by people in a late stage of the life-cycle.

The social selectivity of such movements initiates significant structural changes within the communities involved (Fig. 6). The immediate effect of *population* is not only to increase their population but also to alter their social, demographic and economic structures. Such in-migrants, though acquiring rural residence, still retain urban employment and tend to be relatively young and wealthy, often middle-class in life-style and usually divorced from rural society. The increment in the middle-class element has significant social implications for leadership within a community, and is usually reflected in an increase in the number of voluntary social organisations. Similarly, *repopulation* is age-selective, but such movements tend to take place at a late stage in the family life-cycle and contribute towards an ageing demographic structure. However, although repopulation also involves an increase in the middle-class element resident in the countryside, it does not necessarily mean an increase in urban dependence. In contrast, *depopulation* involves the younger and better qualified elements of rural society moving to the cities, creating an ageing demographic structure and a weakly developed, pyramidal social structure. Such changes are also associated with changes in the value system, the traditional values being slowly displaced. Theoretically, it can be argued that the essential characteristic of rural values is that they are *local* in nature. Each rural society tends to have different sets of values and attitudes, and therefore there is little uniformity in values over a wide area. In contrast urban values are more *national* since they are more uniform irrespective of location. These national values are ones in which prestige is given to those who have been materially successful in the world, and therefore socio-economic characteristics determine their status levels within urban communities. Higher status, allotted to those who have received advanced education and have a non-manual occupation, will determine community leadership. Therefore, the changing value system involves either the addition of the national value system, with consequent conflict, or complete displacement of the local by the national. The rate of such changes markedly affects the personal contacts created by the three types of population movements identified above. *Population* and *repopulation* would appear to accentuate the demise of the local value system, whilst *depopulation* contributes to its eventual collapse. In any event rural society is increasingly being assimilated into the total society.

Such structural and value-system changes have a marked effect upon the behaviour of the population, both inside and outside the community (Fig. 6). Within a rural community the segregation of the inhabitants is based upon the local values, but the effects of the introduction of a more socio-economic value system is to create two forms of society, middle-class and working-class, each of which has its own life-style. Even within a small community, such groups are often socially and geographically more segregated than groups formed by the local value system. In addition, such processes affect the behaviour patterns of individuals beyond the community. In a traditional rural society behaviour is essentially spatially restricted for most members: the employed work locally, kinship and friendship relationships are locally oriented, and migration is generally short-distance. In contrast, the spatial connectors of an urban population are more extensive and vary with individuals. Greater mobility potential allows wider migration and kinship distances, while at the same time there is a tendency for work and residence to become separated and for friendship ties to become more diffuse. Therefore, a new behavioural pattern is created for the whole of society, not only for rural communities. However, the rate of such change is accentuated by personal contacts created by the nature of the population movements into and out of the rural communities. *Population* and *repopulation* would appear to create a more segregated and behaviourally extensive society whilst *depopulation* contributes to a collapsing society. The energy for this social change is provided by value changes which result in structural and behavioural change, each of which is capable of feeding back into the value system and modifying it further. A spatial interpretation of social change within the countryside is considered in chapter seven.

This chapter has examined ways in which the process of social change is affecting the rural community and suggests a framework through which it might be viewed. In doing so it has attempted to break away from more traditional frameworks as exemplified in the rural–urban dichotomy/continuum models. Such models and their associated concepts are now thought to distort and inhibit progress in this field. Though the terms rural and urban often refer only to physical appearance, size and land use, this chapter has suggested a different perspective, as yet little developed, of emphasis upon socio-economic structure, behaviour and value systems in contrast to the more familiar morphological and landscape approaches.

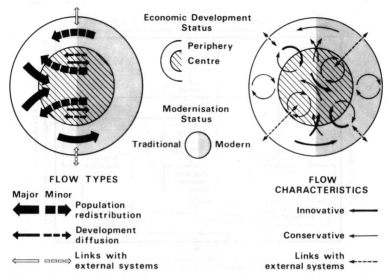

Economic Development Status

Periphery

Centre

Modernisation Status

Traditional ◯ Modern

FLOW TYPES

Major Minor

Population redistribution

Development diffusion

Links with external systems

FLOW CHARACTERISTICS

Innovative ←

Conservative ←

Links with external systems

Figure 9. Migration and the process of modernisation: (*left*) the spatial structure of urbanisation; (*right*) an internal migration paradigm. (Source; Pryor, R. J., 'Migration and the Process of Modernization' in Kosinski, L. A. and Prothero, R. M., *People on the Move*, Methuen, 1975, pp 23–38)

fied in Mabogunje's conceptualisation of rural-to-urban migration in Africa within a systems framework[7] (Fig. 10). This approach 'enables consideration of rural–urban migration no longer as a linear, uni-directional, "push and pull" cause–effect movement, but as a circular, inderdependent, progressively complex, and self-modifying system in which the effect of changes in one part can be traced through the whole of the system'.[8] In this system the rural communities are experiencing a break-up of their isolation and self-sufficiency as a result of economic development. The potential migrant is encouraged to leave the rural village by stimuli from the environment, and the decision as to whether to migrate or not is influenced by a rural control system (family ties, local community) and an urban control system (occupational and residential opportunities, degree of urban assimilation). Once a rural dweller has migrated to the city his role in the system does not end because, by means of a feedback of information to his original village, he can either enlarge or attenuate subsequent

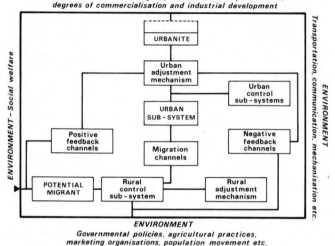

Figure 10. A rural–urban migration system. (Source: Mabogunje, A. L., 'Systems Approach to a Theory of Rural–Urban Migration', *Geographical Analysis*, 2, 1970, pp 1–18.) © 1970 by the Ohio State University Press

migration. All systems contain a driving force, or energy, and in this system it is 'related to the degree of the integration of the rural economy into the national economy, to the degree of awareness of opportunities outside the rural areas, and to the nature of the social and economic expectations held by the rural population'.[9] Although Mabogunje's migration system is designed specifically for Africa, it does reveal that rural–urban migration is 'a continuous process occurring in most countries all the time at different levels of complexity. In this respect the systems approach also serves as a normative model against which one can seek to explain obvious deviations.'[10] In addition, such a system emphasises the need to be concerned not only with why people migrate, but with all the implications and ramifications of the process. Basically, at least four questions are raised by such an approach: (1) why do people migrate? (2) where do people migrate to? (3) who are the migrants? (4) how do people decide to migrate? It is on the resolution of these questions within a rural context that attention is now focused.

Reasons for migrating

Motives for migrating can be explained only in terms of the relative attractiveness of different locations (or place utilities). In 1938 Herberle[11] conceptualised the forces underlying the motive to migrate into those which encourage an individual to leave one place (push) and those which attract him to another (pull). According to Lord Eversley the vast exodus of labourers from the rural districts into the towns of England and Wales during the nineteenth century was due not only to 'the greater prosperity and the general rise of wages in the manufacturing and mining districts',[12] but also 'to a growing disinclination to farm work among labourers in rural districts, to the absence of opportunities for them of rising in their vocation, and to a desire for the greater independence and freedom of life in towns'.[13] Within this listing of the factors explaining migration two undifferentiated sets of forces appear to exist. On the one hand, there are the stimuli to migrate created by changes within the environment, and on the other, changes in the personal motives of the individual.

Changes in the environment can be interpreted as flows from one area to another because of prolonged disequilibria of particular kinds. The most easily recognisable disequilibrium is that created by variations in economic opportunities. Often studies at an inter-regional or inter-county scale have analysed the significance of such factors within a framework provided by the Lowry model.[14] Using a regression analysis, Andrei Rogers,[15] for example, found that the model's four variables—distance, non-agricultural employment, unemployment, and hourly wage rates—accounted for 90 per cent of the variation in inter-county migration in California in 1961. A whole series of similar multiple regression analyses in different parts of the world have upheld the significance of the economic factor in predicting variation in inter-regional and inter-county migration, although the explanatory levels of a number were considerably lower than those recorded for California.[16] For example, Allan Rodgers discovered that

economic variables failed to explain fully the variation in
out-migration from southern Italy between 1952 and 1968.[17]
However, by adding social variables to the data set and subjecting it to a principal component analysis a first component,
which accounted for 37 per cent of the variance, identified
levels of socio-economic health. A simple regression between
net out-migration ratios and the scores on this first component
revealed that nearly two-thirds of the variance in migration
levels in southern Italy was accounted for by spatial differences in socio-economic health (Fig. 11).

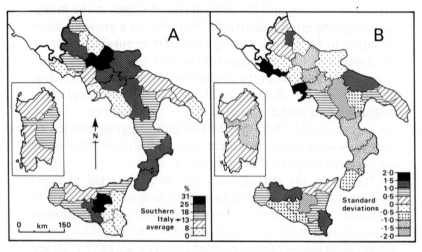

Figure 11.   Migration from southern Italy: A—net out-migration, 1952–68,
as a percentage of 1960 population; B—socio-economic health (principal
component 1). (Source: Rodgers, A., 'Migration and Industrial Development: the Southern Italian Experience', *Economic Geography*, 46, 1970, pp
111–35)

    In the studies cited above the apparent reason for migration
was inferred from the patterns revealed and the attributes of
the areas involved. The actual reasons why people migrate,
however, can only be derived from detailed questionnaire
survey. Despite the problems of getting valid answers to questions about past decisions, some idea as to people's motives in
migrating can be derived from a number of case-studies.

Among such studies there is considerable support for the hypothesis that economic considerations are the major determinants of rural migration. Hannan, for example, stresses the significance of limited local employment in the intentions of young adults to migrate from western Ireland. Overwhelmingly, these intentions were determined by 'beliefs about one's ability to fulfil "economic type" aspirations locally'.[18] Similarly House and Knight's survey of rural north-east England revealed that 72 per cent of those who left the area did so for employment reasons, whilst another 25 per cent migrated upon marriage and 3 per cent moved for educational purposes.[19] Cowie and Giles, in a study of farm labourers' mobility in Gloucestershire in 1950, revealed that 40 per cent of the respondents listed 'long hours' and 'low pay' as their prime reason for leaving agriculture, and this figure rose to 60 per cent among those aged between 16 and 25 years.[20] This, of course, is the age when marriage is being contemplated, which heightens the consideration of long-term prospects in agriculture.[21] Also in the developing countries the role of the economic motive in rural migration has been shown to be significant. For example, according to Prothero 52 per cent of the seasonal migrants leaving Sokoto Province in Nigeria migrated to 'seek money', and another 24 per cent to carry out trade.[22] Among the Mossi from the Upper Volta, Skinner has claimed that so much emphasis is placed upon the economic motive in labour migration that no other reason was mentioned in a major survey.[23]

Despite considerable evidence from both developed and developing countries of the economic factor in determining rural migration, other studies have warned against overstressing it. In less isolated rural communities, where the outlook and activities of the people have been affected by urbanisation, the motives for migration are increasingly related to psychosocial factors. An investigation carried out by Imogene in the new town of Sapele, in mid-western Nigeria, and in a nearby but isolated village of Jesse, tends to support this hypothesis.[24] It has also been claimed that rural migration motives vary with the direction of the movement. In a study of migration in the Welsh Borderland between 1958 and 1968 the present author identified variations in the proportions of the motives of those moving into and out of the region[25] (Table 2). Among the out-migrants economic motives were predominant, clearly reflecting the limited employment opportunities available locally, whilst greater social motivation among the in-migrants probably points to a growing residential function in parts of the region. A number of studies have emphasised the significance of 'housing' and 'community life' in the urban-to-rural flow of migrants in areas adjacent to the cities.[26] Sternstein has revealed a similar pattern of variation in the migration motives of those individuals moving into and out of Bangkok, although it should be pointed out that the greater proportion of these migrants are seasonal.[27]

TABLE 2   Motives for migrating in the Welsh Borderland, 1958–68

Motive	Out-migrants %	In-migrants %
Occupational	32	13
Income	29	9
Social	19	36
Community	12	18
Personal	8	24

After: Lewis, G. J., *A Study of Socio-geographic Change in the Welsh Borderland*, unpublished University of Leicester PhD thesis, 1969

In addition, it is wrong to assume that wherever the flow of migration is small all the needs of the people are being satisfied. It is now well established that there are a number of forces which may prevent an individual from migrating, even when there are high levels of dissatisfaction. Caldwell has shown that many illiterate villagers in Ghana find it difficult to move from conditions of limited opportunities because they lack skills and training for other forms of employment whether in another rural area or in the cities.[28] Of those who had no schooling, less than one-quarter migrated from rural to urban areas, whereas two-thirds of those who achieved secondary education had migrated. More specifically, it has been estimated that over 21 per cent of the residents of the Welsh Borderland in 1968 wished to migrate.[29] These potential migrants were frustrated from achieving their desires by (in order) failure to find suitable alternative employment, family ties, uncertainty and fear of the unknown, cost of moving, and lack of suitable housing elsewhere.

Size and direction

Although the motives discussed in the previous section may initiate a desire to move, they do not determine the destination, which can only be achieved by reference to the location of available opportunities and the degree to which the migrant is constrained by factors such as movement costs. Such a framework was identified in the 1880s by E. G. Ravenstein in his 'Laws of Migration'[30]: after more than eighty years most of these laws are still valid. In a study of migration in upland Wales, H. R. Jones was able to confirm the existence of a significant distance-decay, the absorption of migrants in a leap-frogging fashion, a predominant out-migration partially counterbalanced by an in-migration, and the attraction of those classed as long-distance migrants to the cities of the Midlands and south-east England.[31] In the developing countries, too, there is considerable evidence of both step-wise migration and direct re-location to cities. Examples of the latter include the vast migration into Bombay from its hinterland, as outlined by two independent surveys,[32] and the movement into Nairobi and Mombasa by the Kikuyu, Embu, and Meru peoples from the Kenya highlands, central Nyanza, and the coastal belt.[33] A good example of the former is the migration into the Akim cocoa-growing zone of Ghana by the Krobos tribe. According to Hunter a family purchases a plot of land some days' journey

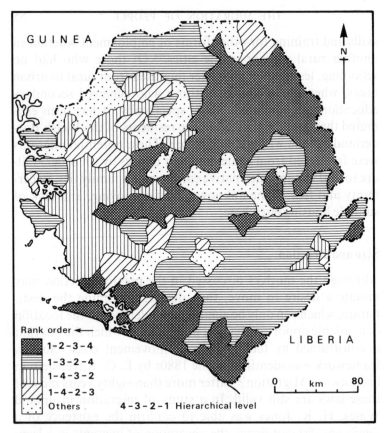

Figure 12. Migration preferences in Sierra Leone; numbers indicate urban(1)–rural(4) continuum. (Source: Harvey, M. E. and Riddell, J. B., 'Development, Urbanization and Migration: a Test of a Hypothesis in the Third World' in Kosinski, L. A. and Prothero, R. M., *People on the Move*, Methuen, 1975, pp 51–65)

from its present home, and after successful cultivation moves farther west.[34] The independence of these two processes in the developing world has been partly corroborated by Riddell and Harvey in a study of migration preferences in Sierra Leone[35] (Fig. 12). The sparsely populated and poorly connected interior regions exhibited a perfect stepwise pattern (1, 2, 3, 4), whilst a certain degree of short-circuiting in the direction of the larger interior cities characterised the pattern of the arboriculture and diamond-mining areas (1, 3, 2, 4). Preference for migration to the capital, Freetown, was restricted to its hinterland, thus reflecting the attenuating effect of distance and the presence of localised employment centres and regional capitals. However, it should not be thought that migration in developing countries is uni-directional; for example, a study of the Matlab district of Bangladesh provides some interesting details on migratory counter-streams.[36] Of those who left the district between 1968 and 1969, 64 per cent migrated to towns and cities, and were replaced by migrants, 48 per cent of whom originated from urban areas. However, the adequacy of the 'laws' as a description of migration flows in the developing countries is weakened by their failure to take into account two distinctive features. The first of these is the re-location of large numbers of migrants over long distances within the rural areas: for example, the major migratory flows in India during the last two decades were the influx of farmers from Bengal into Assam and the large-scale permanent migration to the canal colonies within the state of Punjab.[37] Secondly, widespread seasonal or short-term migration exists in West Africa, where migrants 'leave home to seek work between late September and November, at the beginning of the dry season after the harvest has been taken; they return home again in the following April and May to cultivate their farms with the onset of the rains'.[38]

However, since Ravenstein's seminal work, a number of studies have developed his suggestion that the friction of distance reduces migration contact between areas. Zipf argued that the attraction of a place does not only decline with simple linear distance from a second place but is also dependent upon the size of the places involved.[39] This has been formalised into what is usually called the Gravity Model, whose validity is evident from a number of inter-regional migration studies.[40] But within the majority of these studies it is apparent that a good deal of the variation in the migration still remains unexplained. According to Stouffer this weakness is due to a failure to take into account the fact that 'the number of persons going a given distance is directly proportional to the number of intervening opportunities'.[41] Once again this hypothesis has only partially been substantiated; see, for example, Isbell's study of inter-county and intra-county migration in Sweden between 1921 and 1930[42] (Fig. 13). As a result of these discrepancies between the 'expected' and 'observed' relationships between migration and intervening opportunities, Stouffer refined his theory by introducing an additional variable which he called 'competing migrants'.[43] His revised model postulates that the total number of individuals migrating from A to B is an inverse function of the number of opportunities intervening between A and B, as well as of the number of other individuals competing for opportunities at B.

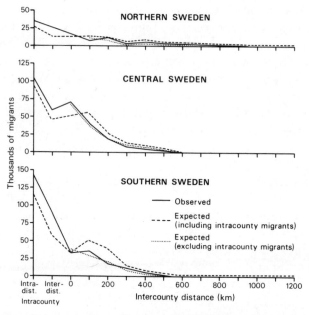

Figure 13. Observed and expected male intercommunity migrants in Sweden, 1921–30, by region of origin and distance of last migration. (Source: Isbell, E. C., 'Internal Migration in Sweden and Intervening Opportunities', *American Sociological Review*, 9, 1944, pp 627–39)

Basically, all such postulates about the size and direction of migration are only refinements of Ravenstein's 'laws'. Even Lee's elaborate attempt to incorporate all the constraints upon migration under the all-embracing concept of 'intervening obstacles' is simply a more detailed expression of what has long been recognised, confirming that the size and direction of migration are guided by distance and intervening opportunities within the context of the individual's aspirations and his ability to overcome a series of intervening obstacles.[44] Clearly, such forces will not operate uniformly for all potential migrants, and hence there is a tendency for a degree of migrant selectivity to exist. It is to the determination of such differential migration that we must now turn.

The selection of migrants

Two of Ravenstein's seven 'laws' of migration indicated the existence of a certain degree of differential migration: that females are more migratory than males, and that the natives of towns are less migratory than those of rural parts of a country. Since the publication of Ravenstein's 'laws', a number of studies investigating the selective nature of migration have been carried out. By far the most significant has been the wide-ranging review undertaken by Dorothy S. Thomas[45] in 1938. Using the evidence produced by Thomas and others, Beshers and Nishuira[46] were able to postulate a series of generalisations concerning migration differentials. These generalisations are: that young adults are the more mobile segment of the population; that males tend to be more migratory than females; that unemployed persons are more likely to move than employed persons; that (within the USA) whites move more than non-whites; and that professional people are among the most mobile groups of the population.

Detailed study of the available empirical evidence on selective migration involving rural areas suggests that not all these hypotheses are upheld in every situation. At an inter-regional scale, studies of the United States, England and Wales, and

France[47] show that age differences are largely responsible for migration differentials, and that factors such as income, education, sex, family size, and marital status operated essentially within a life-cycle dimension. Indeed, Friedlander and Roshier went as far as to claim the existence of two distinct mobility streams associated with family formation in England and Wales in 1960:[48] first, a migration out of rural areas before marriage, and secondly, a movement, predominantly after marriage, out of urban areas (Fig. 14).

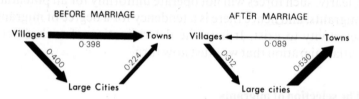

Figure 14.   Migration balances between urban and rural areas in England and Wales, 1960; the net index of migration was calculated on the basis of differences in flows between each pair of places. (Source: Friedlander, D. and Roshier, D. J., 'A Study of Internal Migration in England and Wales, Part II', *Population Studies*, 20, 1966, pp 45–59)

In a study of the Welsh Borderland it has also been shown that the life-cycle dimension differs between migrants moving into and those moving out of the region.[49] Those leaving the Welsh Borderland between 1958 and 1968 were predominantly young adults (aged 15–30 years) and were only marginally differentiated on income, education, sex, and marital status, whilst middle-aged migrants (30–45) were both fewer and more selective, consisting mainly of married couples with higher income and more schooling. In direct contrast, the in-migrants were overwhelmingly of the older age-groups (over 45 years), with nearly 40 per cent in the retirement category, and once again tended to be from the higher income and educational groups. Such migration selectivity reflects the social and economic conditions typically associated with a rural environment. The Welsh Borderland fails to provide sufficient job opportunities, so young adults, even if seeking unskilled jobs, have to leave home. On the other hand, as families retire to the area or buy a 'home in the country' the demographic and social structure of the rural communities is being markedly changed.

Of all the rural dwellers in Western Europe and North America the least mobile are the farming population. According to Gasson[50] the small farmer in the Fens and Hertfordshire is reluctant to leave farming because his present income is adequate, or he foresees difficulties in finding satisfactory alternative employment or has a strong preference for remaining in his present occupation. The farmers are often dissuaded from moving by advanced age and lack of alternatives, but even without these constraints farmers show a strong attachment to their job, as among the Pennine hill-farmers of Staffordshire.[51] Since those farmers who could migrate do not and those who would move cannot, the farming population is unlikely to achieve the mobility levels of the other rural dwellers.

The evidence from the developing countries on the selectivity of rural migrants is more fragmentary and inconclusive than that from the developed countries. Despite Herrick's claim that in Chile the rural migrant differs little from the nonmigrant,[52] a number of inter-regional studies in Southern Asia[53] and West Africa[54] have revealed a tendency for the number of male migrants to exceed that of female migrants, especially in long distance and rural–urban streams. However, the complex nature of migrant selectivity in the rural parts of these countries can only be appreciated after a consideration of a number of local surveys. According to three surveys in Ghana,[55] India,[56] and Bangladesh[57] migrants tended to be single young male adults, a feature which reflects the greater independence of males, the temporariness of the migration, and the type of employment opportunities available in the towns. In Ghana[58] evidence of a reduction in the sex differential in rural-to-urban migration provides additional evidence of a trend toward more permanent migration. The propensity to migrate increased also with the size of the family: for example, in Ghana, the proportion of male migrants rose from 35 per cent among those with one male sibling to 50 per cent among those with five or more male siblings. No doubt this reflects not only chain migration, but also increased pressure on subsistence in rural areas for those in large families. In addition, all three surveys found that a disproportionate fraction of the better educated and members of conspicuously wealthier households were migrants.

Among the rural communities of both the developed and underdeveloped countries Bogue's claim that 'only one migration differential seems to have systematically withstood the test—that for age . . . Migration is highly associated with the first commitment and acts of adjustment of adulthood that are made by adolescents as they mature'[59] has considerable validity. This does not mean that other forms of differential migration do not take place, but rather that they vary in character according to the nature of the rural environment and the people involved. However, despite the failure to identify universal differentials in migration, apart from age, it may be concluded that individuals differently located in space and social structure have different degrees of knowledge about, and are able to benefit to differing extents from, opportunities available at places other than those in which they currently reside. The next section will therefore be concerned with how people decide to migrate in the light of such knowledge.

The decision to migrate

Conceptually, the decision to migrate can be sub-divided into three stages: a first stage, in which a decision to make such a change of residence takes place; a second, in which an alternative location is selected; and a third, in which a decision whether or not to stay is made. The decision will in turn tend to consist of two successive steps (Fig. 15). In the first step a decision is made about the desired general area of residence. If the present home and the current job are highly valued, then migration beyond the commuting field of the place of work is unlikely. On the other hand, if a high value is placed upon a better job or a better environment, in another area, then migration may take place. After this first decision has been made, a second has to be made regarding the location of the home within the general area. This decision is based upon a comparative evaluation of the site and neighbourhood attributes of the present home with those of the potential alternative home. If both the general-area and house-site decisions favour the present situation, people are unlikely to migrate. Of the two types of migrant, total displacement and partial displacement migrants, only the former have to change their location as a result of both steps; the latter base their decisions solely on the site and neighbourhood attributes of home.

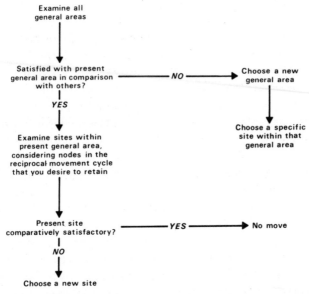

Figure 15.   Generalised locational decision scheme. (Source: Roseman, C. C., 'Migration as a Spatial and Temporal Process', *Annals of the Association of American Geographers*, 61, 1971, pp 589–98)

The comparative evaluation of the present location and potential future location is based upon the knowledge a migrant has concerning each alternative. The procedure by which an individual gathers such information is guided by the extent and content of his information field, or the set of places about which he has knowledge. Such a field can be divided into two: an activity space and an indirect contact space.[60] Activity space is made up of all those locations with which an individual has regular, almost day-to-day contact, resulting in a fairly accurate knowledge of the area involved, although it may be spatially restricted. Such knowledge forms the basis of the partial displacement migrant's decision. In contrast, indirect contact space lies beyond the area of the individual's day-to-day contacts, and partly depends upon information from the mass media and other people about alternative locations. The total displacement migrant's decision is more likely to be based upon this type of knowledge. The nature of such knowledge tends to make his site and neighbourhood decision less efficient than that of the partial displacement migrant's, and so increases the possibility that he himself will make a further partial displacement movement shortly after the initial move.

Within such an information-gathering process there tends to be a decay in the accuracy and content of the information an individual possesses with distance. However, attempts to identify the nature of migration information among rural dwellers are extremely limited. Probably the most meaningful are the preference maps of Gould and White.[61] Implicit within these analyses is a relationship between knowledge and locational desirability. Among schoolchildren in both rural Nigeria and England and Wales a definite preference for their local area and for larger cities was revealed (Fig. 16). However, a tendency among some of the English and Welsh to favour pleasanter coastal and suburban areas emphasises the greater uniformity of the space perception of Nigerian children. Such information will of course play an important role in the decision to migrate and in the selection of likely destinations.

In gathering information there are a series of biases, principally of an attitudinal and connective nature, which distort the distance decay of information. Attitude biases in information sources are those which result from the values placed on the

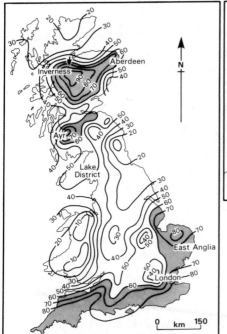
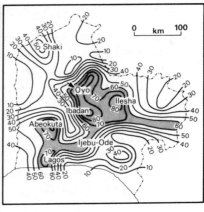

Figure 16.   Residential desirability surfaces: (*left*) as seen by Scottish pupils about to leave school, and (*right*) as seen by 18-year-old students in Oyo, Nigeria. (Source: Gould, P. R. and White, R. R., 'The mental maps of British school leavers', *Regional Studies*, 2, 1968, pp 161–82; Abler, R., Adams, J. S. and Gould, P. R., *Spatial Organisation*, Prentice-Hall, 1971, p 529)

local rural community as well as alternative locations. According to Hannan[62] 'the overwhelming majority of the rural youth in western Ireland expected to migrate to get on in the world'. Similarly, there was a tendency in the Welsh Borderland to regard those who remained as 'failed migrants'.[63] In both communities, long-established out-migration has created a 'migration mentality' which encourages the young to leave their home in search of 'better' opportunities, even when there are local opportunities. One of the few attempts to measure rural attitudes towards locations is Rambaud's survey in France of the residents' interpretation of the concept of a 'town'.[64] 'Snap-type' answers revealed that the rural dwellers viewed the town as a place offering plenty of employment and attractive entertainment which contrasted with the quietness, boredom, and the routine of working in the countryside. In contrast, 'thought-out' answers listed educational opportunities as being the most significant, followed by recreational facilities. These responses illuminate most strikingly the way in which rural life is perceived as being restricted whilst that of the town is seen as containing all the advantages.

Connective biases in information sources are those which result from regular contact, irrespective of distance, with friends and relatives. Such contacts provide the potential migrant with considerable information about the home locations of friends and relatives, and this often becomes the basis for selecting a new place of residence. In addition, friends and relatives can assist migrants by contributing to a reduction in movement costs, and can aid the assimilation of the newcomer into a strange community. The effect of such information feedback is to create a distinctive migration stream between two places. Hillery and Brown have shown that 'the southern Appalachians is not a region in the sense of its parts belonging to the same migration system. Rather it is a collection of fringes, or, as it has often been put, of "backyards"'[65] which are connected to non-Appalachian areas, often distant cities, as a result of migration. 'The kinship structure provides a highly persuasive line of communication between kinsfolk in the home and the new community which channels information about available job opportunities, and living standards directly . . . [to rural] families. Thus, kinship linkage tends to direct migrants to those areas where their groups are already established.'[66] Similarly, Caldwell found that of those migrants who left his case-study area in rural Ghana for an urban destination, less than one-fifth searched for accommodation on their own.[67] In addition, the migrants who remain in the towns maintain contact with their families by sending home money even after long absences from their villages. However, there is a tendency within rural migration literature to overemphasise this type of connection at the expense of other information channels. In the Welsh Borderland it has been shown that between 1958 and 1968 the information source upon which a new community was selected depended upon the type of migration.[68] Since rural-to-rural migration was predominantly local, personal experience was the most significant source. Surprisingly, those who migrated from the rural area to the towns and cities based their information overwhelmingly upon the mass media; the feedback of knowledge by friends and relatives was of little significance. The onset of the mass media seems to have superseded the traditional information source because of its ability to disseminate greater and more detailed knowledge about locational opportunities. The channel of information used in the urban-to-rural migration in the Welsh Borderland was determined by its purpose. Generally, those families who have settled in the region upon retirement based their decision on knowledge derived either from previous residence or holiday visits, whilst those who moved out from the adjacent towns were guided by their personal knowledge. Clearly the manner in which a rural migrant chooses his new home location is as complex as that revealed for the intra-urban migrant.[69]

In this chapter migration has been conceived in terms of a simple rural system. Change in one part of the system has a direct or indirect effect upon all other parts. Within such a system migration is a response to social, political, economic and cultural changes. Despite differential responses to such changes, there is considerable order in the ways in which ruralites decide to migrate and in which their decisions are constrained by a variety of obstacles. Although for analytical purposes migration has been viewed as a dependent variable in this chapter, it is quite clear that it can also be viewed as an independent variable affecting change processes. In other words, given a pattern of population movement, it can have social, economic, political, and cultural consequences for the rural communities.

CHAPTER FOUR

The Diffusion of Ideas and Innovations

Social change results not only from the movement of individuals and groups but also through the diffusion of ideas and innovations. Innovation can initiate change within a community since it incorporates 'any thought, behaviour or thing that is new because it is qualitatively different from existing forms . . . but some innovations by their nature must remain mental organisations only, whereas others may be given overt and tangible expression'.[1] These innovations diffuse, or spread, through a population in both a spatial and a temporal sense. Unfortunately, studies which have attempted to demonstrate the effects of the adoption of an innovation by a community are largely restricted to those of primitive and peasant societies. For example, in Eastern Nigeria when small palm oil presses were introduced during the 1940s, quadrupling yield, improving quality, and raising incomes, the innovation's impact went far beyond the economic: 'Young men became rich, and tensions between generations became severe as a new class of entrepreneurs challenged the traditional bases of obedience. Thus waves of innovation may leave behind them eddies of social change, disruption, and conflict that continue to swirl for a long time after the excitement of the initial impact is past.'[2] Within rural society the diffusion of ideas and innovations is of increasing significance as more complex skills are required for modern living than was the case in the past.

The diffusion of ideas and innovations within rural populations has been of considerable interest to rural sociologists, agricultural economists, and agricultural extension officers who have been concerned with explaining the rate of diffusion in terms of individual economic, social and behavioural characteristics. However, reviews of such work[3] often, surprisingly, fail to mention the considerable amount of research on the diffusion process which has been carried out by geographers over the last half-century.[4] One of the earliest geographical studies, Carl Sauer's *Agricultural Origins and Dispersals* led to the formation of the 'Berkeley' school of geographers whose primary concern was the tracing of man's diffusion of innovations in time and space.[5] Another major influence was F. J. Turner's thesis on the historical extension of the American Frontier: '. . . stand at the Cumberland Gap and watch the procession of civilization, marching single file— the buffalo following the trail to the salt springs, the Indian, the fur trader and hunter, the cattle raiser, the pioneer farmer—and the frontier has passed by. Stand at South Pass in the Rockies a century later and see the same procession with wider intervals between.'[6] Although the Turner thesis has been much criticised it still has considerable value in any attempt to understand the processes of settlement. In the postwar era a number of Swedish geographers, led by Hägerstrad,[7] have linked the social, historical and geographical approaches to diffusion in two types of study: firstly, they have attempted to generalise about the spatial patterning of diffusion; and secondly, they have suggested stochastic processes as a means for explaining these patterns.

Innovation diffusion through time and space

Like the movement of people, the manner in which ideas and innovations diffuse through time and space involves a distance-decay principle, but it differs in three important ways: the idea moves among people and it is not lost at

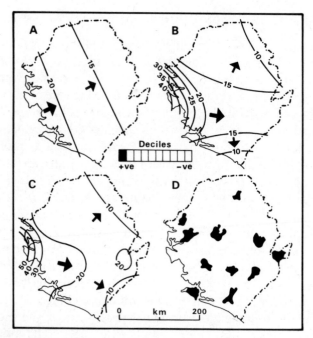

Figure 17. The diffusion of modernisation in Sierra Leone: A—linear trend surface; B—quartic trend surface; C—sixth-order trend surface; D—high positive residuals from sixth-order surface. (Source: Riddell, J. B., *The Spatial Dynamics of Modernization in Sierra Leone*, Northwestern University Press, 1970, p 92)

source; the diffusion is not restricted to routeways; and not every individual contacted adopts the innovation. The recent proliferation of geographical studies of innovation diffusion among rural populations has been concerned mainly with three major themes.[8] First, there is a growing literature concerned with the diffusion of modernisation, particularly in the countries of the developing world. Riddell's noteworthy study of modernisation in Sierra Leone is a typical case.[9] In order to filter the spatial regularity from the detailed pattern a trend surface analysis was carried out (Fig. 17). The highest order surface revealed a progressive decline of modernisation towards the interior of the country, while subsequent surfaces indicated modernisation associated with rail communications and a distance-decay function inland from the capital, Free-

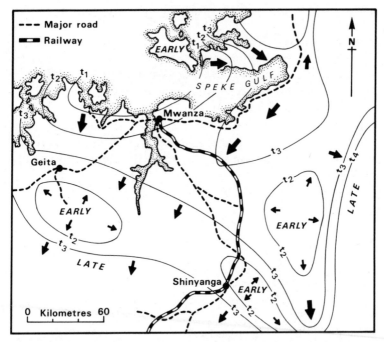

Figure 18. Diffusion of cotton co-operatives, Lake Province, Tanzania. (Source: Gould, P. R., *Spatial Diffusion*, Association of American Geographers, Commission on College Geography Resource, Paper No 4, 1969, p 49)

town; in addition, a bias in the spread of the diffusion along the urban-administrative hierarchy was identified in the map of residuals. A second category of innovation studies includes those specifically concerned with agriculture, a theme typified by Gould's investigation of the spread of cotton co-operatives in northern Tanzania[10] (Fig. 18). Trend surface analysis reveals that the original movement was initiated by farmers in the peninsular and island district of Ukerwe, and then carried by dhow traders and fishermen across the lake to Mwanza; two other early adopting areas were located near the railway line, and another to the west near Geita. The third type of geographical study is that concerned with the adoption of an innovation as a surrogate of social change. Loboda's analysis of the spread of television ownership in Poland is a case in point[11]

(Fig. 19). In 1961 the area characterised by a high degree of television adoption (up to one set for every 80 people) was restricted to the south-west and a small part of the voivodship of Gdansk. By 1965 not only was there an increase in the adoption rate in the south-west, but it had also spread a considerable distance towards the interior. In the last year of the analysis, 1968, a clear decrease of differences in the degree of television dissemination was apparent throughout the whole of Poland.

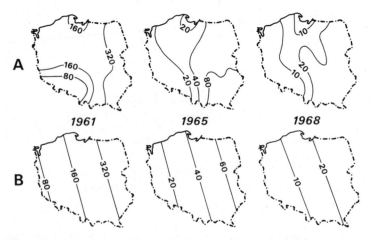

Figure 19.   Direction of television diffusion in Poland: A—trend approximately the real situation; B—idealised linear system. (Source: Loboda, J., 'The Diffusion of Television in Poland', *Economic Geography*, 50, 1974, pp 70–82)

When sociologists such as Coleman[12] and geographers such as Hägerstrand[13] began to develop models to describe the diffusion of ideas and innovations, they saw considerable similarity with the spread of epidemics, for which mathematically derived models already existed. The proportion of adopters plotted against time within a given area gives an S-shaped curve (Fig. 20A) resembling a logistic, or learning curve, which may be expressed as $P = U/(1+e)$ $(a-b.T)$, where P is the proportion of adopters, T is the time periods, U is the upper limits of P, e is 2.7183 (natural log base), a is the parameter which determines the height above the time axis where the curve begins, and b determines the shape of the curve. It is generally considered that the S-shaped form of the diffusion curve results from a low probability of coming into contact with an adopter during the early stages, but as more individuals adopt the probability of contact becomes greater. In the latter stages the probability of contact with non-adopters decreases markedly as saturation level in the diffusion process is reached. This curve can also be used to identify the number of adopters with the passage of time (Fig. 20B). By means of standard deviation units of a normal distribution, Rogers has suggested a fivefold categorisation of adopters on the basis of length of exposure

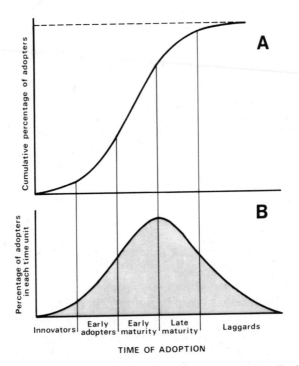

Figure 20.   A—the logistic curve of innovation adoption; B—distribution of innovation adopters

to an innovation before it is fully adopted.[14] In addition, it is increasingly apparent that the spread of an innovation across an area tends to follow a fairly regular spatial sequence. In the innovation diffusion illustrated in Figures 17, 18, and 19 there is, during the early stages, a strong contrast between the innovating area and the distant, remoter areas. This is followed by a marked centrifugal effect with the creation of new innovating centres in more distant areas and a reduction in regional contrasts.[15] These trends continue until the innovation has been adopted by the majority of the population throughout the area involved. According to Hägerstrand 'the main spatial similarity is briefly, that the probability of a new adoption is highest in the vicinity of an earlier one and decreases with increasing distance. Later events seem to be dependent on earlier ones according to a principle for which the term 'neighbourhood effect' would be apt.'[16]

The logistic curve has been found to correspond fairly closely to empirical findings in a number of diffusion studies among rural societies. As long ago as the late twenties and early thirties both Chapin[17] and Pemberton[18] found that cultural development approximated the S-shaped curve. More recently Bose has identified considerable conformity between the expected and observed adoption rates of new farm practices in a number of Indian villages[19] (Fig. 21A), whilst in Colombia Rogers and Svenning have revealed the persistence of the S-shaped innovation curve despite differences in the rate of adoption between modern and traditional villages[20] (Fig. 21B).

However, a number of studies have begun to question the validity of the logistic curve in diffusion studies.[21] It has been argued that the assumptions which have to be made in order to apply the model do not sufficiently reflect reality; for example, the assumptions that an innovation will be accepted after one meeting and that individuals mix without any restrictions are certainly questionable. In addition, Brown and Cox have pointed out that the S-shaped curve can be produced by factors other than those claimed by diffusion theory.[22] It is

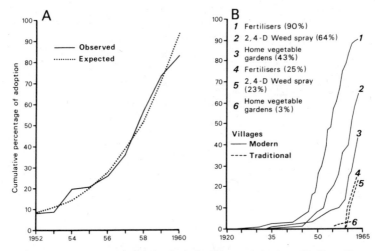

Figure 21. A—adopter distribution of a farm practice in an Indian village. (Source: Bose, S. P., 'The Diffusion of a Farm Practice in Indian Villages', *Rural Sociology*, 29, 1954, pp 53–66)
B—adopter distribution of farm practices in Colombian villages. (Source: Rogers, E. M. with Svenning, L., *Modernization Among Peasants*, Holt, Rinehart and Winston, 1969, p 293)

increasingly clear that both the spatial and temporal theories of diffusion fail to explain adequately the differential rate of innovation. It is necessary, therefore, not only to focus upon the way in which an innovation is adopted but also to assess how the passage of information, the attributes of the individual, and the nature of the innovation itself influence the decision.

Innovation diffusion as a process

The way in which ideas and techniques are adopted is a mental process which an individual goes through from first hearing about an innovation until it is finally adopted or rejected. Figure 22 attempts to summarise the innovation diffusion process within a decision-making framework. The act of adoption or rejection is preceded by a number of events which have a bearing upon the decision: the hearing about the innovation; the learning about its characteristics; the evaluation of the

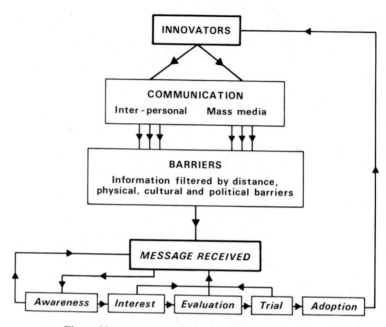

Figure 22.   A generalised innovation decision scheme

factors for and against adoption; and finally, the adoption or rejection of the practice.[23] In 1955 a committee of rural sociologists in North America conceptualised the process into five more specific stages. At the first, or awareness stage the potential adopter learns about an innovation, but lacks sufficient information about it. This provides a basis for the interest stage during which further information is sought. At the next stage, the evaluation, the potential adopter mentally applies the innovation to his present and anticipated future situation, and then decides whether or not to try it on a trial basis. The adoption stage is reached when the individual decides to continue the full use of the innovation. From the initial knowledge of an innovation until its final adoption or rejection can be a few days for some individuals and many years for others. In addition, each of the adoption stages themselves can vary in length. For example, in a study of the adoption period for 2-4-D weed spray by farmers in the Mid-West of the United States, Beal and Rogers observed that the stages of awareness occurred at a more rapid rate than did the stage of adoption: as against 1.7 years between 10 per cent awareness and 10 per cent adoption, there were 31 years between 92 per cent awareness and 92 per cent adoption.[24] In addition, there was a seven-year range in the reported times of awareness.

In recent years a good deal of research has been undertaken, particularly by rural sociologists and agricultural economists, into the efficiency of the current adoption process model used to explain the diffusion process. A number of studies have been concerned with the reliability of different indices for identifying the adoption process. Dasgupta, in a study of the innovation of new farm practices in the central Punjab of India,[25] for example, attempted to assess the relative predictability of five indices of adoption by computing Gutman's coefficient of predictive utility for each of twenty-one variables known to be related to means of adoption. Not surprisingly, not one of the indices was found to be superior to any of the others. At the same time the adoption process model has been criticised for being too simple to fit many of the decisions to adopt innovations. Campbell has even argued for an alternative which allows for more variation in the process by suggesting that it should be constructed around a pair of dichotomies: rational or non-rational decisions, and innovation or problem-oriented ones[26] (Fig. 23).

According to Coughenor 'diffusion may occur even though adoption does not',[27] and he therefore has claimed that the typical diffusion conceptualisation (S-curve) is a measure of adoption rather than of the diffusion process as a whole. In addition, another study has stated a need to incorporate all the stages from awareness to adoption in any assessment of the rate of diffusion, since this allows the researcher to analyse the extent of diffusion at various levels of completeness and therefore provides a more accurate picture of the diffusion process.[28] This argument is well illustrated by Sawhney's analysis of the adoption behaviour of farmers in India.[29] Although the extent of the adoption of artificial insemination was nearly twice as high as for chemical weed control a lower differential

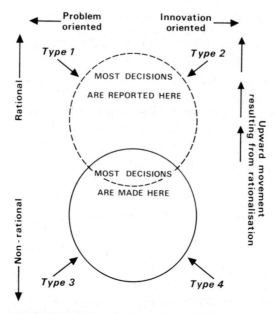

Figure 23. A paradigm of the individual adoption process. This paradigm suggests possible variation in the process, being constructed around two dichotomies: rational or non-rational decisions and innovation- or problem-oriented ones. The combination of these two dimensions produces four ideal-type processes. (Source: Campbell, R. R., 'A Suggested Paradigm of the Individual Adoption Process', *Rural Sociology*, 31, 1966, pp 458–66)

was revealed, however, when all the stages in the diffusion process were incorporated into the analysis. By summing the cumulative proportion of adoption units in each of the five stages a range of indices from zero to 500 is achieved, which yielded a score of 246 for artificial insemination and 184 for chemical weed control.

Communication patterns and innovation diffusion

'Geographical proximity and urban–rural relations are the typical social structures in which channels of communication are thought, in some mysterious way, to inhere.'[30] In order to unravel the mystery a number of theoretical models have been developed by geographers during the last two decades.

Although the process by which information spreads from its source to an individual normally involves a number of channels there is, however, considerable evidence to support the view that within rural societies a two-step flow of information—first by a person with cosmopolite contacts and then via personal contacts—is predominant. Such a flow structure of information was the basis of Hägerstrand's model of the spread of innovation[31] in which it was assumed that information diffused from a limited number of early adopters to adjacent potential adopters declining in frequency with distance. The spatial extent of information transmission, or the mean information field, was determined by the declining probabilities of contact with increasing distance from the early adopters to the potential adopters. Within the geographical literature it is thought that this 'neighbourhood effect' is a major cause of the wave-like spread of adoption through space.[32] A number of studies have confirmed the effectiveness of Hägerstrand's model in simulating actual patterns of diffusion.[33] At a later date, Hannemann and Carroll developed a temporal stochastic diffusion model[34] in which it was assumed that messages about an innovation entered a rural community through two external interpersonal channels: an extension agent and a teacher with urban experience. This model was applied to the diffusion of new ideas among farmers in a rural community in Brazil, producing a simulated cumulative adoption curve which fitted reasonably well with the empirical curve according to the standards of the Kolmogorov-Smirnov two-sample test. Despite the effectiveness of both the spatial and temporal models to simulate the process there has developed more recently a certain degree of reservation about their underlying assumptions. Also it has been argued that both are too simplistic since they are little more than information diffusion models. More specifically Cliff has gone as far as to claim that a 'neighbourhood effect' does not even exist within the data used by Hägerstrand to test his model.[35]

In the questioning by geographers and rural sociologists of the significance of the 'neighbourhood effect' four sources of

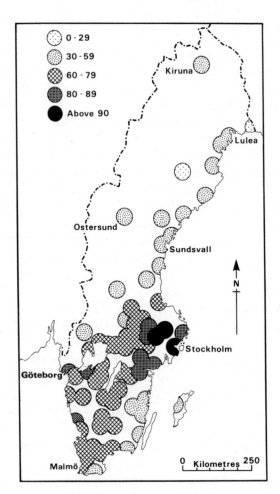

Figure 24. Contact potential in Sweden, 1970. Contact potential is the amount of personal contact required with colleagues outside the plant or office. By aggregation the amount of such contact potentially available at the main centres of population was derived. Stockholm (100) has the greatest contact potential, but though there is a general tendency for values to decline with distance from the capital, Göteborg and Malmö on the southwest coast prove to be surprisingly well placed. (Source: Pred, A. R. and Tornqvist, G. E., *Systems of Cities and Information Flows*, Lund Studies in Geography, Series B, 38, 1973, p 97)

weakness have been emphasised. First, geographers such as Tornqvist, from evidence derived from personal diaries, have argued that regular personal contacts take place over a much wider distance than suggested by spatial diffusion theory[36] (Fig. 24). Further, a number of rural sociologists have been at pains to show the crucial role that the mass media play in the adoption process. Wilkening, for example, concluded from a sample of 341 farmers in a North Carolina rural community that in the acquisition of knowledge about eight selected farm practices 'other farmers and other contacts'[37] were only marginally more significant than the mass media. However, among rural communities in developing countries empirical evidence suggests that local inter-personal channels are still the predominant means of information transmission.[38] In a study of the diffusion of a family planning programme in Bihar state, India, Blaikie argues that despite the use of a variety of information sources personal relationships are still the most significant.[39] Clearly Myren's conclusion to his study of innovation diffusion in a Mexican rural community neatly summarises the differential role of mass media and inter-personal information channels in rural societies at different levels of development: 'the hypothesis about the impact of the mass media can be applied only in areas where media circulate widely, and where, equally important, they command attention and deal with questions of interest to farmers in a comprehensible fashion.'[40]

A second source of weakness within diffusion theory is its failure to incorporate the tendency for different stages in the process to involve different sources of information. This multiple-step approach to the flow of information has been identified in a number of studies, in particular those concerned with agricultural innovation in the United States. In a study of 170 sample farms in Sauk County, Wisconsin, Wilkening found that the mass media, particularly the farm magazine and the radio, were relatively more important in first informing farmers about new practices than in providing the type of information upon which to evaluate and to learn how to perform an operation.[41] This changing role of the mass media and inter-personal communication at each stage of the diffusion process is most clearly illustrated in Beal and Rogers's study of adoption of 2-4-D weed spray by 148 Iowan farmers.[42] It was found that the proportion of respondents mentioning an inter-personal channel increased from 37 per cent at the knowledge stage to 63 per cent at the persuasion stage. In addition, early adopters use information from the mass media more fre-quently through all stages of adoption whilst conversely the laggards are more dependent upon personal contacts. Hence, a mean information field as conceptualised by Hägerstrand does not occur at all stages of the adoption process. Therefore, the extent to which the mean information field will operate, as well as the stage of the adoption, varies from one adopter category to another.

A third reason for the failure of the 'neighbourhood effect' to explain adequately the diffusion of an innovation is the fact that items of information can flow through different com-munication channels. As long ago as 1953 Wilkening reported that among the farmers of Wisconsin agricultural agencies were the most frequently mentioned source of first knowledge about 2-4-D weed control, yet farm managers were the major source of first information about grass silage.[43] However, in a study of the Ziz valley, southern Morocco, Blaikie has argued that information sources about different items can only be in-terpreted within the context of the social and spatial structure of the region.[44] Information about the valley's barrage scheme was obtained by the large landowning farmers by means of their wider travel patterns while the poorer population acquired this knowledge via local sources. At the same time there was a marked decline in information level with increas-ing distance from the barrage scheme which Blaikie in-terpreted as reflecting both a decrease in contacts with those working on the scheme and the low levels of radio listening in the impoverished and unirrigated south (Fig. 25). Similarly, sources of information about an established agricultural inno-vation, that of inorganic fertilisers, also varied with the social

structure of the population. Again the more prosperous farmers had the greatest knowledge of this innovation, as a result
not only of their more widespread movement field but also of
their close association with ORMVAT, the extension agency.
In contrast, the principal sources for the dissemination of information about insecticide, a more recent innovation, were
the extension agencies and the mass media. Evidence such as
this has led a number of researchers to argue that the 'effect of
neighbourhood' might be as significant as the 'neighbourhood
effect' in guiding the diffusion of an innovation.[45]

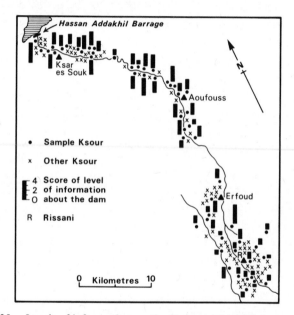

Figure 25.   Levels of information on the Hassan Addakhil dam, southern
Morocco. (Source: Blaikie, P. M., 'The Spatial Structure of Information
Networks and Innovative Behaviour in the Ziz Valley, Southern Morocco',
Geografiska Annaler, 55B, 1973, pp 83–105)

A fourth source of weakness in diffusion theory lies in the
fact that certain types of information are received and trans-
mitted more readily by some people than others. For example,
Lionberger has shown that the flow of information among

farmers in Missouri was guided by kinship groups, social cliques and work groups.[46] This more structured form of communication results from the tendency of individuals to be influenced by their peers, and so there is a gradual trickling down of influence from the upper to the lower strata. In other words, society is made up of a series of loosely-defined overlapping groups the boundaries of which are set by a variety of socio-cultural and spatial factors.[47] In a study of rural Mysore, Mayfield and Yapa not only identified the interlocking nature of these small neighbourhoods by means of both channel density and frequency of usage but also viewed them as the lowest level of a communication hierarchy[48] (Fig. 26). Therefore, if Hudson's view of information flowing with equal probability to all places of equal size within a central place hierarchy is valid,[49]

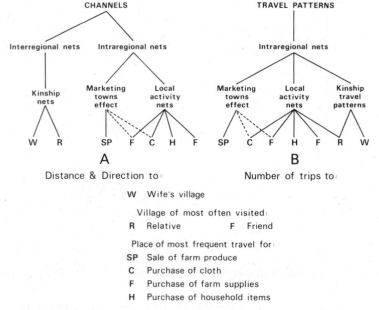

Figure 26. A typology of communication nets in rural Mysore: A—distance and direction; B—trip frequency. (Source: Mayfield, R. C. and Yapa, L. S., 'Information Fields in Rural Mysore', *Economic Geography*, 50, 1974, pp 313–23)

then the smallest neighbourhood need not necessarily be the last to acquire knowledge of an innovation. The passage of information is guided by channels of urban, neighbourhood and social group interaction, rather than through a wave-like spread across an area of homogeneous potential adopters.[50]

Innovativeness

It has long been known that some individuals adopt new ideas earlier than others. The different degree of innovativeness has been used to classify individuals into a series of adopter categories: innovators, early adopters, early majority, late majority and laggards. Many studies of agricultural innovation have revealed considerable selectivity of individuals in their potentiality to innovate. In 1965, for example, the innovativeness of the Mayan Indians living in San Antonio, British Honduras, among whom ancient practices of shifting cultivation were still being followed, were investigated by Feaster.[51] Attitude statements were used to construct a scale of innovativeness, and those variables significantly related to the modification of traditional attitudes—age, education, levels of living, contact with extension agents and aspirations—were identified by multiple regression analysis. The overwhelming majority of studies in both the developed and developing countries confirm the generalisation that early adopters tend to be younger, wealthier, more cosmopolite, literate, less traditional and more media-oriented than the rest of a community.[52] However, attempts to characterise the innovators in rural society are fragmentary in nature and fail to distinguish the relative order of importance and inter-relationships of these characteristics. To deal with this multivariate problem a number of recent studies have used a factor analysis.[53] Though the data lacks comparability and the studies tend to be restricted to traditional communities[54] some general comments may be made about the results. The majority of studies listed in Table 3 identify at least three dimensions which characterise differences in innovation potential. The first dimension

TABLE 3 Factor analysis of innovations

Author and Location	Number of variables	Factors extracted
Deutschmann and Fals Borda[a] (Colombia)	23	1. Economic ability to innovate (farm size) 2. Awareness of innovation (knowledge index) 3. Ability to understand communication (education and literacy)
Rahim[b] (Pakistan)	27	1. Ability to understand communication (literacy, education, and media exposure) 2. Opinion leadership (popularity and formal participation) 3. Cosmopoliteness (media exposure and urban visits)
Whiting[c] (Brazil)	42	1. Modernisation skills (education and mass media exposure) 2. Interpersonal skills (trust, empathy and radio listening) 3. Scale of operations (farm size)
Rogers with Svenning[d] (Colombia)	72	1. External communication (mass media exposure and education) 2. Orientation to change (empathy and age) 3. Innovative leadership orientation (opinion leadership)
Skelty[e] (Mysore, India)	32	1. External communication (farm structure and access to information and supply) 2. Orientation to change (family aspirations and needs) 3. Ability to innovate (owned holdings and index of assets)

Author and Location	Number of variables	Factors extracted
Garst[f] (Kenya)	30	1. Family structure (size, age, and land)
		2. External communication (Membership and contacts)
		3. Innovative leadership orientation (education, offices held and opinion leadership)

After:
a. Deutschmann, P. J. and Fals Borda, O., *Communication and Adoption Patterns in an Andean Village*, Programs Interamericano de Information Poplar, San Jose, 1962
b. Rahim, S. A., 'A Factor Analysis of Modernization Variables Among Pakistani Peasants', unpublished paper, Michigan State University, Department of Communication, quoted in Rogers, E. M. with Svenning, L., *Modernization Among Peasants. The Impact of Communication*, Holt, Rinehart and Winston, 1969, p 324
c. Whiting, G. C., *Empathy, Mass Media, and Modernization in Rural Brazil*, Michigan State University, Department of Communication, Technical Report 1, 1967
d. Rogers, E. M. with Svenning, L., *op.cit.*, 1969, p 326
e. Skelty, N. S., 'A Factor Analysis of Use of Fertilizers by Farmers', *Indian Journal of Agricultural Economics*, 24, 1969, pp 50–61
f. Garst, R. D., 'Innovation Diffusion Among the Gusic of Kenya', *Economic Geography*, 50, 1974, pp 300–12

reflects individual connections with areas beyond the immediate rural neighbourhood in which education and literacy facilitate exposure to the mass media and the development of cosmopoliteness, which in turn leads to greater knowledge and innovation. In addition, social status tends to load on this type of factor, reflecting the fact that those who have contact beyond the community are of a higher social status than those whose lives are locally oriented. A second dimension involves factors which identify an orientation to change among a rural population: where this factor is most clearly apparent, age is the crucial variable. In general, younger rural dwellers have smaller families not only because of their fewer years of marriage but also as a reflection of their modernising attitude. Young ruralites appear dissatisfied with their local neighbourhood, and this manifests itself in a desire to leave as well as a favourable attitude towards change. The third dimension is less distinguishable cross-nationally, though a number of the studies listed in Table 3 reveal the existence of individual factors which identify degrees of opinion leadership as their core. This type of factor was distinguished by the independent assessment of an individual's peers and was significantly correlated with both external communication and orientation to change. Beyond these three dimensions it becomes more difficult to identify from the studies quoted in Table 3 characteristics of the potentiality to innovate. But, of course, before the true significance of the identified dimensions can be confirmed further studies of this type, particularly in the rural world of the developed nations, is necessary.

Social structures vary over space: in particular there is a series of gradients from town to country. What is less clear is the extent to which such spatial variation affects innovative behaviour. Of considerable interest in this context is Fuller's study of the spatial diffusion of fertility decline in Chile[55] which demonstrated that of the several variables which were correlated with birth control practice it was the distance variable which was the single most powerful discriminator between user and non-user of contraceptive techniques. A similar conclusion was reached by Blaikie in a study of the effectiveness of the family planning programme in rural India.[56] Such findings have considerable implications in any future attempt to spread information about birth control methods. Primarily, there appears to be a need to place a greater emphasis on the distribution of change agents or, in specific terms, to relate the distance which a potential adopter travels to obtain knowledge about an innovation to his social characteristics.

Innovation diffusion and expected utility

The students of innovation diffusion have overwhelmingly demonstrated that before an innovation is adopted it must be an improvement on the ideas it supersedes. Kivlin and Fliegel, for example, concluded that the rates of adoption of agricultural innovations among United States farmers was closely related to economic advantage.[57] However, a number of studies have claimed that economic profitability is less important among peasant farmers. Among Punjabi peasants Fliegel found that 'the respondents apparently attach greater importance to social approach and less to financial return'.[58] It would appear that before an innovation is adopted there must be a social environment ripe for change, a feature illustrated by Brookfield's survey of the adoption of commercial coffee growing among the Chimbu peoples of the New Guinea highlands[59] (Fig. 27). However, the relative advantage of an innovation may be heightened by the promotional activities of change agents, for example the provision of subsidies in order to speed up the rate of adoption. The desire of the Indian government to reduce the birth-rate has been encouraged by the provision of a small fee to each male who volunteered for a vasectomy.

Clearly it appears that the rate of adoption cannot be adequately explained in expected utility terms alone. According to Rogers there are at least four innovation characteristics which need to be considered.[60] First, a number of studies have shown that the degree of an innovation's compatability with the existing values, past experiences, and needs of the receiver must be taken into account. This can be illustrated by the adoption of hybrid corn in a small Mexican community in 1947.[61] Within a year nearly half of the villagers had adopted the seed but a year later only a few of the adopters continued to use the new seed. The reason for the rejection of the innovation was not any shortcomings in its yield, but that the corn did not make acceptable tortillas: the innovation did not fit the values of this rural society. Secondly, the rate of adoption may be affected by the relative difficulty of understanding or using an innovation. According to Fliegel and Kivlin the complexity of farm innovations was more highly related (in a negative direction) to their rate of adoption than any other characteristic of innovation except relative advantage.[62] Thirdly, innovations will generally be adopted more rapidly if they can be tested on a trial basis. Once again Fiegel and Kivlin found a correlation between trial ability and the rate of adoption for 43 farm innovations[63] whilst a number of other studies have shown that

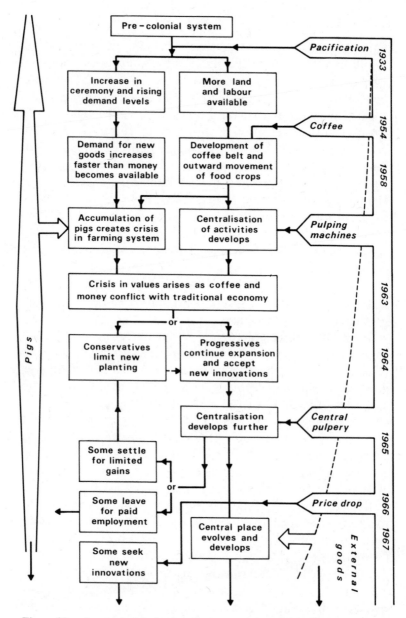

Figure 27.   A model of the innovation path and selected associated changes among the Chimbu, New Guinea. (Source: Brookfield, H. C., 'The Money That Grows on Trees: the Consequences of an Innovation within a Man-Environment System', *Australian Geographical Studies*, 6, 1968, pp 97–119)

early adopters perceive trial ability as more important than later adopters.[64] Lastly, the ease with which an innovation can be observed and communicated to others will also affect its rate of adoption. For example, Erasmus[65] has shown that in a part of Bolivia the visibility of an innovation is particularly important in affecting the rate of adoption, whilst Hrushka[66] in an investigation of the role of demonstration farmers in diffusing new ideas among German villages has rated farm innovations into four categories of observability.

It is readily apparent that any single innovation characteristic provides an inadequate explanation of the differential rate of adoption. Probably the most comprehensive analysis of the inter-relationship between the five innovation characteristics was the one carried out by Kivlin into the rate of adoption of 43 farm ideas by 299 farmers in the United States.[67] The multiple correlation analysis revealed that the most significant relationship existed between the rate of adoption and (1) relative advantage, (2) complexity, and (3) compatability. The combined effect of the innovation characteristics explained only 51 per cent of the variation in the rate of adoption, and none of the characteristics above explained more than 16 per cent of the variance. It has been suggested that this low level of explanation may be attributed to the tendency for different innovation characteristics to be significant at each stage of adoption. Griliches, for example, in his study of the diffusion of hybrid corn in the United States suggested that the early stage was influenced by the cost of innovating and the adaptability of the existing hybrids in a given area.[68] In contrast, the middle stage could be explained by the relative profitability of adopting the new seed, and the saturation stage by long-run demand factors and technological change. A similar case has been put forward, in their study of the spread of soybean production in Illinois by Powell and Roseman,[69] who concluded that the early stages of adoption were influenced by the aggregate level of agricultural commercialisation and related opportunities for innovation, and the later stages by the relevance of the innovation to the total farm enterprise.

Unfortunately, the majority of diffusion studies in rural society have been concerned with technical change involving agriculture in some form or other. The reason for this is easily understood. The nature of agricultural innovation and its path can more often than not be readily identified, and its impact easily comprehended. With other, more inanimate forms of innovation, detailed analysis is fraught with difficulties.[70] Consequently, it has been argued that since the mechanism involved in the spread of one innovation is similar for all innovations, then agricultural innovations can be viewed as surrogates of rural innovations in general. But before this view can be accepted there is a need for more rigorous studies in different rural communities of different types of innovation.

CHAPTER FIVE

Patterns and Process of Settlement

Traditionally, geographers have approached the study of rural communities from the viewpoint of physical space.[1] The settlement of an area is regarded as the physical expression of man's decision to locate either individually or in groups for economic, social and cultural purposes at certain points in space. The focus is upon the community as a place where man resides, and the prime objective is to elucidate 'where are they and why are they there?'.[2] In other words, the concern is with the process of settling the land and the form of the resultant settlement.[3]

Rural settlements have long been a source of interest and research for geographers. A foundation was laid by such eminent geographers as Meitzen and Demangeon, with a further impetus being given by the *Reports of the Commission on Types of Rural Settlement*, published between 1928 and 1931.[4] Unlike studies of urban settlement, those concerned with rural settlement were historically biased and lacked a theoretical framework. 'Such is the complexity of the subject matter, however, that no general laws can yet be formulated, and indeed it is questionable if they should be sought. Hitherto, all attempts to do so have been mere sophistry, leading to generalisations disproved by many exceptions.'[5] But of late there has been a growing reaction, as in human geography generally, against this viewpoint, which has been criticised for a failure to distinguish

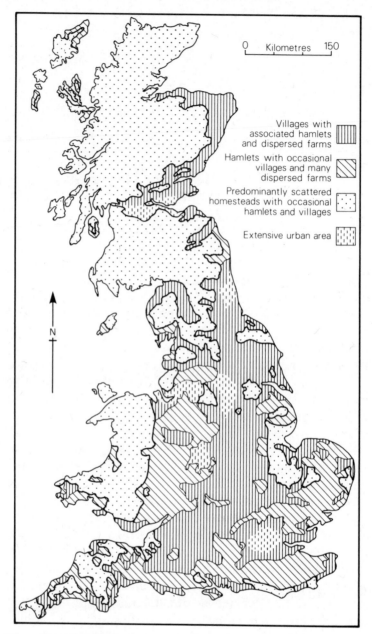

Figure 28. The distribution of rural settlement types in Britain. (Source: Thorpe, H., 'Rural Settlement' in Watson, J. W. and Sissons, J. B., *The British Isles. A Systematic Geography*, Nelson, 1964, pp 360–1)

purely local factors from those of a more general nature, as well as for obscuring the universality of settlement patterns and processes. As a consequence there has been a shift in rural settlement study towards greater quantification and model-building although, when compared with urban geography, these developments are still considerably more attenuated, reflecting their recency and the persistence of traditional approaches by historical geographers[6] and local historians.[7] Although this chapter concentrates largely on the more recent approaches to settlement analysis it does so within the context of the traditional, but still important, body of literature.

Form and Pattern

The early interest in the distribution of rural settlements was facilitated by the ease with which they could be conceptualised as a pattern of points on a map. Despite wide variations in the patterns of rural settlement, two basic forms are recognised, as evidenced in the classifications of Aurousseau[8] and Demangeon[9]: agglomeration or nucleation, and dissemination or dispersal. In general, the former type characterises those areas where the farmers reside in villages and work on the land of the surrounding locality, whilst the latter is more likely to occur when the residences are sited on the farms themselves. However, between these two extremes there are a wide range of intermediate types in different parts of the world.

In any geographical analysis of settlement forms two basic dimensions may be identified: the predominant settlement form within an area, and the origin of that form. A good deal of early work on rural settlement was concerned with the identification of the predominant form within different regions and sub-regions. So widespread and detailed has this work been in Britain that Thorpe was able to construct a settlement map for the whole of the country[10] (Fig. 28). Such maps, however, have been criticised for their failure to distinguish settlement types sufficiently precisely: 'Villages large and

small, hamlets, semi-dispersal and dispersal may appear to be
self-explanatory terms but classification necessarily remains to
some degree subjective. There is no agreed standard of division
between them based on size and form.'[11] In order to overcome
this weakness various indices have been developed in the attempt to measure either the distance between habitations or
their relative degree of concentration and dispersion (Table 4).

TABLE 4   Indices of rural settlement form

Author	*Index*
Bernard[a]	$C = \dfrac{HA}{S^2}$, where C = degree of concentration; H = number of habitations; A = area; and S = number of settlements
Demangeon[b]	$D = \dfrac{P \times I}{T}$, where D = degree of dispersion; P = population of commune less that of its chief settlement; and T = total population
Barnes and Robinson[c]	$D = 1.11 \sqrt{\dfrac{A}{N}}$, where D = average distance of a farm house to nearest six farmhouses; A = total area; N = number of farmhouses
Stone[d]	R = Nh + Nr, where R = continuous or discontinuous settlement; Nh = pattern of permanent habitations within 3 miles along 1–6 major directions from any one permanent residence; Nr = number (1–4) of inter-regional and local routes of transport within 10–20 miles of each residence

After:
a. Bernard, J., 'Une Formule Pour la Catrographie de l'Habitat Rural avec Application au Département de l'Yonne', *Comptes Rendu C. I. G., Paris. 1931*, 3, 1934, pp.
17–32
b. Demangeon, A., 'Une Carte de l'Habitat', *Annales de Géographie*, 42, 1933, pp.
225–32
c. Barnes, J. A. and Robinson, A. H., 'A New Method for the Representation of Dispersed Rural Population', *Geographical Review*, 30, 1940, pp. 134–7
d. Stone, K. H., 'Swedish Fringes of Settlement', *Annals of the Association of American Geographers*, 52, 1962, p 374

One of the most interesting was the index developed by Stone in a classification of settlement forms in rural Spain.[12] After a detailed inspection of a series of topographic maps a simple threefold grouping was suggested:

1. Grouped, with a nucleus: this refers to those settlements, usually centred at a focus of two or more roads, in which habitations are less than three metres apart.
2. Disseminated, without a nucleus: this refers to scattered single habitations (usually at least eight kilometres apart), as well as small clusterings of two to about eight residences with any two being less than 180 metres apart.
3. Disseminated, with a nucleus: this refers to those settlements which are intermediate between the previous two types.

By then calculating the percentage of total dwellings classed into each of the three categories separately, a map of the predominant type of settlement in different parts of Spain was produced (Fig. 29). However, this index, like those listed in Table 4, also suffers from subjectivity, particularly in the selection of the vital size and distance thresholds. Further, the indices used in various studies are not truly comparable because their underlying bases differ, and it is not surprising, therefore, that 'only one is known to have been applied outside the country of origin and only one inside any nation more than once'.[13]

Paralleling such attempts at classifying the form of rural settlement were strenuous efforts to achieve an understanding of their origin. In view of the wealth of available evidence and the detailed nature of the investigations, the problems and controversies related to settlement origins can be most effectively illuminated if we restrict our attention to one part of the world, namely Western Europe.[14] Any attempt to interpret European rural settlement must inevitably begin with Meitzen's[15] detailed late-nineteenth-century work in which he put forward the view that dispersed and nucleated settlements could be related to different ethnic groups. Meitzen argued

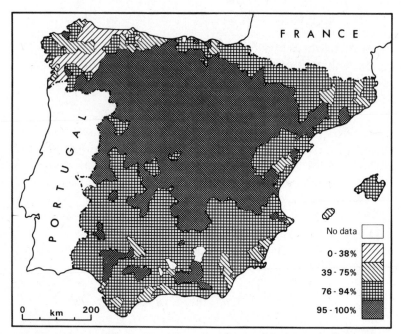

Figure 29. Percentage of total dwellings classed as grouped with nucleus in Spain, 1960. (Source: Stone, K. H., 'Regionalization of Spanish Units of Settlement', *Tijdschrift voor Economische en Sociale Geografie*, 61, 1970, pp 232–41)

that areas of Celtic occupation were characterised by a dispersed, or *Einzelhöfe*, type of settlement while the village, or *Haufendorf*, owed its existence to Germanic conquests; a third ethnic group, the Slavonic peoples, was associated in central and eastern Europe with the street village or *Strassendorf* and the round village or *Rundling* (Fig. 30). This neat division of European settlement into three ethnic categories was largely accepted by students of rural settlement until later work began to undermine this line of thought.[16] In 1939 Evans argued in his classic paper on the Irish open-field system that there was 'abundant evidence that the type of settlement accompanying rundale cultivation before its decay was not the dispersed habitat which generally distinguishes the Irish landscape at the present day'[7] but, rather, 'a secondary dispersion following the dissolution of this type of cultivation'.[18] Thus Evans concluded

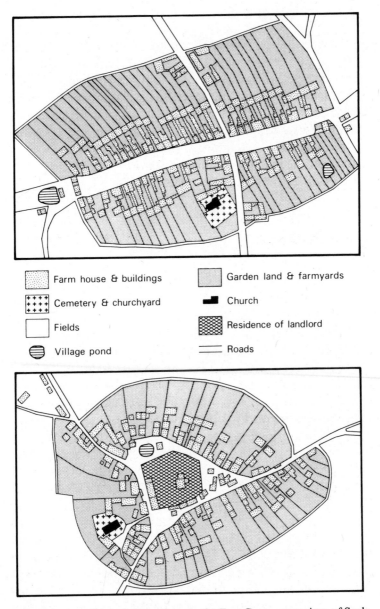

Figure 30. Examples of village form in the East German province of Sachsen: (*above*) Eicha, a street village (*Strassendorf*); (*below*) Licktentanne, a round village (*Rundling*). (Source: Buschan, G. (ed), *Illustrierte Völkerkunde*, vol 2, part 2, Strecker and Schroeder, 1926, p 400)

that 'it is now clear that throughout Western Britain and in many parts of western and south-western Europe, some kind of communal cultivation is of great antiquity—Meitzen's well-known map of *Dörfer* and *Einzelhöfe* needs drastic revision'.[19] The significance of this conclusion cannot be overstated since it emphasises a shift from a static to a dynamic interpretation of settlement form, an approach which has attracted a good deal of detailed and painstaking empirical investigation and, more recently, some attempts at generalisation.

Process of settlement

The process of settlement involves the conversion of an un-inhabited piece of land into one which may be considered settled. The process is more often than not distinguished on the basis of three inter-related components: an increase in the size and density of population; the erection of permanent habitations; and the exploitation of the land by man. In the British Isles detailed reconstructions of the process, based upon a variety of documentary sources, have been carried out for a number of small areas.[20] In summarising the findings for the Celtic west, Bowen likens the process to that of a life-cycle, 'beginning with an original cluster, then passing through a stage of maximum dispersal, and finally returning once more to a cluster pattern'.[21] Interestingly he draws an analogy between this life-cycle in settlement evolution and 'that pattern which modern astronomers would have us believe operates in the stellar universe'.[22] In contrast the majority of studies in North America of the settlement process have adopted some initial frame of reference, in particular Whittlesey's concept of sequent occupance,[23] which emphasises that people of different cultures who have 'lived upon and used the earth'[24] have produced different forms of occupance during succeeding periods.[25] For example, Brown has documented in some detail the cultural innovations and changing perceptions of available resources in a small community, Upsala, in rural Minnesota,

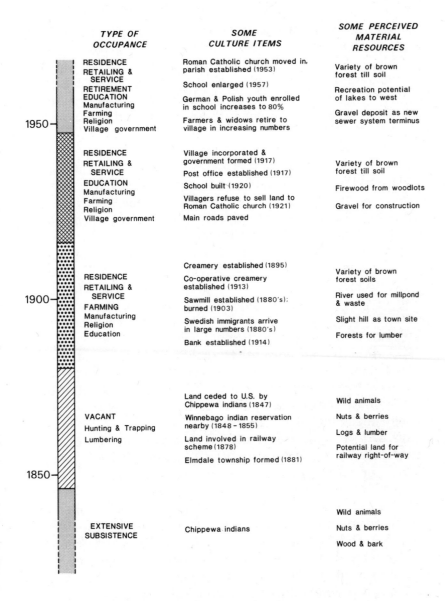

	TYPE OF OCCUPANCE	SOME CULTURE ITEMS	SOME PERCEIVED MATERIAL RESOURCES
1950	RESIDENCE RETAILING & SERVICE RETIREMENT EDUCATION Manufacturing Farming Religion Village government	Roman Catholic church moved in, parish established (1953) School enlarged (1957) German & Polish youth enrolled in school increases to 80% Farmers & widows retire to village in increasing numbers	Variety of brown forest till soil Recreation potential of lakes to west Gravel deposit as new sewer system terminus
	RESIDENCE RETAILING & SERVICE EDUCATION Manufacturing Farming Religion Village government	Village incorporated & government formed (1917) Post office established (1917) School built (1920) Villagers refuse to sell land to Roman Catholic church (1921) Main roads paved	Variety of brown forest till soil Firewood from woodlots Gravel for construction
1900	RESIDENCE RETAILING & SERVICE FARMING Manufacturing Religion Education	Creamery established (1895) Co-operative creamery established (1913) Sawmill established (1880's); burned (1903) Swedish immigrants arrive in large numbers (1880's) Bank established (1914)	Variety of brown forest soils River used for millpond & waste Slight hill as town site Forests for lumber
1850	VACANT Hunting & Trapping Lumbering	Land ceded to U.S. by Chippewa indians (1847) Winnebago indian reservation nearby (1848 - 1855) Land involved in railway scheme (1878) Elmdale township formed (1881)	Wild animals Nuts & berries Logs & lumber Potential land for railway right-of-way
	EXTENSIVE SUBSISTENCE	Chippewa indians	Wild animals Nuts & berries Wood & bark

Figure 31. Sequent occupance in Upsala, Minnesota. (Source: Brown, R. H., 'The Upsala, Minnesota Community: A Case Study in Rural Dynamics', *Annals of the Association of American Geographers*, 57, 1967, pp 267–300)

which has experienced at least five distinct periods of sequent occupance: a first which involved Dakota- and Chippewa-Indian cultures, followed by two eras of frontier colonisation during the late nineteenth century, then an early twentieth-century phase of rural modernisation and, more recently, a greater integration with American society generally[26] (Fig. 31).

Although the concept of sequent occupance was used extensively as a framework for analysing the settling of different parts of the world, it still fails to explain adequately how the process actually operates. In addition, the tendency to focus upon local detail in such empirical investigations precludes the achievement of more precise explanations capable of generalisation. In common with other branches of human geography, recent research on the rural settlement process has become increasingly concerned with isolating the major factors involved, usually by the adoption of a theoretical stance. There are two examples of this model-building approach which are worthy of detailed consideration:

1. *An inductive approach* In an analysis of the colonisation of Pite Lappmark in northern Sweden, Bylund attempted to explain his own observation that '. . . some good land close to established settlements and well suited for colonization may remain unsettled. On the contrary, other localities in remote districts and with inferior natural conditions may have been cultivated surprisingly early.'[27] Within the study area he noted that the settlement process could be subdivided into two stages: the first involved long-distance in-migration of individuals and families, and the second the short-distance migration out from the initial settlements by the sons of the first settlers and then their sons etc, a feature for which Bylund coined the term 'clone-colonisation'. In order to isolate the factors involved, the analysis was taken a stage further by an attempt to simulate the process through time.[28] Since nearly three-quarters of the settlements in Pite Lappmark before 1870 were the result of clone-colonisation it was assumed in the model that the area was initially settled by a few poor

families and the spread of later settlement carried out by their descendants. On this basis several possible ways in which the settlement might have spread were considered (Fig. 32). In the final model greater congruence with reality was achieved when it was assumed that those areas close to a parent settlement, a road, a church, and a market place were of great attraction. Although from a visual comparison between an actual and a simulated map Bylund concluded that it 'cannot be said to be immediately striking as regards the formation of the pattern',[29] this model does begin to dissect the components of the process.

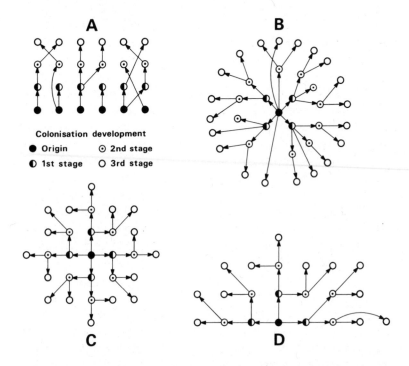

Figure 32.   Hypothetical models of settlement diffusion. The only major difference between the four models is in the number and the location of the mother settlements; A and D assume spread from a coastal location, B and C assume spread from an inland location. (Source: Bylund, E., 'Theoretical Considerations Regarding the Distribution of Settlement in Inner North Sweden', *Geografiska Annaler*, 42, 1960, pp 225–31)

More recently, in a study of the settlement process in Upper Canada, Norton assessed the relative rank and sensitivity of land availability, point of entry, land quality and distance to market in relation to a settler's decision to locate.[30] Settlement patterns for years between 1782 and 1851 were simulated and comparisons with actual patterns by means of correlation analysis revealed greater congruence than in the Bylund study.

2. *A deductive approach* Following the success of the inductive approach in providing a greater insight into the settlement process one major study has adopted a more deductive stance. In an important paper Hudson attempted to integrate the diffusion process inherent within Bylund's model with location theory, as envisaged by the Löschian central place model, in a location theory for rural settlement.[31] In Hudson's theory the settlement process is envisaged as analogous to the spread of plants and animals, and three phases may be postulated: colonisation, spread and competition. In plant ecology the first of these phases involves the invasion of a new area by a species, which in terms of settlement is analogous to the settling of migrants from beyond the local region. The second phase is characterised by the expansion of settlement as a result of secondary colonisation of a clone-type, a feature which is similar to the biological regeneration and short-distance dispersal through root development or the hatching of larvae from heaps of eggs. The final phase is reached in biological terms when, as a result of limitations of the environment, weak individuals are forced out by stronger neighbours, density decreases and the pattern becomes more stable; its counterpart on settlement geography is the tendency for growing numbers of rural dwellers to compete for space, producing a greater regularity in settlement patterns as postulated by central place theory (see chapter six).

Despite the elegance and simplicity of Hudson's deductive theory it has yet to receive the rigorous testing that it deserves. The most comprehensive test has been Hudson's own analysis of settlement change in six Iowan counties between 1870 and 1960, in which it was shown that the regularity of settlement spacing increased with time as a result of changes in the counties' agricultural economy, requiring fewer but larger farms.[32] However, some additional supporting evidence for parts of this theory can be gleaned from two other sources. By reworking Bylund's data on Pite Lappmark, using both trend surface and cell counting analysis, Olsson identified a pattern of contagious distribution which indirectly confirmed the significance of clone-colonisation in settlement expansion.[33] Interestingly, within the context of Christaller and Von Thünen-type locational principles, Siddle has proposed a hypothetical generation of settlement patterns in a subsistence economy which has considerable affinity with Hudson's theory.[34]

Recently this rural settlement theory, like other biologically derived models in human geography, has come under attack from behavioural geographers on at least two counts: first, that to equate human existence with the competition of the plant and animal world, without reference to a specific cultural milieu, is highly dangerous, and secondly, that man does not act like a plant or animal since he has values and attitudes which play a significant role in his locational decision-making. In fact, it has been claimed that to test Hudson's model in Iowa is irrelevant since Iowan farmers are atypical because of 'their high degree of individualism which stimulates them to a greater measure of competition than is usually found among rural societies, and their complex and highly diversified origin which is also rather unusual among rural societies'.[35] The necessity to consider the cultural context in settlement diffusion can be illustrated most effectively from two West African case-studies. Hunter has revealed that settlement dispersal in northern Ghana commences with domestic fission within agnatic lineages from the home farms through land division by inheritance into strips.[36] Figure 33 suggests four modes of settlement dispersal; in the fourth case migration over long distances was necessary since the inherited strips had become too small. This continual dispersal from a core area, usually a defensive hill site, was in turn associated with lineage affiliation. Among the Nike clan in northern Iboland, Nigeria,

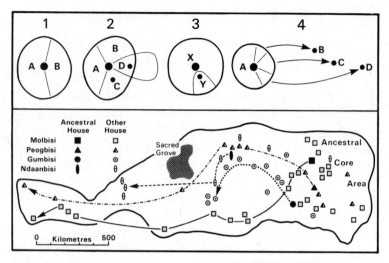

Figure 33.   Settlement diffusion in northern Ghana: (*above*) modes of
settlement dispersion; (*below*) lineage affiliation in settlement dispersion.
(Source: Hunter, J. M., 'The Social Roots of Dispersed Settlement in
Northern Ghana', *Annals of the Association of American Geographers*, 57,
1967, pp 338–49)

Grossman has shown that its frontier zones had been settled,
whilst more fertile and accessible lands were still unoccupied[37]
(Fig. 34). Such a distinctive settlement pattern can only be
understood within the context of the clan's aggressive nature
and its tendency to settle slaves and captives along the frontier
for protection from attack and infiltration. These two studies
show that the choice of new sites for farms is determined by the
distinctive method of settlement of each clan or lineage, according to the way it controls land allocation and tenure, and
emphasise the fact that economic necessity is not always the
prime determinant of settlement dispersal. Similar points are
advocated in many studies of early European settlement:[38] for
example, the manner in which early settlement evolved in the
Balkans reveals considerable affinity with that in Ghana and
Nigeria (Fig. 35). Chisholm has concluded that in the diffusion
of such 'daughter' settlements from the 'mother' settlement
four major changes may be involved: the removal of the need

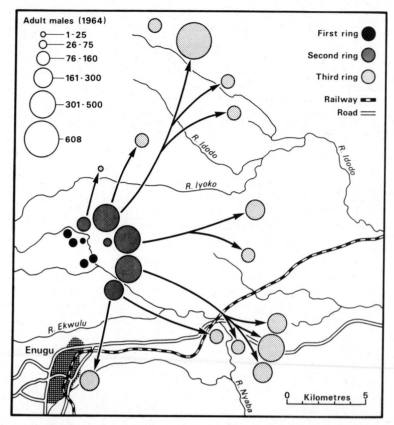

Figure 34. Settlement diffusion in northern Iboland, Nigeria. (Source: Grossman, D., 'Do We Have a Theory For Settlement Geography?—The Case of Iboland', *Professional Geographer*, 23, 1971, pp 197–203)

for defence; improvements in water supply; changes in the land-holding system; and removal of such factors as disease which inhibit earlier settlement.[39]

Spacing of settlements

Although the concept of settlements as points has a long history in settlement geography its analysis was hindered by the absence of a sound theoretical framework and a sufficiently rigorous technique of measurement. The latter was eventually

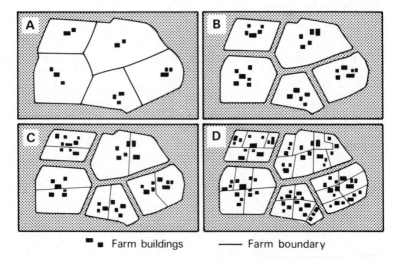

Farm buildings   ——— Farm boundary

Figure 35. Evolution of an irregular clustered village in the Balkans: A—farmsteads of individual families; B—as extended families develop buildings multiply; C—clan hamlets develop as a result of the division of original farmsteads; D—continued sub-division by inheritance results in the formation of an irregular clustered village. (Source: Wilhelmy, H., 'Völkische and Koloniale Siedlungsformen der Slawen', *Geographische Zeitschrift*, 42, 1936, pp 81–97)

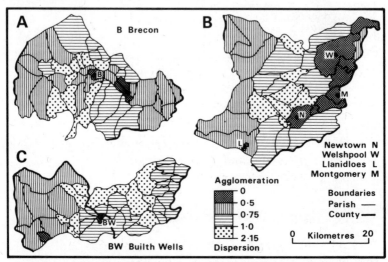

Figure 36. The spacing of rural settlement in the Welsh Borderland, 1968: A—central Brecknockshire; B—eastern Montgomeryshire; C—northern Brecknockshire/eastern Radnorshire.

derived from the work of plant ecologists in the form of the nearest neighbour technique.[40] The central concept of nearest neighbour analysis is randomness: when there is complete absence of a systematic pattern of points in a specified region, the distribution of points is called random; 'a pattern that is not random is either more clustered than random or more uniform than random'.[41] By use of this technique it is possible to test the postulate, derived from Christaller and Lösch, 'that the distribution of places has a long run tendency to move toward a uniform pattern that represents an optimal spatial equilibrium in a dispersed market situation'.[42]

A considerable literature now exists purporting to test whether rural settlements are uniformly or randomly distributed.[43] A study of the Welsh Borderland in 1968 by the author revealed contrasting patterns in the spacing of rural settlements (Fig. 36). By far the most striking feature was the existence of an aggregated settlement spacing on the hill-lands to the west of the region, a feature which can be attributed to the manner in which the area was colonised and, more recently, denuded of its population. Population growth in the Welsh Borderland during the seventeenth and eighteenth centuries created population pressure and many newly established families were forced either to emigrate overseas or to squat on the wastelands and commons of the upland margins. However, these 'new' upland farms were both physically and economically marginal and therefore have failed to adjust to the needs of modern agriculture. As a result farmsteads have been abandoned, particularly those on the hills and valley sides, leaving small clusters of farmsteads along the valley floors as the principal settlements in the area. Similarly, in the southern Corn Belt of the United States, areas of rough topography and low road density were characterised by either random or agglomerated settlement distribution.[44] Conversely, areas with greater topographic uniformity, such as the prairie townships of the western and northern Corn Belt, had a more uniform distribution of farmsteads.

Despite the sensitivity of the nearest neighbour technique in identifying the underlying components of settlement spacing, generalisation is fraught with difficulty since the technique suffers from a number of interpretative problems. The first problem involves the comparability of studies since the R value for a given distribution of points may vary depending on where the boundary is drawn. Hudson has pointed out in some detail that a change of scale can affect the R statistic;[45] for example, a distribution of points at one scale may be regular, but at another it might be clustered. This difficulty is particularly evident if different-sized areal units are used in the same study. This weakness is apparent in the case of the parishes illustrated in Figure 36, although the distortion of the R statistic is attenuated to a certain extent by their relative degree of areal homogeneity. However, it is interesting to note that in a discussion of this problem Kariel concluded that it was 'not so much one of drawing boundaries as of clearly conceptualizing what the researcher is trying to measure'.[46]

The second problem of interpretation involves the tendency for a number of studies to conceive the R statistic as lying on an unidimensional scale ranging from 0.0 to 2.1491. Although this is statistically feasible it is difficult to visualise a rural settlement distribution becoming random as it changes from clustered to uniform. Once again Kariel has proposed a way out of this dilemma by suggesting that there may be two dimensions involved in the statistic, the first relating to the degree of dispersion and ranging from clustered to dispersed, and the second relating to the degree of spacing and ranging from uniform to random[47] (Fig. 37). Therefore, any distribution 'could conceivably be dispersed either randomly or non-randomly, clustered or dispersed randomly, or any other possible combination of these two dimensions'.[48] If this point is accepted then two measures are needed, one for describing the spatial pattern and the other the degree of dispersion.

The third problem with the nearest neighbour technique was that identified by Clark and Evans: 'Since this measure involves only the relationship between a given individual and its nearest neighbour, the majority of spatial relations . . . are

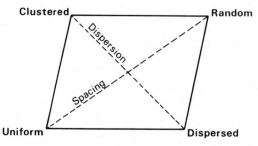

Figure 37. Two dimensions for describing settlement patterns. (Source: Kariel, H. G., 'Analysis of the Alberta Settlement Pattern for 1961 and 1966 by Nearest Neighbor Analysis', *Geografiska Annaler*, 52B, 1970, pp 124–30)

ignored.'[49] One of these is the notion that settlement patterns contain both a random and a regular component; borrowing from the statistical theory of information, Medvedkhov[50] has applied the concept of entropy as a means of separating these two components. By so doing it is possible to determine both the number and percentage of uniformly and randomly distributed settlements, although the accuracy of the results obtained is limited since the calculating procedures are very sensitive to the number and size of the areal units chosen for analysis. Increasingly it is being argued that the concept of entropy is of questionable validity in relation to static distributions, but if research on the settlement patterns of the Canadian prairies is anything to go by then it does provide an effective means of assessing whether a distribution is becoming more uniform with time.[51] Another spatial relationship omitted by the nearest neighbour technique is the direction of the nearest neighbour, a component which is particularly significant when attempting to measure the development of a settlement pattern. Haynes and Enders[52] have suggested that this may be achieved fairly simply by first calculating the angle of degree off north to the nearest neighbours and then testing the distribution of directions by means of the circular normal distribution.[53] Although this distribution has provided a greater insight their analysis of the settlement patterns in the Argentinian pampas has yet to be employed effectively elsewhere.

Optimum settlement patterns

An inherent assumption within settlement theory is the tendency for settlement to evolve towards some optimum pattern within existing economic and social conditions. According to Clawson an optimum situation is one 'which will offer maximum satisfaction to all people involved, and at the least cost for the satisfaction obtained'.[53] But since the existing settlement pattern is slow to adjust to the changing social and economic needs of society considerable imbalances prevail.[54] In order to redress these imbalances a number of countries have set up rural development programmes with the specific task of re-modelling the settlement pattern.

The change experienced by rural society in Western Europe and North America has been so great that rural settlements are in need of considerable re-organisation. The rural settlement pattern of the United States evolved in a 'horse and buggy' society, whilst that in many parts of Europe still retains its medieval origins. The effects of mechanisation in agriculture and the drive towards greater efficiency have increasingly made the small farms and fragmented holdings which characterised most of Europe uneconomic. This problem is not as severe in Britain since the enclosure movement replaced medieval open fields and fragmented plots by large and compact individual holdings. At the same time the effect of a declining farm population and increasingly mobile rural residents is to reduce the viability of villages and small towns: as their businesses decline 'they will be less able to offer services that will attract farmers, who will gradually go to larger towns at further distances. The decline of one kind of store or service will tend to depress the demand for the others; they are all linked together to a degree, since many trips to town are multipurpose.'[55] The effects of the changes are particularly severe on the old and the poor, since the provision of basic utilities for a dispersed population is expensive.

In the Third World the rural settlement pattern is also becoming obsolete, principally as a result of the growth of the rural subsistence population and the increasing desire to provide them with an infrastructure of utilities and services. Although individual countries have tackled the landless labourer problem in a variety of different ways, two approaches, the reform of the land-holding system and the colonisation of wastelands, are by far the most common. Often incorporated into these schemes are attempts to improve service provisions, thus leading to the development of small service centres.

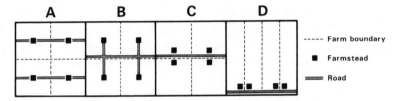

Figure 38.   Road patterns and farm location. The square is the most economical shape for a farm holding, and such a pattern of farmsteads could be provided with roads as shown in A and B. In C the potentiality for social intercourse is greater and the cost of providing roads and public utilities is diminished, but the farmsteads are no longer situated centrally. In D the square is abandoned; further social intercourse is much enhanced, but the farm running expenses again rise. (Source: Chisholm, M., *Rural Settlement and Land Use*, Hutchinson, 1962, p 156)

Before any re-adjustment to a settlement pattern can take place it is necessary to determine the optimum bearing in mind the nature of the existing pattern. Whatever measure is chosen to determine the optimum it is necessary to consider two forces, those operating within a farm and those between the farm and places providing services and markets. Figure 38 illustrates different potential sites for individual settlements. The cost and benefits of these alternatives have to be considered in any re-adjustment of the existing settlement pattern and a number of methods, ranging from the simplistic to the sophisticated, have been employed to determine the optimum. Some idea as to the efficiency of these methods can be gleaned from experiences in rural Britain.[56]

1. *Simple index analysis* In view of the difficulty of defining an optimum settlement size and the cost of carrying out detailed micro-level investigations local authorities have tended to base their judgements for re-grouping settlements upon a rather rough and ready basis. Generally, such criteria as proximity to work, shops and leisure facilities, cost of service facilities, availability of public transport, and the 'character' of a village have been taken into account, but since these have not been measured in any meaningful way the resultant decisions often appear rather arbitrary.[57]

2. *Threshold analysis* This approaches the question of the optimum from a different angle in that it assumes that a rural community has a population threshold below which economic and social life becomes non-viable. In other words, there is a minimum population necessary for the maintenance of local social organisations as well as a viable service provision and public transport. One of the most interesting attempts to determine settlement thresholds was that carried out by Edwards in north-east England in the late 1950s,[58] in which four categories were identified:

a. Settlements with less than 90 adults (120 persons) had only a limited social provision and a rapid declining population.

b. Those with between 90 and 120 adults (120–160 persons) were below the threshold for population growth.

c. Those with between 120 and 140 adults (160–180 persons) had maintained adequate social provision, and were therefore regarded as a minimum size for regrouped settlements.

d. Those above 140 adults (180 persons) had inconsistent demographic histories, but from 450 adults (750 persons) there was population growth with an adequate social provision.

Despite the usefulness of this type of analysis in choosing 'efficient' locations, however, it fails to consider alternative patterns of settlement which may be more viable in terms of community life, operating costs, or some other criteria.

3. *Cost-benefit analysis* More recently there has been a shift in approach towards the use of cost-benefit analysis in the consideration of alternative settlement patterns. An instructive example is the study carried out by Warford in the South Atcham district of Shropshire.[59] The study originated because of the need to provide piped water to all the households and since this was costly it was decided to consider alternative settlement patterns. Fifteen re-groupings of the population were considered and each was compared with extending the piped water to the existing settlements, so that scale economies in water distribution could be realised. Their impact upon the social costs of a number of services, e.g. housing, schools, travel to work, electricity etc., was also analysed. This approach certainly provides a more 'objective' basis for a settlement re-modelling scheme.

The re-modelling of the rural settlement pattern, whether for economic, social or political reasons, is taking place at an increasing scale, in both the developed and the developing world. There has been a massive growth in the geographical and planning literature on this theme, but unfortunately the greater part of it is rather descriptive and lacks a unifying framework. By far the most significant of these studies are those concerned with the difficulties involved in carrying out settlement re-modelling schemes and with the social and economic problems experienced by the people involved. For example, despite widespread land-holding reform in southern Italy the size of the new holdings is too small and their dispersed locations are often regarded by the farmers as too lonely and unsafe. As a result many of the farmers have returned to their former agro-villages creating a scene which has been so succinctly described by McEntire: 'here was a poor, unsanitary village, probably no better in its physical conditions than twenty years before, but crowded with people, while the adjoining countryside was dotted with modern commodious and empty houses'.[60] A similar set of problems has beset those rural areas experiencing a consolidation of their farm holdings:[61] for example, Mayhew has described in some detail the attempt in the Mooriem district near Bremen, West Germany, to replace long-strip holdings by more compact ones.[62] Apart from the cost of providing new roads and services for the new dispersed farmsteads it was often difficult to attract the farmers out of the villages because of 'the traditional association of the farming family to particular farm buildings and land parcels . . . It was not until all the overwhelming advantages of resettlement had been demonstrated by small farmers that some of the established farmers considered making the break with tradition.'[63]

A different set of problems has befallen the colonisation schemes currently taking place in a number of the developing countries. The nature of these problems can be illustrated from schemes in India and Ceylon. According to Farmer one of the fundamental weaknesses in these schemes is poor communications, despite the recognition of their importance in the original master plans.[64] In the case of the Rajasthan Canal project it was recognised that 'a satisfactory standard of communications is a basic necessity for development . . . It is essential as an amenity for its people, is even more essential for development of its economy, for movement of its vast agricultural produce as well as all the varied needs of the community . . .'[65] Although roads were actually built more often than not they were *kachcha* (unmetalled) and, therefore, likely to become impassable morasses in the rainy season. The large colony of Kaki in Assam illustrates another problem. Since it is a linear settlement the villages at the end of the line are remote and inaccessible and communication with and marketing from them is exceedingly difficult. In the case of Kagama New Colony in Ceylon Farmer claims that they are so far from a market that there is no economic incentive for the farmers to attend to the unirrigable portion of their allotments.[66] However, even where roads, whether *pukka* or *kachcha*, have been constructed to serve these new colonies, they are not always subsequently maintained in good or even in passable condition. An additional series of difficulties relates to the market-

ing centres, or *mandis*, upon which these new agricultu
settlements are so dependent. In the smaller schemes the farmers often have to rely on existing *mandis* and even where they
have been planned as part of a major scheme they do not necessarily serve the whole population. A number of these problems
are due to a lack of co-ordination in the layout of the road networks and the marketing centres. In general, the difficulties
being experienced by these new settlement patterns in rural
India and Ceylon reflect not only a failure to co-ordinate each
scheme effectively but also a lack of organisation for their
maintenance.

Despite the considerable geographical literature on rural
settlements the greater part of it is still of an historical nature.
Even when the re-organisation of settlement is being considered the analysis had tended to remain at a descriptive level.
If geographers are to make a more effective contribution to an
understanding of the origins and the reform of existing settlements they need to become more active on two parallel fronts:
first, by developing better theory and more sophisticated
means of measurement, and secondly by actively contributing
to the debate on optimum rural settlement.

CHAPTER SIX

Places
and Localities

The concept of a locality was first introduced into the literature over fifty years ago by a group of American rural sociologists who were attempting to delimit that area in which the economic and social life of the rural dweller took place.[1] More recently geographers have taken up this theme and their research has emphasised the need to consider the rural locality as part of a hierarchical spatial system.[2] The effect of the spread of wealth through rural society has been to raise the ruralite's expectation beyond that available locally as well as to make him considerably more mobile. Thus the rural dweller has to travel beyond his locality for many of his needs, and therefore the rural community has increasingly become tied to other rural communities and to small towns and cities. Such interaction can take at least two forms: first, the population of a rural community may reside within the sphere of influence of a small town or village, and secondly, it may itself provide certain services for a tributary population. However, not all villages have the same level of functions, and therefore a simple functional hierarchy may be envisaged which, in turn, forms a part of a much wider hierarchy involving hamlets and small villages at one end and large metropolitan centres at the other. Thus, independent localities exist only in extremely isolated situations, and at a subsistence level of organisation; since the picture drawn of them by social anthropologists is of a closely knit society they may in systems language be conceived as 'closed' systems.[3]

In general, attempts at delimiting locality boundaries have used some form of economic criteria, in particular those concerned with marketing. Naturally this raises the question of the efficacy of market functions as determinants of a concept which is multi-dimensional. A number of anthropological studies have argued, however, that a close relationship does exist between marketing and the functioning of a social system; for example Belshaw[4] illustrates from a number of peasant societies the crucial role played by market centres in determining marriage patterns as well as the location of cultural festivals. In a wider context, Jones has claimed that social institutions reinforce the significance of a rural community within an overall functional hierarchy.[5] But, before such arguments can be accepted, it should be borne in mind that the success of a social organisation depends to a considerable degree upon the support and leadership of the relevant people.[6] However, when determining rural localities geographers tend either to take marketing functions as surrogates of social ones, or to incorporate the social functions, in an undifferentiated manner, into an overall functional hierarchy.

Villages as central places

Geography traditionally conceives the hierarchical form of localities within the context of central place theory. Although the basic ideas contained in the theory can be traced back to the German geographer, Walter Christaller,[7] in the 1920s, or even earlier,[8] only during the last two decades has there been any rigorous testing of this concept. Although early research, largely into rural communities and small towns in North America,[9] tends to confirm the validity of the theory, more recent studies in other parts of the world have begun to question its general significance. This has led Harvey to go as far as to claim that the 'difficulty of finding empirical evidence for central place theory has proved a major dilemma in human geography, given the generally acknowledged importance of the theory in geographic thinking'.[10]

Since central place theory has been treated in many books it is only necessary here to outline briefly its component parts. According to the theory the importance, or centrality, of a place will depend on the functions—economic, social, and political—it performs, and since the cost and frequency of demand for these functions varies then the number of people necessary to sustain them at a place will differ. This is often referred to as a threshold population.[11] At the same time the cost and time involved in travel will outweigh the need for a function, a feature which has been termed the range of a function.[12] A function with a low threshold and range, that is, a low-order function, will tend to appear in the rural landscape relatively frequently; in contrast, a high-order function will occur only infrequently. Since the occurrence of a function is constrained in this way then in order to utilise space most efficiently those places performing high-order functions would also perform low-order ones. According to Christaller this results in a functional hierarchy of places and a series of hierarchical tributary areas which interlock with one another. The resultant spacing is of a hexagonal pattern since such an arrangement gives the 'best fit' under the conditions laid down by the assumptions. Unfortunately, space precludes any elaboration of Christaller's initial theory or of its further developments, of which the most significant is that by August Lösch in his *Economics of Location*.[13] Although he relaxed many of the rigid rules imposed by Christaller, it is interesting to note that their respective conclusions were relatively similar. Since the Second World War, however, greater attention has been given to the testing of these theories, in particular to the measurement of a hierarchy and the delimitation of tributary areas.

Despite innumerable efforts to measure the functional hierarchy of rural communities the real breakthrough in methodology came in 1958 with the publication of Berry and Garrison's study of Snohomish County, Washington.[14] All the functions found in the study area were incorporated into the analysis and grouped into two basic types of central function: attributes, which by definition could appear only once in a community, and variates, of which a number could exist at any one place. The threshold population, or entry point, of each variate was identified by means of best-fitting exponential growth curves to scatter diagrams of numbers of establishments and population, and when these were subjected to a test of association three groupings of functions were identified. On the other hand, the attributes were correlated with the population size of the communities in which they were to be found, and a test of significance of the ranked coefficients revealed another three categories. Since the two groupings were found to be associated, three classes of central places were postulated. Although the real significance of Berry and Garrison's study lies in the use for the first time of rigorous methods in determining a functional hierarchy, it contains a number of weaknesses, in particular a failure to consider the hinterland population and to distinguish the number and complexity of functions performed by the communities. Despite later adaptations, the replication of Berry and Garrison's methodology elsewhere is fraught with difficulties, and later studies have therefore tended to develop alternative approaches, using either a centrality index based upon the nature of the functions to be found in the study area, or a weighting scale of a selected range of functions.

Of all the centrality measures suggested probably the most effective was that employed by Davies in his study in South Wales.[15] A location coefficient of a single outlet was derived by expressing it as a percentage of the total outlets performing that function. 'Multiplication of the relevant location coefficient by the number of outlets of each functional type present in a settlement gives the degree of centrality imparted to each settlement for every type of function. A functional index is derived by the addition of all the centrality values attained by any settlements.'[16] The settlements can then be ranked on the basis of their functional scores. A major finding of those studies which have used this technique to measure rural centrality is the existence of a disproportionate number of low-order centres in rural areas. For example, O'Farrell

identified four grades among the 143 central places in Tipperary, western Ireland, with the lowest category containing 93
places,[17] and similarly Rowley, in a study in south-west Wales,
showed that 101 of the 115 central places occupied the lowest
of six categories.[18] However, the effectiveness of this technique
as a measure of centrality has been impeded by problems of
data collection. As a consequence a number of researchers
have continued to adopt some weighting procedures, at an
increasing level of sophistication, of a series of selected functions. For example, Wanmali in Miryalkuda taluka, India,[19]
first identified the threshold population of 36 selected functions and by assigning a value of 1 to the function with the
lowest threshold calculated the values of the remainder pro-
portionately. By then multiplying each value by its frequency
of occurrence in all settlements, and summing the scores
achieved by each, a measure of centrality was achieved. The
resultant scores were then ranked. However, a number of researchers have argued that entry point populations are not sufficiently objective, and that median population thresholds are
a better measure.[20] Unfortunately, these are difficult to calcu-
late, if not impossible, when the number of functions is small.
In a study of a part of Nigeria Abiodun attempted to overcome
this difficulty by subjecting her weighted measures to a principal component analysis in order to derive trait complexes.[21]
More recently, and with greater success, Bell, Lieber and
Rushton, [22] in a replication of Hassinger's study of rural communities in Minnesota,[23] employed scalogram analysis as the
basis for distinguishing the clustering of services in central
places.[24]

According to central place theory a positive relationship
exists between the number of functions performed by a community and its population size. However, evidence now exists
from studies of low-order centres that this relationship is considerably more complicated than suggested by theory. In a
study of south-western Iowa,[25] it was revealed that when the
population variable was expressed as a log-function, two relationships were identified: the first included those centres

with a range of 1–8 functions and a population of less than 100, and the second those places with more than 10 functions. Similarly, Abiodun in Nigeria[26] found two log-linear relationships between central functions and population size; in this case the lowest-order centres were to be found with 1–5 functions and 303–1,500 population. The detailed nature of this type of relationship is clearly illustrated from O'Farrell's study in western Ireland in Figure 39.

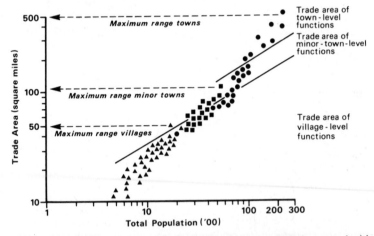

Figure 39.   Relationship between trade area and total population served with levels of the hierarchy in Co Tipperary, Ireland. (Source: O'Farrell, P. N., 'Continuous Regularities and Discontinuities in the Central Place System', *Geografiska Annaler*, 51B, 1969, pp 104–14)

In parallel to the determination of a functional hierarchy considerable research has gone into delimiting the areal extent of a rural locality. Following in the wake of the early American rural sociologists Davies, for example, attempted to delimit for a series of villages in the Welsh Borderland the outer limits of their dependent population[27] (Fig. 40). Since the boundaries of a number of these functions coincide this study lends some credence to the notion of what Hawley has called a 'primary community area'.[28] But since this locality provides only a part of a rural dweller's needs, a greater part of the research has

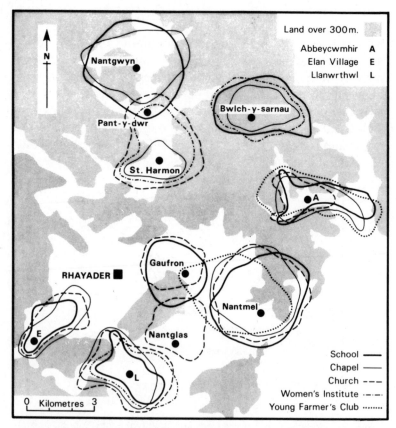

Figure 40. Village neighbourhoods in the Rhayader district, mid-Wales.
(Source: Davies, M. L., *Town, Village and Hamlet in Mid-Wales*, unpublished University of Wales PhD thesis, 1965)

been focused upon the relationship between rural communities and higher order centres. This relationship can be analysed from two viewpoints: outwards from the towns, and inwards from the countryside. In the former type of study the tendency has been to select specific indices which purport to measure the rural dependence upon a town. An early example of this approach is Dickinson's study of small market towns and villages in East Anglia.[29] Despite refinements of Dickinson's methodology in a number of later studies, it is still characterised by a number of basic weaknesses, in particular its dependence upon the availability of suitable data and a tendency to over-generalise the pattern. The alternative approach, that of looking at the town from the viewpoint of the rural area, was initiated by Bracey[30] and developed further with the use of more sophisticated means of measurement in more recent studies.[31] Even this approach suffers from inherent weaknesses, the problem of sampling a representative population and the selection of suitable functions being the most fundamental. These problems are, of course, particularly severe when attempting to relate the size of the rural locality to different levels of a functional hierarchy. For example, O'Farrell in his study in Tipperary[32] selected functional indices such as hardware for village-level functions, banking and footwear for minor-town-level functions, and dry-cleaning and dental services for town-level functions (Fig. 39). In order to overcome the problem of functional selection some recent studies have attempted to elucidate the frequency of visits to various centres and ranked the flows according to the size of the movement as first-, second-, and third-rank.[33] By employing graph theory techniques it is possible not only to 'divide a set of cities into sub-groups which specify a central place and its subordinate hierarchy but also dependent areas of differing functional order'.[34] Figure 41 reveals the movement of Leicestershire's rural population for shopping purposes during a fourteen-day period. Local and regional flows are identified as well as the interdependence of all the communities as shopping centres. The low dependence upon the rural service centres is no doubt a reflection of the population's high mobility rates, and hence the widespread occurrence of multi-purpose visits to major centres such as Leicester, Loughborough and Hinckley. A similar interpretation can be made of the tendency revealed in Figure 39 for the trade area of a particular function to be greater in the case of a high-order centre than of a low-order one.

As the modes of measurement improve, and the number of studies increase, it has become apparent that the central place organisation of rural communities does not conform as closely

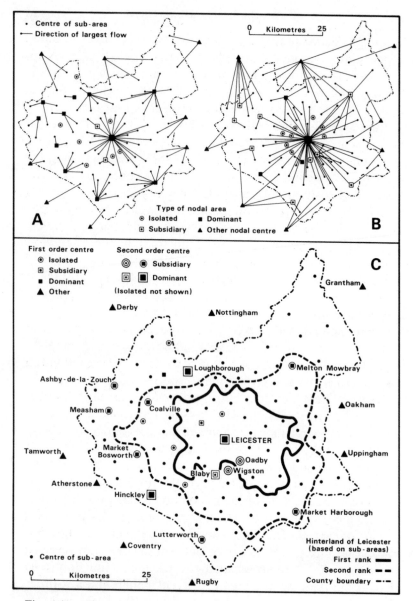

Figure 41. The nodal structure of Leicestershire: A—first-ranking connections; B—second-ranking connections; C—nodal structure. (Source: Lewis, G. J., 'Leicester: Urban Structure and Regional Relationships' in Pye, N. (ed), *Leicester and its Region*, Leicester University Press, 1972, pp 455–78)

to the tenets of classical theory as was initially revealed. There are at least three sources of explanation for this discrepancy:

1. A tendency to regard rural localities as mirror images of functional location. In recent years, however, it has been shown that consumer behaviour does not conform exactly to that predicted by central place theory. As a result there is a need to consider consumer preferences.

2. A tendency to group the majority of rural communities as undifferentiated low-order centres. Increasingly evidence is being gathered which emphasises the fallacy of grouping together all such places because in reality they are often differentiated by the type and nature of the functions they perform. In many ways, Christaller's 'auxiliary central places' are analogous to these communities. In addition, at this level of sophistication, some consideration must be given to the role of periodicity in any meaningful analysis of the centrality of rural communities.

3. A tendency to regard a central place system as standard and unchanging. However, a more realistic interpretation is that it reflects a particular level of economic development and can therefore take different forms in different environments. Even when the system does exist it has become evident that it is constantly in the throes of change as a result of widespread economic and social changes. Clearly in any consideration of centrality there is a need to incorporate a time, or stage, component into the analysis.

Consumer preferences

According to Carter 'classical central place theory often gives the impression of a deterministic, rigid structure, established on the day of creation, to which mere mortals have no option but to conform . . . on the other hand, a given system exists to be perceived in a variety of ways'.[35] Such a questioning of the deterministic explanation of consumer travel patterns in rural society has been thoroughly analysed by Golledge, Rushton

and Clark among the dispersed farm population of Iowa.[36]
They attempted to test the assumption that individuals will
travel shorter distances for those commodities which occur
most frequently. A rank correlation of the order of entry of
commodities by distance to both nearest and farthest place of
purchase revealed correlation coefficients of 0.32 and 0.23,
neither of which was significant at the 0.01 confidence level.
Also it was shown that 'the grouping of central place functions
on the basis of travel behaviour produces a different ordering
of functions on the basis of occurrence of functions'.[37] This
study emphasises the fact that rural dwellers discriminate between central places, and hence more recent research has been
concerned with the manner in which this discrimination manifests itself.

Any consideration of the factors likely to influence consumer preferences must inevitably begin with Harold
Swedner's *Ecological Differentiation of Habits and Attitudes*.[38]
In this study significant differences were revealed between the
farmers and workers of the catchment area of a small Swedish

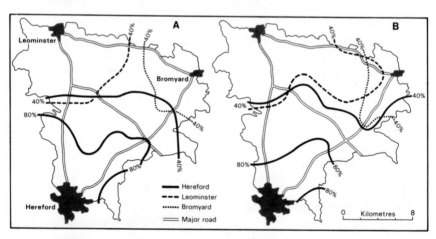

Figure 42. Shopping movement in north Herefordshire: A—manual workers; B—non-manual workers. (Source: Maund, D. J., *Shopping Centres in
Herefordshire*, unpublished University of Leicester BA dissertation, 1968,
p 47)

town with regard to the frequency of their visits to service establishments, the aspiration level for access to such establishments, and the satisfaction with actual distance to the nearest one. These differences were explained in terms not only of time and cost but also of the attitudes and interests of the consumers. Among the residents of a group of Herefordshire villages Maund has also identified sharp contrasts in the shopping habits of manual and non-manual workers:[39] Figure 42 indicates that Hereford has a greater range for manual than non-manual, both at the 80 per cent and 40 per cent levels. Such a behaviour pattern was explicable by the greater use of centres outside the county by the non-manual workers and by the fact that in the case of manual workers journeys to Hereford were multi-purpose, i.e. for shopping and entertainment. Similarly, great differences have been identified in the consumer behaviour patterns of various cultural groups to be found in south-west Ontario, for example between the French- and English-speaking Canadians[40] and between the old-order Mennonites and modern Canadians.[41]

Even within the developing world significant differences have been identified in the consumer travel patterns of the rural population. In her study of south-west Nigeria Abiodun revealed that consumers did not always patronise the nearest available centres[42] (Fig. 43), and explained this nonconformity in terms of three major factors. First, the inadequate transport system often forced consumers to travel farther than would have been necessary if there had been a direct link with the nearest centre; secondly, the continuing historical link between a daughter settlement and its parent town encouraged many to by-pass an alternative higher-order centre; and thirdly, in certain cases the occupation of consumers influenced their travel patterns. In their study of consumer behaviour among a number of villages in a part of Uttar Pradesh, India, Prakasa Rao and Ramachandran recorded a statistically significant relationship between socio-economic status and choice of central place for a variety of goods and services.[43] The rich and medium-class cultivators

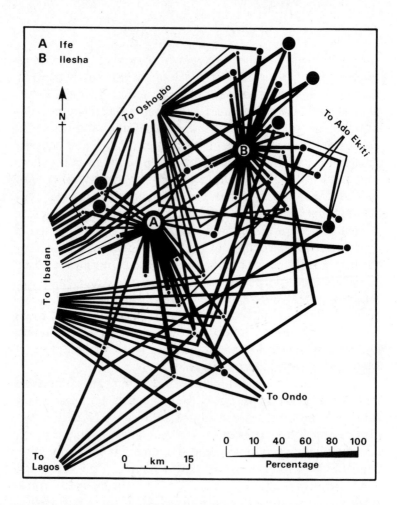

Figure 43. Consumer travel pattern for new clothing (first choice) within the Nigerian cocoa area. (Source: Abiodun, J. C., 'Service Centres and Consumer Behaviour within the Nigerian Cocoa Area', *Geografiska Annaler*, 53B, 1971, pp 78–93)

tended to by-pass Bhopa, a low-order centre, and visit Muzaffarnagar, a higher-order centre, whilst the poor cultivators visited both centres in equal proportions. However, recent research on this theme has been more concerned with the decision-making of consumer behaviour.[44]

Dispersed and periodic central places

Despite the increasing sophistication of the methods employed to identify the central place organisation of rural communities they have, in general, failed to distinguish adequately the nature and type of functions performed by the lowest-order centres. Recent research has shown that the grouping of a large number of low-order centres into one category is an oversimplification of reality, in particular as a consequence of the fragmentation of functional location, the self-sufficiency of certain villages, and the periodicity of central places.

According to classical central place theory, functions of a similar level of importance should 'nest' together at some central location, but recent work on low-order rural centres has begun to question the validity of this aspect of the theory. Evidence from the British Isles indicates that different functions with similar entry points do not always nest together in a single location but rather tend to occur in a dispersed manner, thus forming a locality without a focal point.[45] In order to be able to interpret such a structure it is necessary to conceive a central place not as a single location but as a series which are interdependent upon one another. Clearly this type of locational structure reflects the fragmented manner in which functions decline as a result of depopulation in an already sparsely populated countryside. The relatively high mobility rates of the remaining population allow this dispersed location structure to operate. However, Carter and Lewis have suggested that this type of central place system needs to be interpreted in the light of community structures rather than territorial organisation.[46]

An essential component of central place theory is the existence of a complementary region for each level in the functional hierarchy. However, what is often overlooked is that Christaller, in addition to central places of different orders, also indicated another grouping known as 'auxiliary' central places which did not necessarily have a tributary population. Although the classical central place studies carried out in the

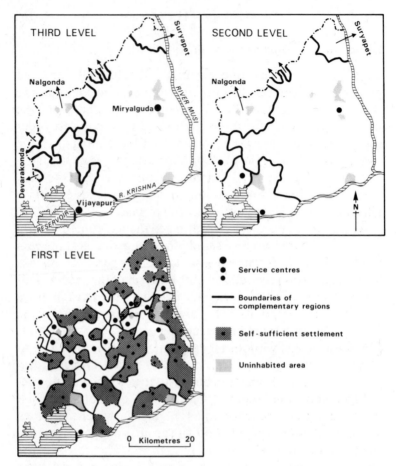

Figure 44.   Tributary population of central places in Miryalguda taluka, Andhra Pradesh, India. (Source: Wanmali, S., 'Central Places and their Tributary Population: Some Observations', *Behavioural Sciences and Community Development*, 6, 1972, pp 11–39)

United States have exhibited the tendency even of villages to have a tributary population, it has been observed in other parts of the world that these 'auxiliary' central places are a common occurrence. The nature of these places can be illustrated by reference once again to Wanmali's study in Andhra Pradesh state, India, where a whole series of self-sufficient villages still exist.[47] In Figure 44 those villages which did not qualify as service centres, i.e. those which possessed 50 per cent of the functions at any level of the functional hierarchy and served at least one more settlement, in addition to their own, for at least 25 per cent of the functions, were classified as being self-sufficient. However, even when the 25 per cent dependency of one settlement was removed, there were eleven villages which did not serve any other. According to Wanmali this distinction in the functional organisation of villages was related to the way the service centres emerged, in particular the way a number of functions, for example primary schools, medical centres, branch post-offices and extension facilities, were deliberately sited at certain villages as a result of government policy.

However, in predominantly peasant societies such central places are even more fragmentary and diffuse, since the place of exchange is periodic rather than permanent and continuous. Periodicity is best represented by a market, which has been defined by Hodder as 'an authorised public gathering of buyers and sellers of commodities meeting at an appointed place at regular intervals'.[48] This system overcomes the low level of surplus production and its corollary, a low demand level for goods and services, as well as the primitive transport technology of peasant societies. It allows the consumer to reduce the distance necessary to travel, often a single day's journey, and enables the supplier to exist by the accumulation of the trade of several different markets. Although the greater part of the literature is concerned with the economic and locational structure of periodic markets, a smaller but significant part emphasises their role in rural social life.[49] According to Skinner 'market structures inevitably shape local social organisation and provide one of the crucial modes for integrating myriad peasant communities into the single social system.'[50]

Following the lead of Stine's work in Korea[51] and Skinner's in China,[52] the size and functional structure of rural markets have been interpreted within the context of central place theory. Although a good deal of evidence exists to suggest that periodic markets are held in nucleated settlements, Hodder has pointed out that in Africa 'the distribution of rural

markets shows little correlation with the distribution or the
size of rural settlements'[53] and therefore concludes that 'traditional markets are not nuclei of settlements but foci of communications'.[54] The frequency with which periodic markets
are held varies considerably, from 3 to 7 days in Latin America,[55] 3 to 9 days in Africa,[56] and 3 to 12 days in Asia.[57] On the
other hand, the spacing of the markets exhibits greater uniformity: a mean distance of 5.01 miles was calculated for markets
in southern India,[58] 4 miles in West Africa,[59] 3.73 in
Guatemala,[60] and 3.65 in Ethiopia,[61] suggesting that despite
differences in population and resource potential the limits on
foot travel are relatively similar throughout the developing
world.

Past and present

A good deal of criticism has recently been levelled against central place studies for their western ethnocentrism. Too often
rural communities from other cultures and other times have
been overlooked; clearly this is an unfortunate oversight since
a full understanding of central places can only be achieved if
they are considered within a wider time–space perspective.[62]
Berry has suggested that the emergence of central places can be
analysed within a development context, and goes as far as to
hypothesise a three-stage sequence: 'the first involves socially
administered exchange. In the second, barter and, later,
money provided the standards of value permitting marketplace transactions in peasant societies. Finally, the peasant
dualism between subsistence and trade has been replaced in
some parts of the world by the specialisation of modern economies, and periodic markets and fairs by a highly articulated
array of market centres.'[63]

The pattern of exchange among peasant communities has
been the focus of detailed investigations by anthropologists for
some time. Following Polanyi's claim that primitive exchange
is subordinate to social customs they have revealed the existence of three exchange systems. First, there is householding,

which has been described as the principle 'of producing and storing for the satisfaction of the wants of the members of the group . . . Production for use as against production for gain . . .'[64] This type of exchange is characteristic of the few remaining hunting and gathering economies[65] and is even found, surprisingly, among some of the sedentary agriculturalists, for example the Tikopia of the British Solomon Islands.[66] Secondly, there is redistribution, in which goods are delivered to, and distributed by, a central authority in order that equity shall be maintained within the society. This type of organisation is still characteristic of the Masai and other cattle-rearing tribes of East Africa.[67] Thirdly, there is reciprocity, in which communities are linked for the exchange of their surpluses. Probably the most frequently quoted example of this type of exchange is the small communities on the Trobriand Islands in Melanesia where those located on the coast are paired with those inland for the exchange of their products.[68] According to Polanyi and others these forms of exchange characterised Europe up to the end of feudal times and are still characteristic of societies in which the market is absent.

However, 'as an economy changes from a self-sufficient to a communal or exchange system, there appear on the landscape facilities for the collection, exchange and distribution of commodities (including goods and services) produced in a spatially separated specialised production place'.[69] These changes are the result of increasing specialisation and the breakdown of self-sufficiency and therefore, in order for demand and supply to be equated, points of exchange become necessary. Initially, these take the form of periodic markets and fairs, the former with local exchange and the latter involving long-distance trade. However, after the establishment of this marketing system it continues to change as a result of increased family participation in the marketing process and the growth in population. Two examples will serve to illustrate this process.

Among the Chimbu peoples of the New Guinea Highlands the introduction of large-scale commercial coffee growing in

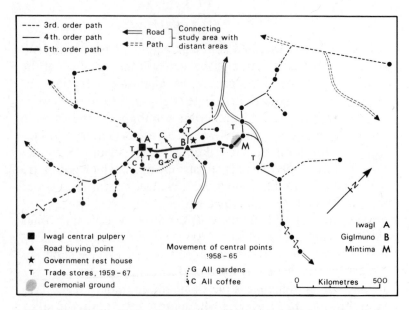

Figure 45.   Some elements in the system of internal circulation and centrality among the Chimbu, New Guinea. Decomposition of the walking network by shortest path to Iwagl, following the most used tracks from men's house sites; distribution of some consumer-oriented functions; movement of central points of distributions. (Source: Brookfield, H. C., 'The Money that Grows on Trees: the Consequences of an Innovation within a Man-Environment System', *Australian Geographical Studies*, 6, 1968, pp 97–119)

1959 resulted in a rise in both demand and income levels.[70] As a result a number of native trade stores were set up along a central artery, which is the shortest-distance path for all members of the tribe (Fig. 45). At two locations along this artery—Iwagl, where a coffee pulpery was sited, and Giglmuno, where the axial path crosses the main highland road—central place functions developed as well as an aggregation of their residential population. The second illustration is drawn from the changes occurring in parts of the Bolivian Altiplano as a result of land reform releasing large numbers of peasants from the bonds of serfdom. Initially, Clark,[71] and more recently, Preston,[72] have identified the emergence, not only of periodic markets, but also of small central-place-type communities for the purpose of exchange and barter (Fig. 46). Clearly the emergence of

Iwagl in the highlands of New Guinea and Baltalass on the Bolivian Altiplano is in many ways analogous to the genesis of central places at the site of grist mills in nineteenth-century Iowa.

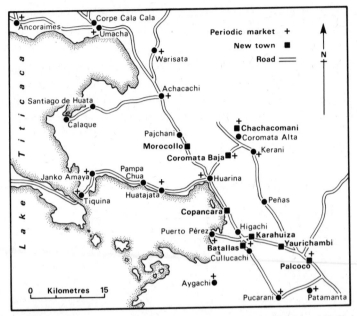

Figure 46. New central places and periodic markets in highland Bolivia. (Source: Preston, D. A., 'New Towns—a Major Change in the Rural Settlement Pattern in Highland Bolivia', *Journal of Latin American Studies*, 2, 1970, pp 2–27)

Once a modern central place system is established in the countryside it continues to change, first as a result of increasing wealth and individual mobility and secondly from the increasing effects of towns and cities upon the rural dweller. In the developed world the coming of the railway and the motor car with their effects upon mobility levels coincided with a demand for more specialised goods and services as a result of an increase in wealth. The impact of these changes was to create a differential growth in the centrality of the rural communities and hence a selective thinning of the central place patterns. This process was involved in the decision to change the type and reduce the number of central places planned for the most recent polder on the Zuider Zee reclamation project in the Netherlands (Fig. 47). This theme has been a focus of considerable research in rural North America, in particular by a group of rural sociologists. Overwhelmingly, their research has emphasised that between 1900 and 1930 there was a decline in the retail and service activities of places with populations of under 2,500. However, since that date, according to Hodge's study of service centres in Saskatchewan,[73] there has been an emergence of central places of intermediate size (300–1,400 population) and a loss in function in both larger and smaller centres. On the other hand, Chittick, in a study of Illinois villages between 1940 and 1960, noted that a decline in the number of goods and services varied inversely

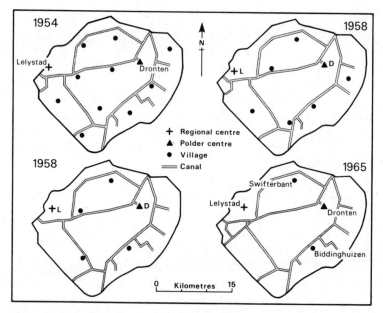

Figure 47.   Changes in plans for settlement development in East Flevoland polder, Netherlands, 1954–65

with population change.[74] In a more detailed study of the period 1939–70 Johanssen and Fuguitt revealed that in Wisconsin the majority of the villages experienced a decline in their central place functions, a change which was related more to access to larger centres than to village size or population size.[75]

A second form of change, the spread of towns and cities into the countryside, is of increasing significance throughout the developed world. This involves at least three processes. First, there is growth in the population size of rural communities adjacent to the major towns and cities which does not necessarily result in an extension of their central place functions. What tends to happen is that the expanding population travels either to the central city or to suburban centres for its various needs, which has the effect of weakening the relationship between population size and functional specialism. In a circular zone of 10-mile radius from Leicester a correlation coefficient of only 0.43, at 0.05 per cent level of confidence, was recorded between village population size and function. Secondly, in those rural areas within the orbit of major cities a specialisation of functions tends to occur as a result of new locational forces and forms of interdependence. In his study of rural Hertfordshire Pahl concluded that a change from hierarchical to segregated structures is one of the distinguishing features of a metropolitan fringe.[76] Thirdly, increasingly the growth of such a fringe communities is controlled by planning legislation, generally within the dispersed city concept. The overall consequence of these processes is to make rural dwellers more than ever dependent upon the towns and cities for an increasing range of their needs, and thus to reduce the significance of rural localities in their everyday lives.

Although rural localities have been analysed in this chapter within the context of a central place system, the need to consider other systems has also been emphasised. In many parts of rural North America and Western Europe the increase in the interdependence between town and village has been such that

the standard central place locality has been considerably attenuated. At the same time it has been argued that in many parts
of the developing world other forms of exchange and interaction take place without a central place system, or at least
independently of it. Therefore, since not all forms of interaction flow through a central place system, it is questionable
whether it is the mechanism 'through which development
occurring in functional space can be projected into geographical space'.[77] Rural development must take into account
the nature of rural localities rather than assuming that they fit
into the standard central place system. 'It appears that the
creation of institutions in geographic space to make them
more accessible is not enough, but those involved will have to
study social space, and devise ways of penetrating it, to make
the programmes more acceptable to all.'[78]

CHAPTER SEVEN

Social Ecology

During the past decade the social ecology of communities has
been of particular concern to urban geographers who, building
upon the classical models of urban ecology, have introduced
more sophisticated measurement techniques as well as more
behavioural modes of explanation.[1] In marked contrast little
attention has been paid to the social ecology of rural communities, an omission which can only partly be explained by
the human geographer's preoccupation with urban studies. Of
equal significance has been the influence of the writings of
Louis Wirth[2] and the uncritical acceptance of concepts such as
the rural–urban dichotomy and continuum,[3] which have had
the effect of making the rural society appear as an aspatial and
homogeneous whole. At the same time the questioning of the
Le Play 'place-work-folk' formula as a means of explaining
different types of social relationships has also indirectly
contributed to the omission of the spatial component in rural
community studies.[4] According to Le Play the resources of a
location control the nature of the work available, which in turn
influences the type of family organisation and the pattern of
social relationships. However, this theory has been severely at-
tacked, initially by Gans[5] and, more recently, by Pahl,[6] on the
grounds that it fails to explain why similar social relationships
occur in both town and country, lending considerable support
to the sociologists' belief that space is an insignificant determinant of behaviour. Similarly, Pahl has also claimed that
change is occurring at all locations,[7] though he fails to acknowledge that such agents of change as the diffusion of innovations and the migration of people are socially and spatially

141

selective and therefore contribute to different rates of change
within an area. As an antidote to these aspatial viewpoints, in
the first part of this chapter a spatial framework for the analysis of the ecology of rural communities is suggested, and then
its efficacy under varying rural conditions is examined.

A spatial perspective

As a result of the spread of urbanisation and modernisation
rural society has experienced considerable change during
the past century. The components of this change were outlined in chapter two, elsewhere it has been suggested that
considerable order exists in the manner of rural social change,
resulting in the emergence of distinctive patterns in the ecology
of rural communities.[8] The prime agents of rural change,
differential movements of people and innovations, are initiated
by towns and cities in their role as centres of change. This
approach is analogous to that of a number of post-war
social ecologists whose work has been largely ignored by
geographers. According to one, W. T. Martin, the extension
of urban influences within the countryside involves two
broad principles of spatial change.[9] First, the gradient principle emphasises the distance-decay effect of cities on their
surrounding rural areas: 'the extent of urban influenced
changes in rural areas varies inversely with distance to the
nearest city and directly with the size of that city'.[10] In addition,
Martin argues that the slope of the gradient becomes less steep
with increasing technological development. Secondly, the differentiation principle claims that urbanisation transforms previously undifferentiated areas by the introduction of
functional specialisation and an increased inter-dependence of
their differentiated parts: 'the expanded community with its
multi-nucleated pattern gains its unity, unlike its predecessor,
through territorial differentiation of specialised functions
rather than through mass production in centrally located institutions.'[11] In brief the principle states that 'the extent of
specialisation of function and differentiation of sub-areas in a

rural territory varies inversely with distance to the nearest city and directly with the size of that city'.[12] Although Martin views these two principles as being complementary, they are partly independent because the demonstrated tenability of the first provides no basis for evaluating the second. However, where the differentiation principle operates then the first holds true at least for the characteristic in question.

The emergence of these spatial variations can be interpreted within the context of interaction and residential location theories. The changing attitudes and values of rural residents result not only from an expansion of the mass media but also from a greater interaction among individuals at increasing distances. At the same time changes in the population of rural communities are the result of greater individual freedom to migrate into or out of the countryside. With the extension of the urban employment field greater residential locational choice has been provided within the rural area in three ways: a move closer to the workplace (involving migration); remaining within the present location (involving commuting); or a move farther from the workplace (involving migration and commuting).[13] For the rural resident, long distances tend to create a higher probability of migration because of the high cost and lengthy time involved in daily commuting, and conversely, at short distances, the economic justification for migration and the burden of commuting is considerably attenuated. On the other hand, the urban dweller considering rural residence faces a similar set of locational decisions.

A time–space framework for analysing the way in which these processes create inter-community variation within the countryside has recently been suggested.[14] In Figure 48 a traditional landscape, Surface A, with one urban centre surrounded by smaller communities at a pre-industrial phase, is envisaged under isotropic conditions. During this phase a marked functional differentiation exists between town and country, since market circulation is minimal, and so rural communities exist in relative isolation. However, on Surface B, a number of differentiating features have appeared. The *no understand within Girvan still at A surface*

process of industrialisation has begun and the resultant market industrial functions, located in the town, attract labour from the more accesssible rural communities. At the same time, this tendency is reinforced within the rural area by a fall in demand for labour as a result of technological innovation in agriculture. During this phase migration is on a permanent rather than a commuter basis, since transport facilities are still poorly developed. Consequently, some communities, especially those nearer the town, begin to experience depopulation (II). In addition, the new captains of industry, benefiting from the success of industrialisation, start to move out into the countryside. Rural residence is seen as an enhancement of status but is initially used only for entertainment and leisure. Clearly depopulation is much greater in volume than repopulation, and these two movements are made up, in the main, of two socially discrete categories of people. Despite these changes traditional communities still exist during this phase, but at increasingly remote locations. The next phase, Surface C, emerges with the rapid advancement in technology which underpins the urban industrial revolution. Depopulation is still a marked characteristic of most communities, even the traditional ones, although repopulation is accelerating, a feature made possible by early retirement among a growing class of high-income executives and a rapid improvement in the transport system. In those circumstances the spatial extent of repopulation (III) has reached a distance beyond daily commuter range. Such a movement tends to take two forms: first, a number of people return to their home area to retire and as such have retained some affinity with the local value system; secondly, a number of newcomers, upon retirement, seek residence in those localities made familiar by regular holiday visits. These individuals would, of course, have less affinity with the local value system. The fourth zone (IV), that most accessible to the town, is characterised by housing estates and expanded dormitory villages, and therefore is attracting the younger middle-class families who are prepared to commute daily to work, not only from the town but also from other parts

due to strong
Kinship ties

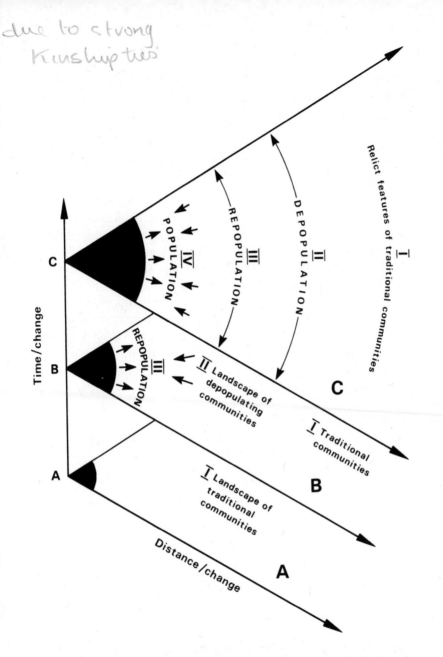

Figure 48.   A time–space order of urbanisation. (Source: Lewis, G. J., and Maund, D. J., 'The Urbanization of the Countryside: a Framework for Analysis', *Geografiska Annaler*, 58B, 1976, pp 17–27)

of the rural areas. The landscape envisaged in Figure 48 is differentiated on social class and life-cycle criteria, and exhibits
an order related to distance from an urban centre. The zones
marked I to IV are conceived not as discrete categories but
rather as tendencies. The processes involved will be present at
all locations but it is their relative proportions which vary with
distance from an urban centre.

So far the discussion has illustrated the nature of inter-
community variation within the context of a rural area dominated by a single urban centre. In reality, since many urban
centres of differing magnitude exist, the processes of socio-
spatial differentiation do not operate in as simple and
straightforward a fashion as that illustrated in Figure 48. In a
rural area with three urban centres, one of conurban dimensions and two of lower order, the greater connectiveness and
range of functions of the conurbation will naturally widen the
population zone and narrow the one experiencing depopulation (Figure 49). Within these zones the smaller centres will
have their own local influence. In Figure 49 centre 1 appears

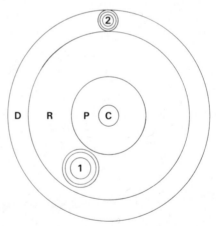

Figure 49. Urbanisation at a regional level: C—conurbation; P—
population zone; R—repopulation zone; D—depopulation zone. (Source:
Lewis, G. J., and Maund, D. J., 'The Urbanization of the Countryside: a
Framework for Analysis', *Geografiska Annaler*, 58B, 1976, pp 17–27)

within the repopulation zone of the conurbation, but at the same time has its own population, repopulation, and depopulation zones. In this case retired people will be found alongside young commuters. Although sporadic visits to the conurbation are relatively easy, daily commuting would be time-consuming and expensive. In contrast, centre 2 is located in the conurbation's depopulation zone, and along with its own population zone it provides a significant growth point in a region of population decline.

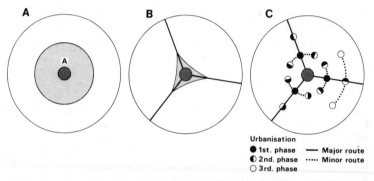

Figure 50. Spatial patterning of urbanisation: A—isotropic surface; B—route distortion; C—existing nodes on distance/access principle. (Source: Lewis, G. J. and Maund, D. J., 'The Urbanization of the Countryside: a Framework for Analysis', *Geografiska Annaler*, 58B, 1976, pp 17–27)

As with many spatial models it has been assumed so far that interaction takes place within the context of least effort, and therefore that population growth will take place first at those locations most accessible to the urban centre (Fig. 50A). In reality, however, movement takes place along defined routes which link a centre to its hinterland, and so a directional bias controls the spread of population (Fig. 50B). In addition, it is likely that population will take place at existing nodes in order to take advantage of the economies to be gained from existing services (Fig. 50C). As the process continues so other locations will be affected.

These illustrations serve to demonstrate some of the complex inter-related web of relationships which characterise the socio-spatial structure of rural communities. At no time was there any attempt to introduce the effects of a hierarchy of competing urban centres which would certainly further complicate the model (Fig 51). However, despite these shortcomings, it is now opportune to seek to assess the extent to which the spatial structure identified manifests itself under various criteria in different rural environments.

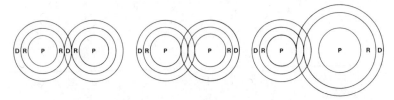

Figure 51.   Urbanisation of the countryside and urban competition: (*left*) equal-order urban centres with depopulating zones interlocking; (*centre*) equal-order urban centres with depopulating and repopulating zones interlocking; (*right*) different-order urban centres. (Source: Lewis, G. J. and Maund, D. J., 'The Urbanization of the Countryside: a Framework for Analysis', *Geografiska Annaler*, 58B, 1976, pp 17–27)

Agriculture and commuting

A striking feature of post-war rural life in Western Europe and North America has been the growth of population in those communities within daily commuting distance from a major town or city. Such communities are being inundated by families, often dissatisfied with urban and suburban living, at a faster rate than that at which farmers are dying or leaving the land to take up urban employment or migrate to the city.[15] As a result, urban commuters are superseding local agriculture farmworkers and a new type of community, neither rural in function nor urban in location, is evolving.

The increasing divorce between place of residence and place of work has been documented in some detail for a number of developed countries. For example, in several papers Lawton has shown that since 1921 in England and Wales urban commuting has spread into the countryside at an ever-increasing distance from the major cities and towns.[16] By the year 2000 Berry has predicted that nearly the whole of rural America will be within daily commuting distance of the major employment centres.[17] However, the aggregate nature of such studies precludes discussion of the journey to work at a community level. In one of the few attempts to identify the significance of commuting for village communities an intensive field investigation of nearly seventy villages in a part of rural Wales in 1965 showed that the majority of the villages were almost completely dependent upon the small town of Aberystwyth for employment and that this dependence declined with distance from the town. A close inspection of Figure 52, however, reveals that this gradient-like relationship did not operate uniformly throughout the study area, since the effects of main road location, the availability of public transport, and the policy of the local authority in controlling village development were additional determinants of the commuting. A similar pattern of commuting has been identified among both the rural and industrial communities of Queensland[19] and the small villages of Herefordshire.[20]

Until recently only a limited amount of research has been carried out on the rural farm population in the hinterland of towns and cities. Since the gradient principle claims that the land adjacent to a city is the most valuable it would, therefore, be expected that farms would be smaller and farming more intensive in such locations. In one of the earliest attempts to investigate this principle, that by Bogue for the rural farm population in the United States[21] (Fig. 53), the general form of the gradient was an initial steep decline in density, followed at about a hundred miles from the nearest metropolis by a more gentle slope. But probably the most striking feature was the variation in the density gradients between the major regions, which no doubt underlines basic differences in their agricultural potential. At the scale of a single state, Anderson and Collier found similar density-gradient relationships in

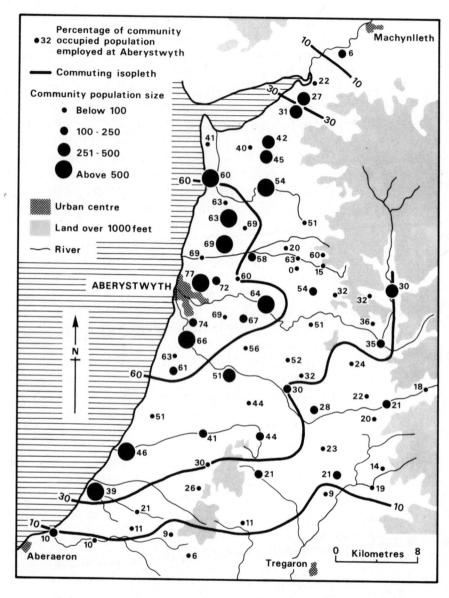

Figure 52. Commuting to Aberystwyth, Wales, 1964. (Source: Lewis, G. J., 'Commuting and the Village in Mid Wales', *Geography*, 52, 1967, pp 294–304)

Missouri.[22] Though farm size seemed to decrease with distance from the urban centres the nature of the gradient was far from simple and straightforward. According to Anderson and Collier, the form of the gradient was also a function of the type of farming prevailing in different parts of the state. Within the Corn Belt, farms increased in size with distance from the nearest farm or city, whilst outside, farms decreased in size with increasing distance. In addition, the farm size gradients were steeper with distance from the nearest city (25,000 population or more) than from the nearest metropolis. The finding of these two studies, along with a number of more recent investigations,[23] cast some doubt on the adequacy of the gradient hypothesis alone to explain variations in rural farm population densities; clearly the nature and structure of agriculture still play a significant role.

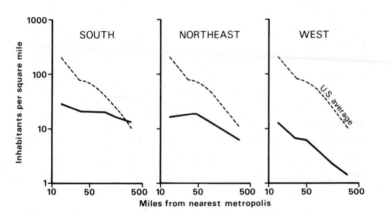

Figure 53. Density–distance relationships for rural farm population in the United States, 1940. (Source: Bogue, D. J., *The Structure of the Metropolitan Community: a Study of Dominance and Subdominance*, University of Michigan, 1949, p 47)

Population characteristics and change

The effect of depopulation and, more recently, population and repopulation, has been to alter markedly the demographic

characteristics and size of rural communities. As these changes
are of geographical interest it is rather surprising that it is a
group of sociologists working on the American Mid-West who
have contributed most to their study.[24] In general, their research has shown that villages adjacent to towns and cities are
more likely to grow in population than those at more distant
locations. A typical example of this type of work is
Doerflinger's study of village population change in Iowa between 1950 and 1960,[25] in which a significant relationship between village growth and distance from urban centres, in
particular those with a population of 2,000 or more, was identified. This suggests that Mid-West villages are sharing in the
same decentralisation of residences, services and retailing that
is going on around many cities in Western Europe and in other
parts of North America. In parallel, there also exists research
which emphasises the importance of the initial size of places in
determining village population change. Fanelli and Pederson
have shown that in Missouri between 1900 and 1950 the larger
villages were likely to have increased their population at a
faster rate than the smaller ones,[26] while a similar trend among
the villages of Wisconsin between 1950 and 1960 has been interpreted by Fuguitt within a probability process.[27] Often this
form of village growth is explained by the increasing centralisation of trade and services due to the rural dweller's greater
levels of mobility and desire for more varied services which can
only be supplied at large centres. In this situation, larger villages have a competitive advantage over smaller ones and
therefore grow much faster.

   When attempting to explain patterns of change in village
populations more recent research has, however, questioned
the validity of treating distance from a city and village size in
isolation, since in reality they tend to operate simultaneously
and at different levels of significance in time and space. For
example, Rikkinen, in an analysis of village and township
population change in Minnesota in each decade between 1930
and 1960,[28] has shown how the relative significance of these
two factors changes with the passage of time. Between 1930

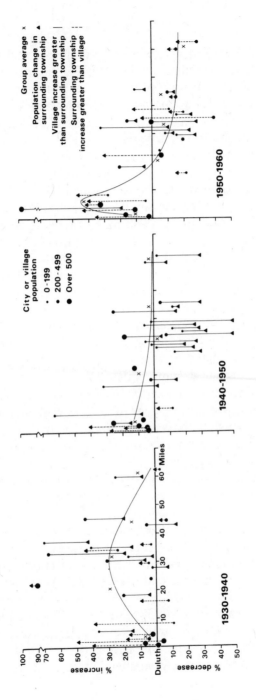

Figure 54.   Village and rural population change with distance from Duluth. (Source: Rikkinen, K., 'Change in Village and Rural Population with Distance from Duluth', *Economic Geography*, 44, 1968, pp 312–25)

and 1940 the village service centres dominated at distances of between 25 and 45 miles from Duluth, and the growth in population of the townships lessened as the distance from these centres increased (Fig. 54). During the succeeding decade, distance from Duluth became the dominant factor in determining population growth, in particular among the townships. Small villages began to lose their service functions everywhere, and at a distance of more than 20 miles from Duluth only three of the larger centres experienced some growth. However, the loss in population among the small villages was less severe than that of the surrounding townships. By the 1950–60 decade the relative growth of both villages and townships had become curvilinearly related to distance from Duluth. A positive correlation existed over a distance of about seven miles from the city, while beyond this distance the relationship was negative. It was also emphasised that only the largest service centres experienced some growth during this period; on the other hand, the small villages had lost their residential attractiveness to such an extent that their population had declined even faster than that of the townships. This study is of considerable significance since it isolates the changing nature of village population growth with the passage of time, as well as emphasising the need to consider the centralisation of activities within rural areas and their decentralisation from urban centres in any explanation of village growth.

Up to a point the findings of Rikkinen's study confirm the claim of a number of researchers that village population growth forms a U-shaped distribution. For example, Borchert found that village population growth in a part of the Mid-West took the following spatial order: those close to the city were the most likely to grow rapidly, then those in remote areas, and finally those in intermediate locations.[29] However, Fuguitt concluded from an investigation involving the whole of the United States between 1950 and 1960[30] that, while the U-shaped distribution characterised villages with over 2,000 residents, there was little difference between remote and intermediate locations among smaller villages. But in the zones adjacent to the cities the small villages were growing as rapidly as the large ones. A number of other studies have emphasised the role of the size of the nearest town or city in determining village population growth. In two significant papers, Hassinger has revealed that in Minnesota villages located around towns which were only slightly larger experienced only a slow rate of growth, whereas large towns made growth more likely.[31] A replication of this study by Butler and Fuguitt in Wisconsin

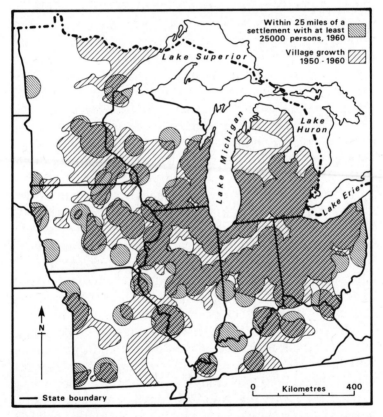

Figure 55. Village population growth in Mid-West, United States, 1950–60. (Source: Hart, J. F. and Salisbury, N. E., 'Population Change in Middle Western Villages: a Statistical Approach', *Annals of the Association of American Geographers*, 55, 1965, pp 140–60)

upheld its findings for the period 1940–50,[32] but for the succeeding decade it was found that villages nearest to towns, irrespective of size, were the most likely to grow in population. It
would appear that the widespread nature of commuting had
muted the effect of competition between towns and villages of
similar sizes located in close proximity.

In an attempt to disentangle the relative significance of village size and distance from towns in explaining village population change Hart and Salisbury in their study of the Mid-West
states adopted a more statistical approach[33] (Fig. 55). A regression analysis revealed that only 8 per cent of the variation
in village population change could be explained by village size,
and the map of residuals on the regression of change on size
indicated distance to be of greater significance (Fig. 56). In
turn, distance explained only 16 per cent of the variation in
change, and the multiple correlation of change with size and
distance no more than 22 per cent. As a result of these low
levels of explanation the authors then considered the likely effects of variation in the socio-economic conditions of the
states. The analysis of variance showed that the villages had
grown more rapidly in some states than in others, and a Q test
identified a statistically significant grouping of states, thus
suggesting the operation of the differentiation principle. Similarly, in the wider context of the United States as a whole
Fuguitt and Thomas found, for the period 1950–60, a correlation of 0.72 between average percentage change in the population of villages and small towns (1,000–100,000 residents)
and the total percentage change in the economic region in
which they were located.[34] Even at the intra-state scale Fuguitt
has noted the significance of the differentiation principle in
Wisconsin between 1950 and 1960.[35] Of those villages with less
than 2,500 population in counties with a declining non-village
population, 55 per cent also lost population. In contrast, in
those counties with a growing non-village population of 20 per
cent, only 1 per cent of the villages declined. Since towns and
villages are closely inter-related, then whole areas may share a
more or less commmon level of population change. These

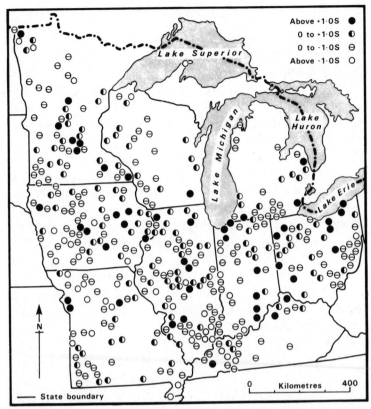

Figure 56. Distribution of residuals from the regression of village population change in the Mid-West, United States, 1950–60, on the size of the village population in 1960. The regression equation was $C = 82.16 + 1.12\sqrt{P}$. Class intervals are in units of one standard error of estimate. (Source: Hart, J. F. and Salisbury, N. E., 'Population Change in Middle Western Villages: a Statistical Approach', *Annals of the Association of American Geographers*, 55, 1965, pp 140–60)

three studies have provided sufficient evidence to make it necessary to consider local and regional environments in any meaningful interpretation.[36]

It is well established that the principal determinant of population change at a local scale is migration. Since migration is highly selective, then the demographic characteristics of those communities growing or losing population will be altered.

Based upon a sample of 570 villages with a population of less than 2,500 residents in the United States, Fuguitt and Field found that they were characterised by an excess of older people and a smaller number of persons per house than was the case in larger places.[37] In addition, these characteristics were more typical of declining than growing villages. Such differential demographic structures may be attributed to selective migration, in particular the tendency for young adults to leave the smaller communities at a faster rate than the larger ones. In turn, since these movements are also spatially selective then variation within a rural area's demographic structure will emerge.[38] For example, Rikkinen has revealed that in rural Minnesota young adults were most likely to be found near Duluth, with older people at greater distances away.[39] By means of a cohort analysis he identified the manner in which such a gradient had evolved. Since the 1930s the influence of distance from Duluth had played an increasing role in ordering the age structure of the population, with the 25–35 age cohorts in particular moving into the zone adjacent to the city and out of the more distant ones. On the other hand, the older groups (40–50, 50–60) were considerably less mobile, particularly those resident adjacent to the city and at remote locations. Despite the interesting nature of this study its conclusions must remain tentative because of a dearth of similar age cohort analyses.[40]

Social structure

The social structure of a community is a multi-dimensional phenomenon which varies both in time and space. Evidence to support this statement comes from the research carried out, initially by sociologists and, more recently, by geographers, on inter-community variation within towns and cities. Unfortunately, the nature of such differentiation within rural society is not so well researched, although a group of American rural sociologists, in response to the acute economic and social difficulties that beset the Southern and Mid-West states during the 1930s, did attempt to delineate social areas within those regions.[41] Only of late has the geographer begun to show interest in this theme. Despite the limited nature of the literature it tends, however, to be characterised by two scales of analysis—village and county—and two levels of measurement sophistication—simple multi-measure indices and factor analysis.

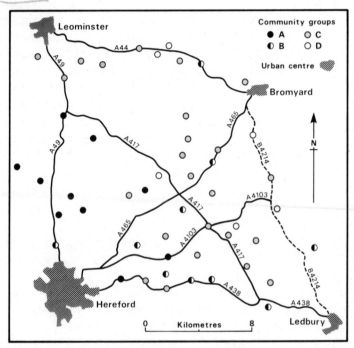

Figure 57. A socio-economic classification of villages in north Herefordshire from A (most urbanised) to D (least urbanised). (Source: Maund, D. J., *The Urbanization of the Countryside: a Case Study in Herefordshire*, unpublished University of Leicester MA thesis, 1976)

An instructive example of the use of multi-measure indices at a village level was Maund's study in north Herefordshire.[42] Derived from a detailed field investigation thirteen variables were initially considered, and only the most connected, as revealed by a matrix of their inter-correlation, formed the basis for identifying the basic dimensions of differentiation, i.e. farmers, commuters, social classes I and II, local employed, established residents, and social organisations. By then summing the villages' rank order on each of the six variables and subjecting the resultant aggregate ranking to a Spearman's coefficient of association between adjacent ranks a fourfold grouping of villages was revealed. From Figure 57 it can be seen that the most urbanised villages, category A, cluster between the urban centres of Hereford and Leominster, whilst the least urbanised villages, category D, are located towards the centre of the study area and around the higher-order villages. In marked contrast, the villages of categories B and C are found scattered throughout north Herefordshire. In general, the location of these villages confirms the processes discussed in the previous section since it is category A villages which are experiencing an influx of migrants, whilst severe depopulation and a falling birth-rate characterise category D villages. Although this distribution is broadly gradient-like certain significant deviations, in particular those caused by private landlord and local authority ownership, can be discerned.

In contrast, the pioneering studies carried out in the American Mid-West were at a county level and based on published census sources. The initial study was that of Lively and Almack of the counties of Ohio in 1938.[43] The basic dimensions of differentiation were identified by grouping the initial 83 variables into six categories, and within each the variables were subjected to a correlation analysis in order to isolate the most connected. This procedure was repeated until only three variables remained: gross cash income per farm, rural place of living index, and rural population fertility. Since these were independent of each other, and yet related to a large number of other variables, the authors regarded them as the most significant for differentiating the counties. In a later paper Hagood, Danilevsky and Beum adopted these three dimensions along with those of latitude and longitude in their delineation of homogeneous social areas in Ohio.[44] Figure 58

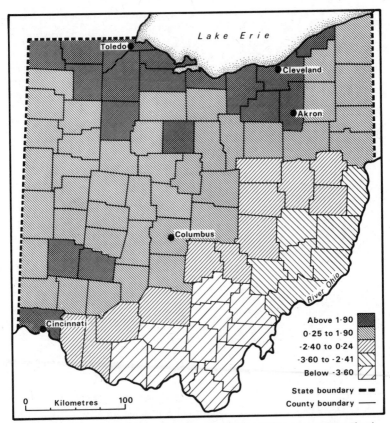

Figure 58. The socio-spatial structure of Ohio, 1930, on a county basis. Categories stretch from high levels of living (above 1.90) to low levels of living (below 3.60). (Source: Hagood, M. J., Danilevsky, N. and Beum, C. O., 'An Examination of the Use of Factor Analysis in the Problem of Sub-regional Delineation', *Rural Sociology*, September 1941, pp 216–33)

reveals a simple gradient extending from a zone of high levels of living which stretches north-east to south-west across the state, with the highest adjacent to the metropolitan centres and the interior cities, to a zone of low living standards along the foothills of the Appalachians. In a similar study of Louisiana, Bertrand found that the urban–rural gradient was less developed.[45] After isolating seven variables—school expenditure per student, proportion of land in farms, age index, race index, level of living of rural non-farm population, level of living of

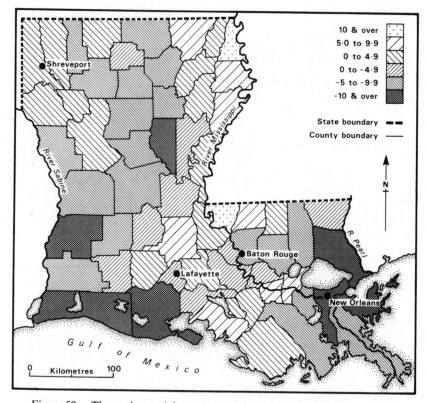

Figure 59. The socio-spatial structure of Louisiana. High positive scores identify areas with low levels of living, high fertility, high proportion of negroes and high proportion of land in tenanted farms; high negative scores measure the opposite set of characteristics. (Source: Bertrand, A. L., *The Many Louisianas, Rural Social Areas and Cultural Island, 1950*, Louisiana State University Agricultural Experiment Station Bulletin, 496, 1955)

rural farm population, fertility ratio—from a correlation matrix of the 23 initial variables a composite index of differentiation was derived. When compared with Ohio the distribution of these indices in Louisiana revealed greater variability in the levels of living and ethnic structure of the population (Fig. 59). Positive scores pick out those areas characterised by a high proportion of negroes, low levels of living, high fertility, and high proportion of land in tenanted farms, and in general coincide with the Red River valley, the north

Louisiana uplands, the middle Mississippi delta, and the Sugar Bowl counties along the coast. On the other hand, negative scores are limited to an area around New Orleans and Baton Rouge, and a larger zone stretching from north-central Louisiana towards its south-western boundary. These are areas with high levels of living, low proportions of negroes, and high proportions of non-farm populations.

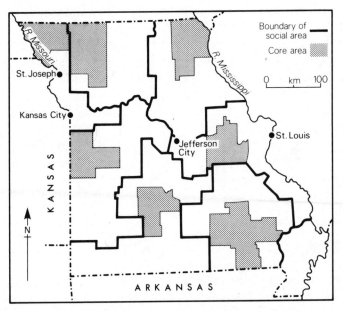

Figure 60.   Rural social areas of Missouri, 1950. (Source: Gregory, C. L., *Rural Social Areas in Missouri*, University of Missouri Agricultural Experiment Station Bulletin, 665, 1958)

A number of these early attempts at measuring inter-community variation within rural areas were also concerned with delineating core areas and their peripheries. The approach adopted is well illustrated by Gregory's study of the social structure of the counties in Missouri.[46] (Fig. 60). The basic underlying factors of differentiation—farm levels of living index and percentage of farms operated by tenants—

were used to compute the coefficients of association between each pair of adjoining counties and from the highest two quartiles of these scores eight groupings of sub-areas were derived. A further coefficient of association computation between each possible pair of sub-areas identified four major core areas. In the south-east, the Mississippi lowlands were characterised by a high density of population, predominantly young and negro, with a low standard of living and educational attainment, and were differentiated from a similar area, the Ozark mountains, by location and the low proportion of negroes in the latter. In contrast, the core area to the north-west had relatively low population densities, low birth-rates, high educational levels, and a prosperous agriculture, within the context of the gradient-like influence of St Joseph and Kansas City. Between these poor and prosperous areas lay the fourth core, intermediate both in location and social characteristics. Once again these patterns emphasise the inadequacy of the gradient principle alone in explaining inter-community variation within rural society.

Factorial ecology

In urban geography multivariate, or factorial, techniques have replaced multi-measure indices as a means of identifying social areas. These techniques have the advantage of being able to isolate clusters of related variables objectively as well as measuring their contribution to the variance within the data. Experience within the urban context has shown that care needs to be taken when using factor analytical methods, particularly in the choice of type of technique, the selection of the data input, and the scale of the analyses.[47] The only study to date of the factorial ecology of rural communities is that of south-east Leicestershire in 1971. A principal axis factor analysis of 51 variables for 114 parishes derived seven components which explained nearly 65 per cent of the original variance. The first component, essentially of a socio-economic character, differentiated villages of a low status (negative scores), located to the

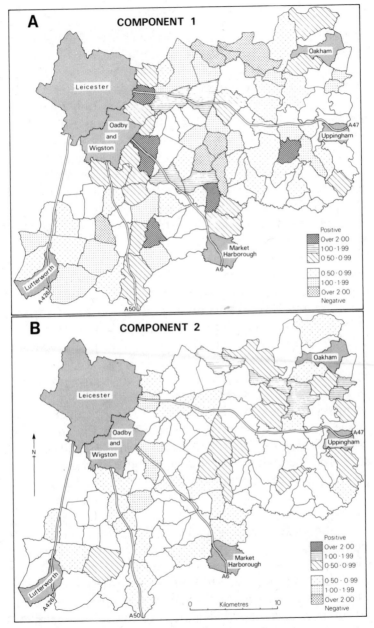

Figure 61. A factorial ecology of south-east Leicestershire parishes, 1971:
A—socio-economic status (component 1); B—mobility (component 2)

east and south-west of the county from those of a high status (positive scores), which were scattered between the urban centres (Fig. 61A). Villages with a population of a medium status were located adjacent to Leicester and along accessible routeways to the south and east. This distribution highlights a tendency for high-status people to seek 'unspoilt' villages, whilst those of a medium status sought accessibility, in particular to Leicester. The mapping of the second component revealed a decline in mobility with distance from Leicester, a pattern which was partly distorted by the high levels of mobility among the communities located along the major routeways and adjacent to the three small towns on the county's border (Fig. 61B). The third component identified the functional changes experienced by these rural communities during the past thirty years. On the one hand, there were those villages, located to the east, which were still agricultural, and on the other, there were the commuter villages, located adjacent to Leicester and along accessible routeways. The fourth component appeared as a measure of the life-cycle dimension, since it differentiated those villages occupied by high percentages of elderly and middle-aged adults from those with high percentages of children, large households, and owner-occupancy. In general, there appears to be a gradual increase in age with distance from Leicester. Despite the preliminary nature of this study the results obtained are of significance, in particular the high degree of comparability between urbanising villages and communities within cities and the existence of a gradient-like pattern in the distribution of a number of the factor loadings.

An alternative means of analysing the ecology of rural communities was suggested by Harvey and Bhardwaj in a study of Rajasthan, India.[48] The study involved 700 villages in four minor civil divisions (*tehsils*), and since these *tehsils* were at different levels of urbanisation and varying intensities or irrigation, mathematical combinations of contrasting pairs provided the bases for testing hypotheses about differences between the sub-units (Table 5). Since there are four administrative units—A, B, C, D—pairwise analysis of the *tehsils* (AB, AC, AD, BC, BD, CD) allowed the study of both the differences within the region and the factors responsible for them. On the basis of 14 variables derived from the 1961 census of India a factor analysis identified the significant differences between pairs of *tehsils* and stepwise discriminant analysis identified the relative order of importance of the variables in creating significant differences. With the introduction of irrigation to certain *tehsils* the region became dichotomised on the basis of land capability, secondary activities, and the extent of literacy, and where urbanisation was extensive the villages were characterised by an intense circulation of peoples and commerce, a feature which was most prevalent in those irrigated areas close to established towns. However, in those intensively irrigated areas where the urban system was less developed, the villagers had to rely on irregular contacts with a market centre and therefore to store their surpluses. In the less irrigated areas there was not only a low agricultural production but also an out-migration of the active population. On the evidence of this study it appears that this type of analysis provides an effective means of measuring the impact of different processes upon the ecology of small communities.[49]

TABLE 5
Typology of tehsils

		IRRIGATION	
		Intensive	Less intensive
DEGREE OF	More	A	B
URBANISATION	Less	C	D

After: Harvey, M. E. and Bhardwaj, S. M., 'Spatial Dimensions of Modernization in a Rural Environment—Rajasthan, India', *Tijdschrift voor Economische en Sociale Geografie*, 64, 1973, p147

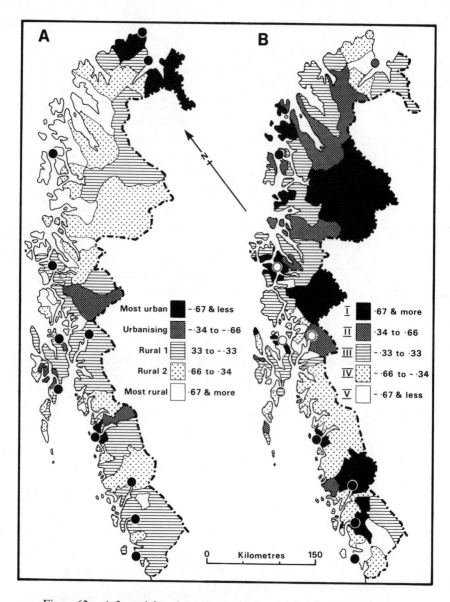

Figure 62. A factorial ecology of north Norway, 1947–65, by townships: A—urbanisation (factor 1); B—demographic change (factor 2). (Source: Sommers, L. M. and Gade, O., 'The Spatial Impact of Government Decision on Postwar Economic Change in North Norway', *Annals of the Association of American Geographers*, 61, 1971, pp 522–36)

As a result of a growing interest in regionalisation among geographers and planners and the increasing availability of suitable data a spate of factor ecological studies at a county or regional scale have been published of late. Despite variations in purpose, data input, and choice of technique it is surprising how closely the basic dimensions identified in a number of these studies conform. For example, in a factor analytical study of 40 economic and demographic variables for the period 1947–65 for 125 townships in northern Norway, Sommers and Gade identified four factors which explained 83 per cent of the total variance.[50] The negative scores of the first factor, labelled urbanisation, picked out zones around the towns of the region, and the positive scores the physically isolated islands, fjords, and valleys (Fig. 62A). In many ways the second factor, demographic change, mirrored the first (Fig. 62B). Negative scores identified those townships, generally dependent upon fishing and agriculture, which have been most seriously affected by out-migration. On the other hand, positive scores picked out not only the areas around the towns but also those involved in the extractive industries. The remaining two factors were concerned with the economic functions of different parts of the region. Similarly, within the context of the interacting processes of economic development and modernisation Pryor has derived the factor ecological structure of peninsular Malaysia in 1970.[51] Three factors—urbanisation, forest area and sex ratio, and household size and distance from Kuala Lumpur—accounted for nearly 60 per cent of the variance. By transforming the urbanisation factor score for each district into a percentage of the highest score, that of Kuala Lumpur (100), an urbanisation surface was constructed (Fig. 63). This reveals steep gradients surrounding the development corridor of the Klang and Kunta valleys as well as Georgetown, with lower and more moderate convex contours identifying the location of less important centres. However, the majority of these 'regional' studies have gone a stage further than those of rural Norway and Malaysia by attempting to delineate 'homogeneous' regions. One of the more

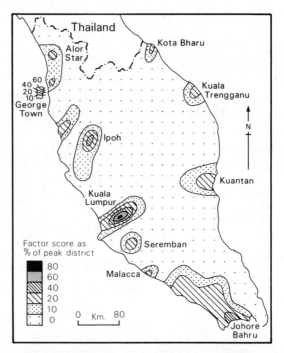

Figure 63. Urbanisation surface in peninsular Malaysia, 1970. (Source: Pryor, R. J., 'Urbanization in Peninsular Malaysia: a Factor Analytical Approach', *Australian Geographical Studies*, 13, 1975, pp 13–32)

interesting was that carried out by Horton, McConnell and Tirtha for the whole of India in 1964[52] (Fig. 64). From a grouping of the five principal components homogeneous regions were derived, and their spatial distribution was strongly suggestive of contagion, i.e., contiguous administrative districts tend to have similar socio-economic structure and the likelihood of membership of the same class decreases with intervening distance. Although it is dangerous to generalise about the 'regional' social structure of rural society on the basis of three studies it is, however, apparent that an urban-to-rural gradient superimposed over regional differences exists in all three situations. Once again the degree to which this generalisation holds true for all rural societies still remains to be proven.

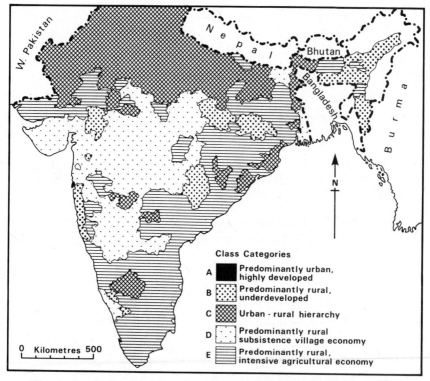

Figure 64. Categories of socio-economic structure in India. (Source: Horton, F. E., McConnell, H. and Tirtha, R., 'Spatial Patterns of Socio-economic Structure in India', *Tijdschrift voor Economische en Sociale Geografie*, 61, 1970, pp 101–13)

This chapter has been essentially speculative, since the social ecology of rural society is theoretically and empirically weakly developed. Many of the concepts introduced have been borrowed from other branches of the discipline, and quite often it has been necessary to rely upon rural sociology for their empirical verification. Although the spatial differentiation and gradient principles provide a framework for an understanding of the socio-spatial patterning of rural communities their true significance is far from proven. There is no doubt that ample opportunities exist for the geographer, armed with a battery of sophisticated measurement techniques, to tackle these and other related problems.

CHAPTER EIGHT

Community Life: A Synthesis

An alternative means of studying a community is to view it as the smallest spatial system which encompasses the principal features of a society. Basically, this social systems approach involves two processes of community development: that reflecting a common cultural or psychological bond among the members, and that reflecting a social interaction. In the 'ideal' community these two processes are inter-related and focused upon a locality, within which the bases of social distinction, or segregation, are locally derived criteria. However, this 'ideal' situation has been disrupted and modified as a consequence of urbanisation and modernisation.[1] With an increase in the linkages between the local community and a wider society new values and norms of behaviour have been introduced. Individual activity spaces have become more widespread and diffuse, so weakening the coherence of the community. New values may either replace completely or co-exist alongside the 'traditional' ones, thus effectively shifting the basis for evaluating intra-community distinction from local to nationally derived criteria. In many rural areas this process appears almost complete, whilst in others many of the 'traditional' features of rural life still persist. These traditional features are, in the main, susceptible to change, but where they are essential to the functioning of a community there is little scope for modification.

As a result of these changes several overlapping and conflicting systems can exist within the same community, thus reducing the effectiveness of a social systems approach. In order to overcome this weakness there has been a tendency among researchers to seek out those communities, whether they be 'primitive' tribal group in Zaire or 'isolated' crofting township in Scotland, where the 'ideal' conditions are thought to be best preserved. Others have sought to dispense with the social systems concept altogether by arguing in favour of 'an interest community which, within a freely communicating society, need not be spatially concentrated for we are increasingly able to interact with each other, wherever we may be located'.[2] However, the empirical evidence shows that even for a highly mobile individual a part of his activity space is still locally prescribed.[3] It is probably nearer the truth to say that there are, on the one hand, those communities where the majority of the members' activities are spatially restricted, and, on the other, those where most activities are performed outside the locality. Margaret Stacey has attempted to conceptualise these different forms of social system into a holistic framework, aptly entitled a 'local social system'.[4]

A local social system

A local social system was characterised by Stacey as a set of inter-relationships existing within a geographically defined territory. 'If there are no connections between the major social institutions in the locality, that is connections which are specific to the locality, there is *no* local social system.'[5] As well as defining this concept Stacey also made 31 propositions as to its form and structure, but since not all of these are directly relevant to an understanding of community life, only those which are will be discussed here.

The initial condition for the formation of a local social system is that the majority of the population will have been resident in the locality for some period of time (1).[6] This system is said to exist when the majority of the residents play multiplex roles to each other (4), and the 'more institutions are present in the locality ... the chances of multiplex role

playing are increased' (5).[7] As with any social system, a local
one has beliefs shared by the majority of the population which
manifest themselves through multiplex role-playing and overlapping group membership (14). In addition, 'there tends to be
a convergence of the elites . . . that is, a tendency to the development of a total social system in the locality' (28), and for 'the
social relationships of people in the population to which the
local social system relates' to include 'those of conflict as well
as co-operation' (29).[8] A local social system will also have connections with other systems beyond the locality, that is, 'not
that the local system as a whole is part of a wider system, but
that its parts are parts of a wider system' (20).[9] Where the majority of the local residents do not share common beliefs,
groups, and institutions a local social system does not exist
(15), and so those 'elements of other social systems may show
no systematic connections *within* the locality, or partial connection only' (19).[10] 'Given that in any one locality there are
persons not involved in the local system (16) and that elements
of other systems will be present (18) the local social system will
be sensitive to any changes which take place in these social
systems outside itself. This sensitivity is increased because of
the connection of parts of the local social system with parts of
wider social systems.'[11]

   Although in the paper in which these propositions were set
out they were not supported by empirical findings they are an
admirable framework for initiating research and interpreting
existing studies. It is within such a context that the concept of a
local social system is used in this book. In the remainder of this
chapter it provides a framework for synthesising the vast
literature produced by what have become known as rural community studies, and in the next chapter it offers a means for
organising some of the more analytical approaches.

Rural community studies

The origin of rural community studies can be traced back to the early part of this century when a more scientific approach was adopted within social anthropology.[12] Initially they were restricted to primitive societies on the premise that the mechanism of societal development could best be understood in a relatively simple situation.[13] More industrial societies were not treated to anthropological analyses until much later;[14] for example, the first major study in the British Isles was that by Arensberg and Kimball of a small community in Southern Ireland in 1938.[15] Since that date rural community studies have proliferated in both the developed[16] and the developing world.[17]

Although the majority of these studies are concerned with presenting a holistic picture of life in a rural locality, inevitably each one has emphasised different aspects of community life. Very few have attempted to test any specific hypotheses, though a number have at least interpreted community structures within a social change perspective. Most of the studies are innumerate, even to the point of not including basic demographic statistics. In general, the focus of interest is small isolated communities; for example, of the twelve studies carried out in Wales between 1940 and 1968, eleven were of communities located in its northern and western regions[18] (Fig. 65). Usually a community study involved the researcher in residence within a community for a period in excess of twelve months and the collection of information by means of 'participant observation'.[19] Also it is apparent that a researcher's cultural background strongly influences his perception of community life. The controversy as to whether a greater insight is achieved 'from within' or 'from without' can be illustrated once again from the studies of Welsh rural communities. Those studies undertaken by Welsh-speaking researchers, 'from within', are preoccupied with religion and the values it represents,[20] whilst those by non-Welsh speakers, 'from without', give greater attention to secular activities,

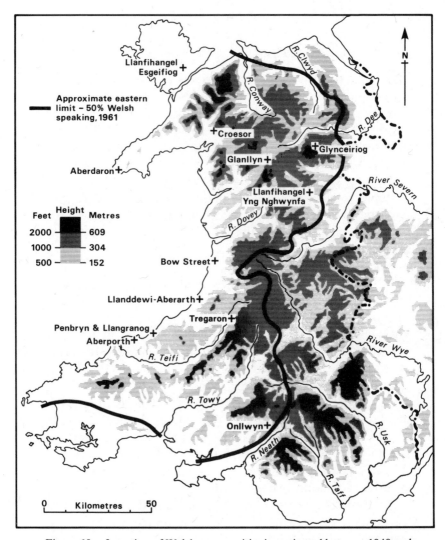

Figure 65. Location of Welsh communities investigated between 1940 and 1968

like, for example, the football club, the carnival, and local government.[21] As a result of these differing viewpoints and weak methodologies any attempt to generalise from their findings is a hazardous and difficult task.[22] In fact, Ruth Glass has gone as far as to describe community studies as 'the poor sociologist's substitute for the novel'.[23] However, this type of criticism is a little too sweeping, since the majority of these studies contain a wealth of detailed and useful information.[24] Furthermore, many of their shortcomings can partly be overcome if their findings are interpreted within a framework such as Stacey's local social system. In this way a greater degree of comparability and generalisation may be achieved. In view of the vast rural community literature available, the ensuing discussion will be restricted to evidence from two countries only, one from the developing world—India—and the other from the developed world—the British Isles.

Rural India

It is widely acknowledged that the majority of mankind is still ecologically and culturally tied to the land at a relatively low level of technology. According to Shanin this 'peasant' way of life is characterised by the following:

1. The peasant family farm as the basic unit of multi-dimensional social organisation.
2. Land husbandry as the main means of livelihood directly providing the major part of the consumption needs.
3. Specific traditional culture related to the way of life of small communities.
4. The underdog position—the domination of peasantry by outsiders.[25]

Although peasant societies are generally associated with the developing world it should not be overlooked that they still exist in parts of Europe.[26] However, despite the persistence and widespread occurrence of this way of life, it is increasingly being affected by urbanisation and the spread of mass culture. In other words, the introduction of a money economy and urban values is destroying many of the attributes of a peasant culture.

Of all the developing world peasantry probably that of India has been subjected to the most intensive scientific investigation. Since the pre-war pioneering studies of Emerson[27] and the Wisers,[28] and the immediate post-war ones of Dube,[29] Srinivas,[30] and Mayer,[31] there has been a proliferation of attempts to provide a many-sided picture of Indian rural life. Therefore, in any attempt to synthesise their findings within a local social system framework it will, as in the British case, be impossible to refer to all of the studies and so a certain amount of selection is necessary.

In any discussion of Indian rural life it is necessary to begin by posing Dumont's question: 'Is the village indeed the social fact which it has for long been assumed to be?'[32] In other words, this question focuses on the controversy as to whether caste or locality is the principal determinant of co-operation or conflict within an Indian village community.[33] On the one hand, there are those researchers who support Redfield's view that 'the principal elements of the countryside networks of India consist of familial and caste associations that persist through generations. The associations connect one set of villages with another or some of the families in one village with families corresponding in culture and social status in other villages. It is as if the characteristic social structure of the primitive self-contained community had to be dissected out and its components spread about a wide area.'[34] But, on the other hand, there are those who point out that this view ignores the 'bonds which form the occupational interdependence of hereditary groups, from the continued sharing of common experience—flood, famine, epidemic, feast, fast, and festival—and from an investing of territorial areas with religious values. Caste unity and village unity are both real: members of the same caste are distinguished territorially, while members of the same village are distinguished on the basis of caste.'[35] More recent studies, however, regard this controversy as unreal since the impact of urbanisation has made the Indian village a part of wider society and weakened the caste system's hold on rural life.[36] In chapter six it was revealed that Indian villages were becoming linked to towns and cities for their market and service needs; other studies have shown that political relations extend beyond the village since the villagers now belong to national parties and partake in local government affairs.[37] The effect of these developments has been to weaken the traditional association between caste, class, and power. For example, Pareek and Trivedi have identified by means of factor analysis that the status of farmers in villages near Delhi was determined by the dimensions of occupation, income and education.[38] Among the villages of Mysore and Maharashtra it has been claimed that castes exhibit a greater deviation from their traditional occupations in a market than in an agricultural village.[39] This difference was explained by the occurrence in market villages of occupations which were open to all castes. Similarly, in an attitude survey of villages in Allahabad, Sinha concluded that the residents of a 'developed' village were more prepared to accept change than those of an 'undeveloped' village.[40] This type of evidence illustrates the point that where a money economy has been accepted caste restriction upon social mobility has weakened considerably.

The impact of these processes upon community life can most effectively be illustrated from Beteille's study of Sripuram, a Tanjore village.[41] Basically, it was revealed that the socially and ritually dominant caste, the Brahmins, had lost a good deal of their economic and political power. The introduction of a money economy meant that the purchase of land was freed from the ties of caste, and therefore many non-Brahmins had become landowners. At the same time the non-Brahmins and the Adi Dravidas (untouchables) had become more socially mobile as a result of the spread of universal education. Above all, within local politics power had shifted to the more numerous non-Brahmin castes since the introduction of 'one man one vote' after Independence in 1947 had given the numerically dominant caste this new power base. What appears to be happening is that the local social system, based on caste, is being overlaid by systems of an economic and political nature, thus effecting a complex overlapping structure.

The nature of the social distinctions which have evolved

within rural communities as a result of these economic and political changes has been documented in some detail by Epstein for two villages, one with irrigated land and the other without, near to the town of Mandya in Mysore.[42] The dry village, Dalena, is an enclave in an irrigated area, a development which spurred a number of villagers on to efforts leading to their own economic progress. A few purchased irrigated lands in the vicinity of their villages. But since available irrigated land was limited and incomes low, some of the more enterprising peasants began to develop Dalena as a small service centre for neighbouring irrigated villages, and others became daily commuters to the factories at Mandya. These diverse activities took Dalena peasants beyond the sphere of their own village, resulting in their living in two social worlds.[43] 'On the one hand, through their daily contact with the town they introduce urban values into the village, and on the other hand, through their desire to become full time farmers and acquire prestige in the village they support the traditional system.'[44] According to Epstein these desires both strengthen and weaken the local social system, since the introduction of urban values undermines the traditional ones, yet at the same time the desire for local prestige upholds the traditional system. On the other hand, at Wangala, the development of irrigation has preserved the farming economy by providing an increased number of jobs locally, and therefore has indirectly aided the preservation of the local social system. 'Dalena's social system changed radically, because the diversification of its economy changed economic roles and relations within the village. Wangala's persisting social system has incorporated many of the cultural changes now characteristic of wider society: similarly, Dalena's changed system still shows the effects of traditional relations and values.'[45] Interestingly, following a revisit to these villages in 1970 Epstein has stated that despite an increase in population and a change in their appearance both communities remain relatively unchanged. 'In line with its past developments, Dalena's entrepreneurs have continued to extend their ventures outside their own village; by contrast

Wangala's investment has remained almost wholly within the borders of the village.'[46] However, looking into the future the effect of population pressure was seen as a major cause of change and conflict within both communities. For example, at Dalena 'an increasing economic diversification reflected in an intra-peasant class cleavage and a further deterioration in the economic conditions of the local A.K.s (untouchables). These economic changes are likely to be reflected increasingly in more radical socio-political changes.'[47] Similarly, in Wangala, 'the few wealthiest peasant farmers will become richer, while caste middle-farmers will become poorer and A.K. labourers may be reduced to a minimum subsistence level. Except for a limited number of peasant farmers who may secure regular urban employment and commute from their village home, intra-village agriculture will remain the dominant economic interest and activity of Wangala residents. This economic introversion will be reflected in continued political isolationalism.'[48]

This continuing stability of the Indian village's social structure can also be illustrated by its unchanging social morphology. Despite the weakening of the caste system's control over social behaviour, it does still play a significant role in determining spatial segregation within the village. For example, Beteille has identified three social areas in Sripuram[49]: the Brahmins, because of its religious significance, formed a closely knit group adjacent to the river; because they were considered outside Hindu society the Adi Dravida resided on the edge of the village; and the non-Brahmins occupied small blocks, based on individual castes and sub-castes, scattered around the village. Similarly, Sinha maintains that social areas based on caste are apparent in both undeveloped and developed villages,[50] an observation which is supported by the morphology of Dalena and Wangala as depicted in Figure 66.

Among the vast literature on rural India there appears to be general agreement that the growth of a money economy and the decline in the power of the aristocracy is the source of the majority of changes within community life.[51] But from the

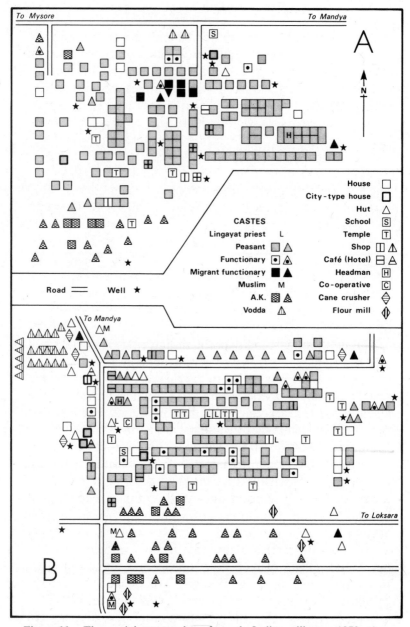

Figure 66. The social geography of south Indian villages, 1970: A—Dalena; B—Wangala. (Source: Epstein, T. S., *South India: Yesterday, Today and Tomorrow*, Macmillan, 1973, pp 80 and 85)

limited number of studies referred to in the preceding discussion it is evident that the direction of change, whether the villages be developed or undeveloped, agricultural or commuter, is far from clear. In addition, this type of evidence should make any student of rural life extremely sceptical of the generalisations made by sociologists such as Lerner in his study of *The Passing of Traditional Societies*.[52] In rural India the spread of commerce, literacy, and mass culture is considerably less dramatic than many authorities would have us believe. However, an understanding of these changes at a micro-level is vital in any assessment of the effects of economic development on rural life.

Rural Britain

Nowhere is rural change more in evidence than in the British Isles. Since the Second World War the movement towards universal car ownership has increased the accessibility of villages at ever increasing distances from towns and cities. As agriculture and associated trades decline the rural population has been able to seek employment in towns and cities without migrating. Urban dwellers who desire 'rural' residence as wealth increases and those who find accommodation difficult to acquire in the city are able to migrate to the countryside and commute daily to work. The effect of these increased linkages and movements between town and country has been seen to change the traditional rural way of life in several respects. Fortunately, since the 1930s the changing nature of rural communities in the British Isles has been documented in some detail. Evidence contained in these studies indicated that despite considerable change the majority of the rural communities were still characterised by a local social system. When compared to the Indian rural community the local social system in rural Britain, however, is considerably more complex and difficult to interpret. The social structures of the communities are more complex and the activity patterns of the residents more spatially extensive, thus creating a whole series of 'social worlds' within the same community. Also the rate of change can be exceedingly rapid, as has been so succinctly illustrated by Ambrose in his book *The Quiet Revolution*.[53]

Despite the widespread nature of these changes the occurrence of a simple local social system has been identified among some of the more isolated rural communities. The nature of this system can be illustrated most effectively from the classic studies of Arensberg and Kimball[54] and Rees[55] in western Ireland and north-east Wales respectively. Both communities were agricultural in function with the family being the principal economic and social unit. The major controlling force in community life was the kinship tie since it acted as 'a framework of reference points which help the individual to identify other people. It explains the stability of the community by linking its members with those of the past.'[56] The extent of such kinship ties in another upland Welsh rural community is illustrated in Figure 67. These kinship connections played a vital role in determining the relationships between families, the informal communication network, and the allegiances to local social organisations. In other words, they were an agent of social control since an individual's behaviour reflects not only on his own reputation but also that of his relatives. According to Rees the immobility of the population could be related to the solidarity of the family, the bonds of kinship and the individual's status among his neighbours, since 'all tie him to his locality and make life incomplete elsewhere'.[57] Within this local social system there did exist, however, certain discontinuities. Since the varied activities of a Welsh rural community 'reflect a system of values which attach some importance to non-economic accomplishments'[58] two distinct ways of living, or *buchedd* (the Welsh term), result: that which gives value to religious adherence and allegiance to local social organisations, and that which supports the tavern and dance and shows little respect for education. Similarly, Arensberg and Kimball argue that 'Irish rural life and small farm subsistence is largely a matter of the anatomy of two institutions . . . the family and the rural community', which form a 'master

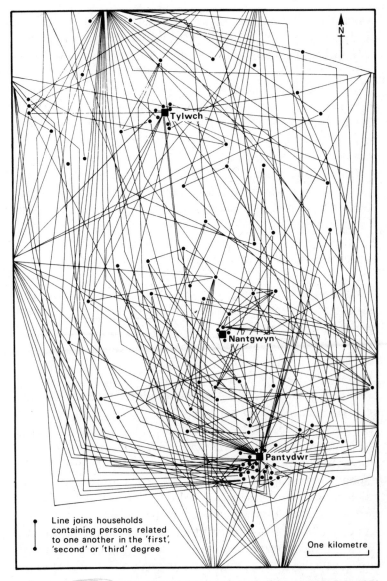

Figure 67. Kinship connections in the Dulas valley, mid-Wales, 1970. (Source: Carter, H. and Lewis, C. R., *Dulas Valley Enquiry: a Survey of Demographic and Community Characteristics*, University College of Wales, Aberystwyth, Department of Geography publication, 1970, p 13)

system articulating five major subsidiary systems'[59]—i.e. the relationship of the familistic order, age-grading, sex organisation, local division of labour, and economic exchange and distribution.

Despite the success of these early community studies, they have been criticised for misinterpreting rural life in at least four different ways. First, a number of studies like that by Williams of Gosforth in Cumberland[60] argue that rural communities are characterised by two distinct local social systems—the large independent farmer and the wage-earner—rather than a single system. Secondly, a number of writers have claimed that a rural local social system is stable rather than static. In a later study Williams has shown that in Ashworthy, a pseudonym for a small parish in Devon, the system was in a constant state of 'dynamic equilibrium' since 'community life . . . is subject to piecemeal changes, is constantly in a state of internal adjustment between one part and another'.[61] In exceptional circumstances this stability can be maintained if a local landed estate restricts any development within a community, a feature exemplified in Figure 68A by Rockingham, a small Northamptonshire village. Thirdly, the view that the rural community is an isolated social system has also been severely criticised. In an interesting reconstruction of the social structure of a small Welsh rural community at the turn of this century Jenkins revealed the existence of important economic and social ties with small towns and villages at some distance.[62] Fourthly, several researchers have questioned the notion of an unchanging rural community. Probably a more appropriate conclusion to the evidence contained in the studies of Arensberg and Rees is that which Williams reached in his study of a Cumberland parish: 'Gosforth has changed more in the past two or three decades than it did in the previous centuries, largely as a result of the increasing influence of urban culture . . . Against this the traditional way of life is static and can offer nothing to replace the loss in community feeling which is a result of these developments.'[63]

Later studies have taken up the theme of a changing rural

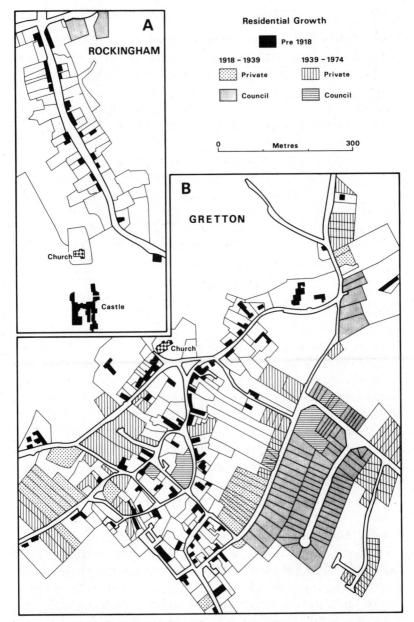

Figure 68.   Residential development in two Northamptonshire villages.
(Source: Lewis, G. J. and Strachan, A. J., *The Corby Village Survey*, University of Leicester, Department of Geography publication, 1974)

community and have revealed that the local system has been modified in several different ways. One of the most readily apparent is the collapsing social system which results from a failure by members of a community to maintain social life as a result of depopulation.[64] According to Mitchell these communities are characterised by a small and elderly population and a limited number of social institutions.[65] However, the system continues to exist as a result of a high degree of cooperation among its members and a sharing of social institutions with adjacent communities.[66] But with a continual fall in population and a decline in social institutions the local social system is in a constant state of collapse.[67] In certain communities this trend has been accelerated by an increase in 'second-home' ownership,[68] in others ameliorated by a reduction in migration potential as a result of the existence of such constraints as low income levels and high home-ownership rates.[69]

Among those communities located within commuting distances of towns and cities the influx of population has provided the basis for other types of local social systems. Only of late has much attention been given to these communities, the majority of which are characterised by three distinguishable features.[70] First, immigration into the community is selective; on the one hand, private housing developments attract mobile, middle-class commuters, and on the other, local authority housing attracts mostly working-class families. Secondly, the introduction of the urban commuter changes the principal function of the community; it becomes nothing more than a dormitory for the city. Thirdly, there is a tendency towards a social and spatial segregation of the population, a feature which may be identified in the morphology of a small Northamptonshire village (Fig. 68B). Characteristically, it is made up of three units: an old village core, the local authority housing estates, and the private housing estates built specifically for the commuter. The effect of these developments is to create a dual local system, often referred to as the 'established and newcomer' system.[71]

More recently a number of authorities have claimed that
this dichotomy is much too simplistic and according to Pahl a
more realistic distinction is based on six groups:[72]

Pop^n Structure division

1. The traditional village landowners.
2. The professional and business groups who have been
attracted by the 'rural way of life'.
3. The retirement group, often former urban workers.
4. The urban commuters who have been forced to seek rural
residence because of high prices of housing in the city.
5. The working-class who reside either in older housing or
on local authority estates and commute elsewhere to work.
6. Local workers who include tradespeople, agricultural
workers and craftsmen, and may be regarded as the remnants
of the traditional villagers.

The effect of this diversification of a rural community's
social structure is to transform its value system from a local
one into one of a national character. Socio-economic values, in
terms of wealth and property, become the major distinguishing feature and the highly 'respected' villager is no
longer the person who plays a significant role in local affairs
but rather one who makes a contribution at a regional or even
national level. As a result of these developments a dual social
system based on class lines rather than length of residence
becomes the distinguishing feature. In general, there is a low
degree of interaction between the middle class and the working
class; so effective is this distinction that each group tends to develop its own separate social organisations.[73] The social activity space of the middle classes extends beyond the locality
thus reflecting interest rather than propinquity; since some of
them live in a kind of dispersed 'non-place' world the rural
community is regarded as simply a 'place to sleep in'. In contrast, the social activities of the working classes are more spatially restricted and so locality remains a fundamental factor in
their way of life.

Bld connected.

Not all of the rural communities which have experienced an influx of urban commuters are characterised by a class-based local social system. From detailed studies in rural Wales[74] it is evident that an overlapping social system characterises the majority of the rural communities. In these communities four groups can be distinguished:

1. Local agricultural and tradespeople.
2. Urban commuters, attracted by rural residence.
3. Urban commuters and local workers, originating from nearby rural areas.
4. The retirement element, largely individuals and couples returning to their home area. *usualey relative*

Although a national value system had been introduced by the middle classes, the majority of the newcomers, however, *eg* still had affinity with the local values. Those originating from *G'rave* nearby rural areas and the retirement group still had affinity with the local area and even the commuter, since he sought rural residence, had the desire to retain the 'traditional' way of life. This has resulted in a complex series of overlapping social systems as illustrated in Figure 69. In this North Cardiganshire rural community four elements overlap: the nationally derived occupational and house-type status, and the locally derived religious and participation status. Since these communities are relatively small the survival of local social organisations depends on their ability to attract members from all walks of life. In other words, they have to be interest- rather than class-based activities. What we have been discussing here is essentially a community which has not been overwhelmed by the middle-class commuter and which therefore still retains many of the values characteristic of a local social system.

It would appear that irrespective of location the rural community is becoming increasingly integrated into wider society, and that the local repercussions of this change are determined by its social, economic, and geographical background. The

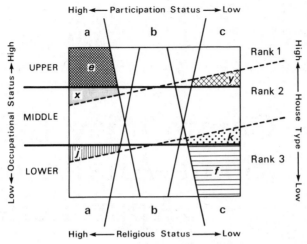

Figure 69. Overlapping status systems within a North Cardiganshire village: e—highest overall status; f—lowest overall status; the remaining letters (x, y, j, k)—a series of intermediate overlapping status positions.

spread of urbanisation is removing many of the distinctive features of rural life, resulting quite often in a confrontation between old and new. In this chapter an attempt has been made to provide a more meaningful interpretation of the changing rural ways of life by introducing Stacey's local social system. Bearing in mind the subjective nature of the concept it does have the advantage of forcing the researcher to interpret the diverse findings of community studies within a socio-spatial framework. However, it could be argued that this has been an unreal exercise since not only are many of the community studies out of date but also the development of new techniques of analysis has made their methods outmoded. Although this may possibly be true it must be said that they still have a place in social geography since they have identified significant and meaningful questions, many of which still remain unresolved. The next chapter, therefore, will introduce some of the more analytical methods recently adopted to provide answers to these questions.

CHAPTER NINE

Community Life: Some Analytical Approaches

Many community studies carried out by anthropologists and geographers during the past three decades have contributed significantly towards an understanding of the nature and changing form of rural life throughout the world. Despite various attempts to place their findings within a conceptual framework the subjective nature of their data precludes true comparability. However, one major theme which the majority of these studies emphasise is that a 'true' community is characterised by a high degree of affinity and interaction among the residents of a locality; on the other hand, if there is little agreement among the residents then discontinuities and segregation result. Recent community studies have attempted to tackle this theme by adopting a more analytical approach. So far the studies have been piecemeal and lack a sound conceptual base. This chapter, therefore, will attempt to introduce some of these newer approaches: since the evidence is limited, it must be speculative rather than definitive, but only those methodologies successfully employed in studies of rural communities are introduced.

Concept of integration

When discussing discontinuities within a locality community studies have been concerned essentially with the concept of integration. This concept involves the degree of social interaction among the residents of a locality; the greater the degree of interaction the more integrated the community. Clearly, the concept of integration is imprecise and many-faceted but it does involve at least two elements: first, the process by which an individual becomes integrated into a community, and secondly, the dimensions involved in that process.

The process by which an individual becomes integrated into a community is often referred to as assimilation. A considerable literature, beginning with Thomas and Zaniecki's classic study of *The Polish Peasant in Europe and America*,[1] has described and analysed the nature of assimilation. The majority of studies have been concerned with the prejudice and discrimination experienced within an urban context by migrants, particularly their exclusion from certain spheres of activity and the problems created by the differences in norms, values, and customs between them and the host population. However, this process can be applied equally to rural communities. The assimilation of a newcomer into the receiving community, according to Germani, involves three, often interrelated, sub-processes:

1. Participation: 'how many and in which roles [he is] performing within the institutions, social groups and various sections of the host community'.[2]

2. Acculturation: 'the process [and the degree] of acquisition and learning by the migrant of ways of behaviour (including roles, habits, attitudes, values, knowledge) of the receiving society'.[3]

3. Adjustment: 'the manner in which the migrant is able to perform his roles in the various spheres of activitiy in which he participates'.[4]

There have been many attempts to identify the stages through which an individual goes during his assimilation into a host community.[5] Broadly speaking, there are two major theories—'melting-pot' and 'ethnic-pluralities'—which attempt to explain the assimilation process. The first theory looks essentially towards the eventual absorption of the migrant into the host community; the second assumes that differences will harden into permanent distinct groups. Between the two, different levels of assimilation may be envisaged.

On the basis of the sub-processes involved in the assimilation process at least five major dimensions may be identified. The sub-process of participation involves not only relationships with institutionalised and formalised structures, such as schools, churches etc., but also involvement with voluntary groupings. Also this sub-process can include the informal contacts and acquaintanceships which can develop among individuals within a spatially restricted locality. Acculturation is achieved when there is a high degree of solidarity among the residents, in terms of values and attitudes, towards the community. The third sub-process, adjustment, is more difficult to measure, but at least two representative dimensions may be recognised: the level of satisfaction with the community and the extent of an agreed identification of the community. 'A community, if it is to have meaning outside the purely theoretical realm, must have position; the interested person must be able to locate it in a geographic context.'[6] The degree of consensus among residents towards these five dimensions will determine the nature and form of a community. Where there is a high degree of consensus then an integrated community will characterise the locality but if there is little agreement then discontinuities and segregation will result, thus producing a disintegrated community.

Participation in voluntary groupings

One of the most significant indicators of social interaction is the extent to which residents participate in voluntary organisations pertaining to a locality. These organisations are of two basic types: local-based activities such as football, drama, discussion meetings etc., and accomplishments with social goals, often referred to as action programmes, for example school expansion, church repair, rural conservation etc. In any attempt to compare participation levels among rural communities or to relate them to explanatory variables, some form of quantification is involved. Usually, community participation is measured by allocating scores to each resident on the basis of the activity in which he takes part, and then by summing the scores for all residents a participation index for the whole community is derived. An early example of a participation scale was that suggested by Chapin some thirty years ago;[7] in this scale the items and their weightings were: membership, 1 point; attendance, 2; contributions, 3; membership on committees, 4; and position as an officer, 5. An obvious weakness in this scale is its failure to take into account the degree of individual involvement, since, as Kaufman claims, 'the best single index of participation is membership classified as to degree of activity'.[8] Therefore, more recent research has focused upon deriving scales of participation within a multi-dimensional context.

As a result of these measurement problems any attempt to generalise about participation levels within rural communities is difficult. However, some idea as to the nature of differential participation levels may be gleaned from studies conducted in the counties of Suffolk,[9] Sussex,[10] Northamptonshire[11] and Pembrokeshire.[12] In line with the *Community Attitude Survey* carried out by the Royal Commission on Local Government in England (1969),[13] all four surveys emphasise that female participation was slightly higher than that of males. The greatest difference was in one of the eight villages surveyed in south Pembrokeshire, where only 22 per cent of the females as compared with 54 per cent of males did not support at least one local voluntary organisation. In general, the studies confirmed the widely held view that the middle classes were more actively involved in rural community activities than the working classes, though some interesting evidence to the contrary was found in some of the Northamptonshire villages. In those villages where the middle classes were predominant there were only a few voluntary organisations, indicating possibly that the diverse interests of its members precluded the functioning of activities to suit all tastes. Although it was evident that length of residence provided a biasing effect, in particular the tendency for participation to increase with the years of residence, this was far from uniform in all localities. In the Pembrokeshire villages there was a reduction in support for local organisations after 30 years' residence, possibly reflecting advancement in age, whilst in the Sussex village of Ringmer the relationship was even more irregular, since families of 3–6 years' residence revealed higher rates of participation than those of 7–10 years'. This irregular relationship may be related to the fact that commuter villages such as Ringmer have a large number of young families and so a number of organisations designed specifically for their needs have been established. Involvement in these types of organisations can be immediate since they are not restricted by local values and traditions. But the studies in Suffolk, Northamptonshire and Pembrokeshire concluded that those communities adjacent to a town had lower participation rates than those at some distance away; those of a medium size (around 1,000 population) with a socially mixed population had the highest participation levels. Where the population was larger activities tended to be segmented along class lines, thus reducing the number of voluntary organisations which involved the whole community. These features emphasise the point that two factors were preeminent in determining community participation levels: a minimum population threshold necessary to sustain a variety of activities, and accessibility to alternate forms of activity. Other explanatory variables were important but where two or more were significant they often cancelled each other out, for example social class and length of residence.

An alternative means of delineating community participation involves the behaviour of residents in community action programmes, an approach which has the advantage of focusing upon issues significant to the whole community and therefore likely to be sensitive to any latent community involvement. An interesting attempt to investigate this type of participation was that of Wilkinson in two small rural communities in the United States.[14] In this study participation was measured in two ways: first, by the number of programmes supported by the residents, and secondly, by the nature of their role in each programme. Differential roles were identified according to a fivefold category—awareness, organisation, decision, resource mobilisation, and resource allocation—and each was quantified on a scale of one to five repectively. Although the prime focus was methodological, a number of significant findings were made, in particular that which classified participants into four basic types: first, those who provided much of the continuity for community involvement by supporting all action programmes; secondly, those who made a less diffuse contribution by supporting only a limited range of programmes; thirdly, those who were involved in similar actions, so indicating task specialisation; and fourthly, those who were involved with a single programme only, so representing a minimum involvement in community action.

Despite advancement in measurement techniques, it is apparent that the concept of participation is far from fully understood. Many of the generalisations derived from community studies have not withstood the test of rigorous analysis, thus suggesting a much more complex issue than hitherto realised. For example, Ambrose has gone as far as to claim that 'certain personality attributes. . . might have greater explanatory power and that the well-known distinction 'joiners' and 'non-joiners' incorporates aspects which have not here been identified.'[15] In other words, more questions have been raised than answered.

Informal contacts and acquaintanceships

Another form of participation involves the nature and intensity of relationships among the members of a community. The majority of studies have interpreted this within the context of informal contacts and acquaintanceships, and argued that kin and friendship relationships were the major determinants. In their attempt to describe and explain more precisely the social processes involved in these relationships social scientists have conceived them in terms of a network (Fig. 70). Although 'the image of "network relations" to represent a complex set of inter-relationships in a social system has had a long history'[16], it has until recently been used in a metaphorical rather than an analytical sense. This change of approach can be traced largely to the mathematical sociologist Barnes, who through a study of the small Norwegian community of Bremnes introduced the concept of a social network.[17] 'The image I have is of a set of points some of which are joined by lines. The points of the image are people, or sometimes groups, and the lines indicate which people interact with each other. We can, of course, think of the whole of social life as generating a network of this kind.'[18] According to Barnes social relationships are made up of 'ties of friendship and acquaintance which everyone . . . partly inherits and largely builds for himself'.[19]

But, of course, in both anthropology[20] and geography[21] the network concept has been used in a variety of different ways.

Of the various network structures distinguished in mathematical graph theory the digraph appears to be the most

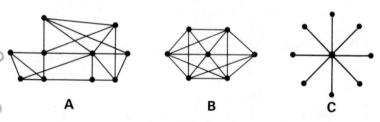

Figure 70.   A—a social network; B—close-knit; C—loose-knit

meaningful in any investigation of community life. Within this network structure there are no loops since no lines link a point back to itself directly without passing through some other point. The main focus of Barnes's interest was upon the morphological characteristics of a network and its significance for social behaviour, rather than the communication-flow through a network. Despite the existence of considerable terminological confusion within the literature, a social network's morphology may be identified in at least four ways: connectivity, or the extent to which connections which could exist among individuals actually *do* exist; accessibility, or relative accessibility between each individual and all other individuals on the network; diameter, or the number of links between the two most widely separated individuals; and shape, or the ratio between the number of links and the diameter of the network. Clearly these are concerned with the structure of a network only and therefore say nothing about the nature and form of the social communication involved. In recent years a number of anthropologists have become increasingly preoccupied with these social 'flows' since their frequency, strength and content are regarded as the most significant component of a social network. According to Mitchell these flows may be interpreted in five ways: content, or the basis of the interaction; directedness, or whether the communication is single-stranded or reciprocal; durability, or the recognition by people of sets of obligations and rights in respect of certain other identified people; intensity, or the degree to which individuals are prepared to honour obligations; and frequency, or the level of contact among individuals.[22] Following Barnes's seminal paper on Bremnes, the concept of a social network has been used in a variety of ways, resulting in a good deal of confusion and misunderstanding. This led him to write a review paper in which he argued that it was 'preferable to use the term "network" only when some kind of social field is intended, for there has been some confusion about ego-centric and socio-centric extracts from the total network'.[23] An ego-centric network is one based upon the social relationships of a single person and has the advantage of allowing the possibility of isolating first-order, second-order, etc. relations within a network (Fig. 71). On the other hand, a socio-centric network is defined by a specific social situation and therefore includes all members of a community, thus making it more appropriate for analysing community life.[24]

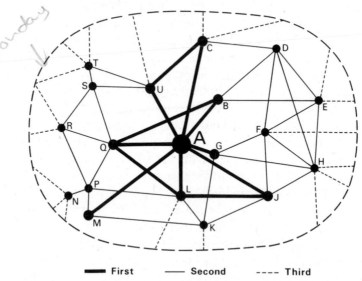

Figure 71. An ego-centric network, illustrating first-, second- and third-order relations

In her classic study of conjugal roles Elizabeth Bott distinguished two types of social network[25]: close-knit, in which the amount of interaction was high, and loose-knit, where it was low (Fig 70). This distinction was used by Srinivas and Beteille to describe social change in rural India,[26] arguing that Indian rural communities were experiencing a transformation from a close-knit to a more loose-knit network. In broader terms, the multiplex relationships between individuals in a tribal society and the more single-stranded relationships in an industrial society equate with the distinction between close- and loose-knit networks respectively. Put more simply, in an industrial society 'Alpha originates action with his contact

Beta for purpose 1, with Gamma for purpose 2, with Delta for purpose 3, and so on. In a tribal society, Alpha makes contact with Beta sometimes for purpose 1, sometimes for purpose 2, sometimes for purpose 3, and so on.'[27] Clearly the three individuals have more in common with one another in the second than in the first case.

Like a number of concepts in the social sciences that of a social network still awaits extensive measurement with carefully derived empirical data. One of the few studies to employ this concept was an attempt to see whether 'commuter' villages in Pembrokeshire had looser-knit friendship networks than 'agricultural' villages.[28] In order to test this hypothesis the linkages were measured in two ways: first for their degree of connectivity, using the equation $\frac{n(n-1)}{2}$ where n refers to the number of persons involved; and secondly for their degree of accessibility, which was computed for each person by means of the index $\Sigma_j d_{ij}$, where d_{ij} refers to the number of links between persons j and i, and then for the whole network on the basis of the average number of persons reached over all the links in the network. In general, the analysis confirmed the hypothesis; the 'commuter' villages recorded degrees of density ranging from 18 per cent to 29 per cent and accessibility from 0.3 to 1.9, whilst the 'agricultural' villages had scores of 53 per cent to 76 per cent and 1.8 to 2.7 respectively. However, upon a closer inspection of the results it was apparent that the initial hypothesis was too simplistic since other significant explanatory variables were involved, in particular the location, population size, religious structure, and linguistic background of the villages. In view of the dearth of studies like the one quoted here in Pembrokeshire it is little wonder that the discussion in this section has been largely conceptual and technical.

Community solidarity

If a locality is to function as a community its resident members must possess a common set of values and norms of social behaviour. 'When community attitudes cluster about a distinct core of values and common social norms of behaviour distinct from those possessed by the larger society of which the community is a part, community solidarity may be assumed to be high; when opinions are disparate ... solidarity may be said to be lacking.'[29] By means of a schedule containing forty statements about social behaviour in eight different areas of activity in rural communities in Iowa, Fessler provides an early attempt to measure such community solidarity. The results for two representative communities are

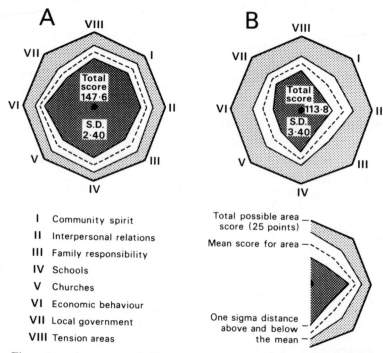

I   Community spirit
II   Interpersonal relations
III Family responsibility
IV   Schools
V   Churches
VI   Economic behaviour
VII Local government
VIII Tension areas

Total possible area score (25 points)
Mean score for area
One sigma distance above and below the mean

Figure 72. Community solidarity in two Iowan rural communities. A low standard deviation of scores indicates a high degree of consensus. The distribution of statements into eight areas of community behaviour made possible the construction of an octagonal profile of each community revealing the evaluation of the community by its members, the degree of balance between areas of behaviour, and the degree of consensus in each area. (Source: Fessler, D. R., 'The Development of a Scale for Measuring Community Solidarity', *Rural Sociology*, 17, 1952, pp 144–52)

illustrated in Figure 72. Since the sigma distance on either side of the mean for each activity was relatively uniform in Community A, it was regarded as a community with a high degree of solidarity. On the other hand, the residents of Community B exhibited a greater diversity of opinion towards each activity, thus indicating a weaker community solidarity.

More recent research has adopted a more semantic approach to the measurement of community values and attitudes. One of the basic techniques is the Semantic Differential, a psychological technique which makes use of linguistic encoding as an index of meaning. As illustrated in Figure 73A, the method involves the provision of the subject with a concept to be differentiated and a set of bi-polar adjectival scales against which to do it. The connotative meaning of concepts such as this can be considered as points in a 'semantic space, a region of some unknown dimensionality and Euclidian in character', and which, 'defined by a pair of polar (opposite in meaning) adjectives, is assumed to represent a straight line function that passes through the origin of this space, and a sample of such scales then represents a multi-dimensional space'.[30] A graphical representation of a semantic space of four concepts differentiated by two bi-polar adjectival scales is illustrated in Figure 73B.

The potentiality of this technique in an analysis of community satisfaction has recently been exhibited by Maund's study in rural Herefordshire.[31] A 20 per cent sample of the heads of households in four representative villages, selected on the basis of their differing social structures, were asked on a five bi-polar adjectival scale to indicate their views on twelve concepts related to rural life (village expansion; local government re-organisation; local employment: commuting; people leaving the village; people moving into the village; local planning; national planning, friends; travel; cities; countryside). Although the results obtained are of considerable interest space must restrict our attention to the more significant. The two predominantly middle-class villages, Sutton and Ashperton, despite differences in size and location, were characterised

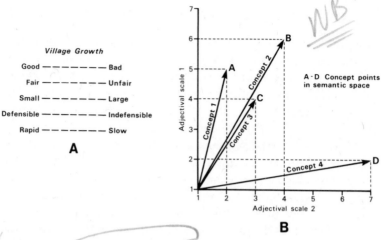

Figure 73. The semantic differential: A—an example of the testing procedure; B—a graphical expression of a semantic space

by a segregated attitude system: on the one hand, opinions which were locally oriented and generally satisfied with the community, and, on the other, those exhibiting greater dissatisfaction and a more national character. In contrast, the remaining two villages, Stoke Lacey and Eggleton, which were characterised by a high proportion of manual residents, recorded attitudes which clustered around the central point of the majority of the concepts. In the case of Stoke Lacey this occurred despite a recent influx of non-manual newcomers, possibly indicating them to be disinterested 'reluctant' migrants. The concepts which produced greatest differences were those of 'commuting' and 'cities', whilst 'village expansion' and 'local government re-organisation' failed to produce any discontinuities. The dominant differentiating variable within Sutton, Ashperton and Eggleton was length of residence, and at Stoke Lacey it was social class. Life-cycle was of low significance in all four communities. Bearing in mind the summary nature of these conclusions it is, however, readily apparent that the Semantic Differential technique has considerable potential. However, as Maund has pointed out, there is a need for greater attention to the selection of concepts and the size of the sample before this technique, or associated ones, can provide a meaningful basis for interpreting the nature of community values and attitudes.

Community satisfaction

If a new resident is to become adjusted he must develop some degree of satisfaction with the community. The greater the consensus of satisfaction among the residents of a locality the greater its feeling of community. The first attempt to measure community satisfaction was that undertaken by Vernon Davis as long ago as 1945.[32] He developed a multi-item scale to assess the degree of satisfaction held by rural residents towards their village community and concluded that satisfaction was strongly related to village population size, moderately to intelligence, and weakly to age and sex. Some twenty years later Jesser[33], by means of a satisfaction index based upon Davis's work, analysed the community satisfaction of 'professional' residents in a part of the rural United States. Briefly, Jesser found that satisfaction was strongly influenced by levels of community participation and previous migration histories as well as population size, whilst income, education, sex, age and place of birth had little effect. A number of recent rural surveys in England and Wales have been particularly concerned with opinions towards village life. In a study in Northamptonshire villagers were questioned as to their attitudes towards seven local issues[34]: the village as a place to live; preference for village over town life; village friendliness; shopping facilities; newcomers; voluntary social organisations; and village improvements. In general, the survey revealed a favourable attitude towards village life, irrespective of population size and social structure. Even those villages with a high proportion of urban immigrants still manifested an overwhelming preference for village life, indicating that while some of these immigrants may in a sense be 'reluctant', they do not appear to feel the need to return to town life. The majority of the respondents thought that their village was a friendly one, and there seemed to be no particular grievances held by those interviewed in answer to the question as to how the village could be improved, although there was considerable dissatisfaction with local shopping facilities, particularly in those villages with a number of manual and non-manual commuters. Interestingly, the general opinion of village life revealed in this study confirmed many of the views expressed in similar studies of villages in Kent,[35] Hampshire,[36] Cambridgeshire,[37] and Suffolk.[38]

Despite the usefulness of the evidence contained in these studies its value is weakened by a failure to conceptualise sufficiently rigorously people's satisfaction with their community. As a result of efforts to overcome this weakness two significant developments may be discerned in the more recent literature. Firstly, a number of studies have been concerned with devising more rigorous means of scaling the items selected to measure community satisfaction. For example, by means of factor analysis Johnson and Knop[39] were able to distinguish differences in satisfaction between rural and urban townships in North Dakota in a multi-dimensional fashion. The urban residents were most satisfied with those items which measured service and employment provision, whereas the rural people were more satisfied with local voluntary organisations and the general environmental milieu. In parallel, a second type of investigation has begun to question the use of simple objective information to measure community satisfaction. Campbell and Converse have been at pains to emphasise that in many communities dissatisfaction with objective conditions has increased despite improvements in these conditions.[40] Conversely, numerous other studies, particularly in urban areas, have revealed high levels of satisfaction with communities which were essentially slums.[41] Marans and Rodgers have shown that in a series of small rural communities in the United States the assessment of perceived environmental attributes was the major influence on the respondents' sense of community[42]. Building upon this study Rojek, Clements and Summers found in Putnam County, Illinois,[43] considerable supporting evidence: for example, the existence of significant differences between rural and urban satisfaction levels with respect to medical and commercial services, but not to public and educational services. In all of these studies the emphasis is upon the need to consider values, attitudes, and expectations since they serve as intervening filters between the 'environment as it is and the environment as it is perceived' in the formation of community satisfaction.

Community identification

Another aspect of community adjustment is the degree of commonality among the residents as to the perception of the community. Despite increasing interest among human geographers in space perception, little attention has been given to community identification. This means that the spatial component of community identification, particularly within a rural context, has been left to a few sociological and psychological studies, for example those dealing with the delimitation of the perceived community and the factors influencing community identification. An interesting example of the first is Drabick and Buck's study of four small rural communities in three adjacent townships in south-east Pennsylvania.[44] Five groups of residents from within and from around each township were invited to discuss the spatial limits of their community, and then to co-operate in outlining its location on a map. In order to express consensus in a numerical form it was decided that 'at any point about a center at which more than half of the boundaries . . . occurred within a distance of three-quarters of a mile, consensus was presumed to exist'.[45] If consensus existed at all points around a centre, 'it could be expressed in terms of a circle, as 360 degrees. Consequently, it was possible to convert the degrees of a circle into a 0 to 100 equivalent and express the amount of consensus occurring measured by a circular protractor, as a consensus index number'.[46] The results obtained revealed that the two communities with relatively stable populations recorded high consensus indices, whilst those with rapidly expanding and diversifying populations had a low consensus index. Surprisingly, population size had little influence on the levels of community identification.

In contrast, other studies have been more concerned with the relationship between community identification and certain explanatory variables such as residential location and social class. A representative example of this type of study is that by Young and Larson of a small locality in upstate New York.[47] Among the study's findings the most significant was the categorisation of community identification into three basic types: first, there were those village and open-country dwellers who regarded the central village as their community; secondly, there were those who identified a larger area which included both the village and its surrounding locality; and thirdly, there were the 'non-identifiers', a collection of individuals who failed to express any feeling of belonging to the village-centred community in which they resided. Interestingly, it was also shown that in an area of less than one mile from the village only about 20 per cent identified with a place other than the village. With greater distance from a village, residential location became the major determinant of the type of community identification. Even within all three occupational categories (farm operator, wage worker, and self-employed non-farmer), those living close to the village centre were the least likely to be 'non-identifiers'. In addition, within each distance zone from the village there was little difference among the occupational groups regarding community identification.

The ability of local residents to identify with a rural community and to delimit its boundaries is, of course, the result of shared knowledge, attitudes and values. It has been suggested that for individuals to achieve consensus they must have the ability to 'maintain orientation toward one another and toward the object of their communication'.[48] Unfortunately, the nature of the empirical evidence on rural community identification precludes a meaningful assessment of this statement. For this to be achieved there is a need for the geographer to specify the spatial framework more precisely as well as develop

ie venting techniqué

more rigorous means of analysis. Among those techniques adopted successfully by behavioural geographers, particularly within an urban context, are preference scales, personal construct theory, and close procedures. Only when these or similar techniques are applied will the form of rural community identification be fully revealed and the significance of explanatory variables such as residential location, community size, social structure, etc. be truly assessed.

A recurrent theme throughout this chapter has been the existence of a number of elegant concepts which are still in need of rigorous testing in the field. However, with the introduction of more behavioural techniques of analysis into human geography, future research will be able not only to develop sounder hypotheses but also to test them with greater rigour, thereby working towards the establishment of a general theory of the geography of community life.

Conclusion

This book has sought to examine the ways in which the process of social change is affecting the rural community and to suggest a geographical framework through which it might be viewed. Since research is an on-going process a conclusion is out of date by the time the ink has dried on the paper; therefore, a passage such as this is more often than not an irrelevancy. But in view of the tentative and speculative nature of this book some concluding comments are needed. At least three themes suggest themselves for consideration: the role of the geographical perspective in rural community study; the changing nature of the countryside; and the question of relevance in academic study.

Despite an increasing amount of geographical research on the countryside in general, there is still relatively little on the rural community. This short-fall is particularly evident in the consideration of the rural community as an ecological system and as a social system. The latter approach has been of particular interest to the anthropologist and the rural sociologist, and over the years they have developed concepts such as the 'local social system' which are of interest to the geographer. Also in their explanation of community phenomena social scientists have often incorporated, though implicitly, concepts such as locality, distance and location: this points the way to a major field of inquiry requiring detailed geographical investigation. On the other hand, geographers as well as other social scientists have paid little attention to the ecological approach to rural community study. Certainly a major obstacle, until recently, has been the absence of sufficient data and readily understood techniques to measure what is, essentially, a multi-dimensional concept. However, in recent years urban geographers have gone some way towards measuring this concept by the use of small area data and the adoption of multivariate techniques; therefore, those interested in rural communities might well adopt similar or allied methodologies and thus at least begin to grapple with the complexities of the ecological structure of rural society.

A major theme of this book has been that of social change. Too often the view has been fostered in newspapers, magazines and books, and on the radio and television, of a traditional, static rural society. In reality this is far from being the case; like urban society, rural society is constantly in the throes of change. All rural communities are now linked to a wider society: what happens elsewhere has significance for the most isolated community. The most widespread of these changes is the increasing significance of dormitory and recreational functions within the countryside, thus emphasising the need to consider the rural community as a part of a system of communities. By focusing on the rural side this book has simply isolated one part of the system.

Linking these first two themes is the question of academic relevance. As in all social sciences, during the past few years geographers have been involved in discussions as to the relevance of their work to the outside world. Most have agreed upon the need for research to be focused upon the identification of social and economic problems and to suggest means for their alleviation. Some researchers have gone a stage further by arguing the need for geographers to become actively involved in the issues since only by participation can decisions be influenced. A minority disagree entirely with these liberal viewpoints, claiming that only by revolutionary means can contemporary inequalities be removed: it is interesting to note that the greater part of the research of such 'radical' geographers has been concerned with urban problems. Clearly this bias needs to be redressed since rural society suffers from as many problems as urban society. This point can be illustrated at two scales of analysis. First, many parts of the countryside in the developing world are at a distinct disadvantage compared with the towns and cities. In a recent report on mid-Wales, one of the remoter regions of Britain, it was stated that 'the heavy dependence . . . on agriculture and the absence of industries showing a high level of earnings is reflected in a level of income per head of population which is much lower than the national average . . . [and also] there is the problem of providing relatively expensive services . . . since it is difficult to achieve efficiency when services are spread over an extensive region with a low density of consumers'.[1] Secondly, at a world scale, rural problems need to be understood against a background of underdevelopment. The people of the developing countries 'have a life expectancy about one-half that in more developed countries . . . have six times as many people per doctor . . . their daily food intake is about one-third less . . . only about one in five is literate . . . the lowest income classes in North America are better off than the average in less developed countries'.[2] These are but a few of the problems facing rural society today; like urban problems they merit attention and understanding. Only after an understanding of the anatomy of rural society has been achieved can meaningful improvements be effected. Understanding involves analysis; here one such perspective has been attempted—the geographical.

Notes

Introduction

1 See, for example, Hauser, P. M. and Schnore, L. F., *The Study of Urbanization*, Wiley, 1965; Breese, Gerald, *The City in Newly Developing Countries*, Prentice-Hall, 1969

2 Galeski, B., *Basic Concepts of Rural Sociology*, Manchester University Press, 1972

3 Halpern, J. M. *The Changing Village Community*, Prentice-Hall, 1967

4 For a discussion see Thorpe, D., *The Geographer and Urban Studies*, Department of Geography, University of Durham, Occasional Paper Series, 8, 1966; and Davies, W. K. D., 'Approaches to Urban Geography: An Overview' in Carter, H. and Davies, W. K. D. (eds), *Urban Essays: Studies in the Geography of Wales*, Longmans, 1970, pp 1–22

5 For a brief introductory survey of the geography of the countryside see Clout, H., *Rural Geography*, Pergamon Press, 1972

6 Freeman, T. W., *One Hundred Years of Geography*, Duckworth, 1961

7 For example, Houston, J. M., *A Social Geography of Europe*, Duckworth, 1953; Chisholm, M., *Rural Settlement and Land Use*, Hutchinson, 1962; Roberts, B. K., *Rural Settlement in Britain*, Dawson, 1977

8 For example, Found, W. C., *A Theoretical Approach to Rural Land-Use Patterns*, Edward Arnold, 1971; Tarrant, J. R., *Agricultural Geography*, David and Charles, 1974; Morgan, W. B. and Munton, R. J. C., *Agricultural Geography*, Methuen, 1971

9 For example, Hägerstrand, T. (translated by Pred, A.), *Innovation Diffusion as a Spatial Process*, University of Chicago Press, 1967; Brown, L. A., *Diffusion Process and Location: A Conceptual Framework and Bibliography*, Regional Science Institute, 1968; and Hudson, J. C., *Geographical Diffusion Theory*, Northwestern University Studies in Geography, 19, 1972

10 For example, Saville, J., *Rural Depopulation in England and Wales, 1851–1951* Routledge and Kegan Paul, 1957; Lewis, G. J., *Human Migration* D342.9, Open University Press, 1974; and Kosinski, L. A. and Prothero, R. M. (eds), *People on the Move*, Methuen, 1975

215

11 For example, Pahl, R. E., 'Trends in Social Geography' in Chorley, R. J. and Haggett, P. (eds), *Frontiers in Geographical Teaching*, Methuen, 1965, pp 81–100

12 Febvre, L., *A Geographical Introduction to History*, Knopf, 1932, p 37

13 Haggett, P., *Locational Analysis in Human Geography*, Arnold, 1965

14 Park, R. E., *Human Communities—The City and Human Ecology*, Free Press, 1952, p 14

15 Frankenberg, R. E., *Communities in Britain*, Penguin, 1966, p 45

16 'A Retrospect' in Bowen, E. G., Carter, H. and Taylor, J. A. (eds), *Geography at Aberystwyth*, University of Wales Press, 1968, pp xix–xxxvi

17 Rees, A. D., *Life in a Welsh Countryside*, University of Wales Press, 1950

18 Davies, E. and Rees, A. D. (eds), *Welsh Rural Communities*, University of Wales Press, 1960

19 See, for example, Malinowski, B., *A Scientific Theory of Culture*, University of North Carolina Press, 1944; Radcliffe-Brown, A. R., 'On the Concept of Function in Social Science', *American Anthropologist*, 37, 1935, pp 394–402; and Firth, R., *Elements of Social Organisation*, Watts, 1963, pp 1–41

20 See, for example, Brookfield, H. C., 'Questions on the Human Frontiers of Geography', *Economic Geography*, 40, 1964, pp 283–303; and Grossman, D., 'Man-Environment Relationships in Anthropology and Geography', *Annals of the Association of American Geographers*, 67, 1977, pp 126–44

21 For a discussion see Watson, J. W., 'The Sociological Aspects of Geography' in Taylor, G. (ed), *Geography in the Twentieth Century*, Methuen, 1957, pp 463–99; Buttimer, A., 'Social Geography' in Sills, D. L. (ed), *International Encyclopaedia of the Social Sciences*, 6, 1968, pp 134–45; and Eyles, J., 'Social Theory and Social Geography, *Progress in Geography*, 6, 1974, pp 22–87

22 *Social Progress Through Community Development*, United Nations Bureau of Social Affairs, 1955, p 5

23 Thorns, D., *The Quest for Community*, Allen and Unwin, 1976

24 Pahl, R. E., *op. cit.*, 1965, p 81

25 See Jones, E., *Readings in Social Geography*, Oxford University Press, 1975; and Jones, E. and Eyles, J., *An Introduction to Social Geography*, Oxford University Press, 1977

26 See, for example, Herbert, D. T., *Urban Geography. A Social Perspective*, David and Charles, 1972

27 See the studies contained in Berry, B. J. L. (ed), 'Comparative Factorial Ecology', *Economic Geography*, 47, 1971, pp 209–367; Clark, B. D. and Gleave, M. B. (eds), *Social Patterns in Cities*, Institute of British Geographers, Special Publication 5, 1973; and Herbert, D. T. and Johnston, R. J. (eds), *Social Areas in Cities*, vols 1 and 2, Wiley, 1976

28 See, for example, Loomis, C. P. and Beagle, J. A., *Rural Sociology: the Strategy of Change*, Prentice-Hall, 1957; Bertrand, A. L. (ed), *Rural Sociology: an Analysis of Contemporary Rural Life*; Halpern, J. M., *op. cit.*, 1967; Smith, T. L. and Zopf, P. E., *Principles of Inductive Rural Sociology*, Davis, 1970; Rogers, E. M. and Burdge, R. J., *Social Change in Rural Societies*, Prentice-Hall, 1972; Galeski, B., *op. cit.*, 1972; and Jones, G., *Rural Life*, Longman, 1973

29 For an early discussion of this theme see Forde, C. D., 'Human Geography, Sociology and History', *Scottish Geographical Magazine*, 55, 1939, pp 217–34

30 Davis, K., *Human Society*, Macmillan, 1948, p 311

Chapter One

1 Wibberley, G. P., 'Changes in the Structure and Function of the Rural Community', *Sociologia Ruralis*, 1, 1960, p 120

2 Cloke, P. J., 'An Index of Rurality for England and Wales', *Regional Studies*, 11, 1977, pp 31–46

3 For a detailed discussion see *United Nations, Department of Economic and Social Affairs, Population Studies*, 44, 1969

4 Carter, H., *The Study of Urban Geography*, Arnold, 1972; and Berry, B. J. L. and Horton, F. E., *Geographic Perspectives on Urban Systems*, Prentice-Hall, 1970

5 Wibberley, G. P., 'Rural activities and rural settlements', mimeographed paper presented at the Town and Country Planning Association's Conference, London, 16–17 February 1972, p 2

6 Best, R. H. and Rogers, A. W., *The Urban Countryside*, Faber, 1973, p 26

7 Halpern, J. M., *The Changing Village Community*, Prentice-Hall, 1967, p 44

8 Morrill, R. L., *Spatial Organisation of Society*, Duxbury, 1974, p 83

9 An early use of 20,000 as a lower size limit in the study of urban population appears in Davis, K. and Hertz, Hilda, 'The World Distribution of Urbanization', *Bulletin of the International Statistical Institute*, 33, 1965, part IV

10 Best, R. H. and Rogers, A. W., *op. cit.*, 1973, p 27

11 Haggett, P., *Locational Analysis in Human Geography*, Arnold, 1965, pp 106–7

12 Saville, J., *Rural Depopulation in England and Wales, 1851–1951*, Routledge and Kegan Paul, 1957

13 Halpern, J. M., *op. cit.*, 1967, p 44

14 Galeski, B., *Basic Concepts of Rural Sociology*, Manchester University Press, 1972

15 Bertrand, A. L., *Rural Land Tenure in the United States*, Louisiana State University Press, 1962, p 36
16 Weller, J., *Modern Agriculture and Planning*, Architectural Press, 1967
17 Shanin, T. (ed), *Peasants and Peasant Societies*, Penguin, 1971
18 Franklin, S. H., *Rural Societies*, Macmillan, 1971
19 Fuguitt, G. V., 'The City and Countryside', *Rural Sociology*, 28, 1963, p 246
20 Mehta, V., 'A Letter from New Delhi', *Observer Review*, 19 January, 1975, p 23
21 For a summary see Ashton, J. and Long, W. H. (eds), *The Remoter Rural Areas of Britain*, Oliver and Boyd, 1972; and Cherry, G. E. (ed), *Rural Planning Problems*, Leonard Hill, 1976
22 Russell, A. J., *The Village in Myth and Reality*, Chester House, 1975
23 Blythe, R., *Akenfield, Portrait of an English Village*, Penguin, 1972, p 18
24 Fairbrother, N., *New Lives, New Landscapes*, Penguin, 1972, p 22
25 Bracey, H. E., *People and the Countryside*, Routledge and Kegan Paul, 1970; Thorburn, A., *Planning Villages*, Estates Gazette, 1971; and Green, R. J., *Country and Planning*, Manchester University Press, 1971
26 For a general review see Whitby, M. C., Robins, D. L. J., Tansey, A. W. and Willis, K. G., *Rural Resource Development*, Methuen, 1974
27 For example, Higgs, J., *People in the Countryside*, National Council of Social Service, 1966; Hofstee, E. W., *Rural Life and Rural Welfare in the Netherlands*, Government Publishing Office, 1957; and Hart, J. F., 'Urban Encroachment on Rural Areas', *Geographical Review*, 66, 1976, pp 1–17
28 For an interesting attempt to determine the quality of rural life by means of information contained in village scrapbooks kept by branches of the Women' Institute Federation see Jennings, P., *The Living Village*, Hodder and Stoughton, 1968
29 Dickinson, R. E., *City Region and Regionalism*, Routledge and Kegan Paul, 1947, p xii

Chapter Two

1 Chisholm, M., *Human Geography: Evolution or Revolution*, Penguin, 1975
2 For a discussion of recent trends in geography see Taaffe, E. J., 'The Spatial View in Context', *Annals of the Association of American Geographers*, 64, 1974, pp 1–16
3 Golledge, R. G., Brown, L. A. and Williamson, F., 'Behavioural Approaches in Geography: An Overview', *Australian Geographer*, 12, 1972, pp 59–79

4 Jones, E., 'Cause and Effect in Human Geography', *Annals of the Association of American Geographers*, 46, 1956, pp 369–77

5 Harvey, D., 'Social Processes and Spatial Form: An Analysis of the Conceptual Problems of Urban Planning', *Papers of the Regional Science Association*, 25, 1970, pp 47–69

6 Hillery, G. A., 'Villages, Cities and Total Institutions', *American Sociological Review*, 28, 1963, p 779

7 Minar, D. W. and Scott, Greer, *The Concept of Community: Readings with Interpretations*, Aldine, 1969, p 140

8 Rogers, E. M. and Burdge, R. J., *Social Change in Rural Societies*, Prentice-Hall, 1972, p 264

9 Minar, D. W. and Scott, Greer, *op. cit.*, 1969, p ix

10 Brownell, B., *The Human Community: Its Philosophy and Practice for a Time of Crisis*, Harper and Row, 1950, p 209

11 Hillery, G. A., 'Definitions of Community: Areas of Agreement', *Rural Sociology*, 20, 1955, pp 111–23

12 Hillery, G. A., *ibid*, 1955, p 111

13 Reiss, A. J., 'The Sociological Study of Communities', *Rural Sociology*, 24, 1959, p 118

14 Morgan, W. B. and Moss, R. P., 'The Concept of Community: Some Applications in Geographical Research', *Transactions of the Institute of British Geographers*, 41, 1967, pp 21–32

15 Hawley, A. H., *Human Ecology: A Theory of Community Structure*, Ronald Press, 1950, p 246

16 Reiss, A. J., *op. cit.*, 1959, p 127

17 Park, R E., 'Human Ecology', *American Journal of Sociology*, 42, 1936, p 15

18 Duncan, O. D., 'Social Organization and the Ecosystem' in Faris, R. E. L. (ed), *Handbook of Modern Sociology*, Rand McNally, 1964, p 77

19 Murdoch, S. and Sutton, W. A., 'The New Ecology and Community Theory: Similarities, Differences and Convergencies', *Rural Sociology*, 39, 1974, pp 319–33

20 Jones, E. and Eyles, J., *An Introduction to Social Geography*, Oxford University Press, 1977, pp 5–25

21 Pahl, R. E., 'The Rural-Urban Continuum', *Sociologia Ruralis*, 6, 1966, p 322

22 Webber, M. M., 'Order in Diversity: Community without Propinquity' in Wingo, L. (ed), *Cities and Space*, The Johns Hopkins Press, 1963

23 Clark, D. B., 'The Concept of Community: a Re-Examination', *Sociological Review*, 21, 1973, pp 397–416

24 Reiss, A. J., *op. cit.*, 1959, p 127

25 Sanders, I. T., *The Community: An Introduction to a Social System*, Ronald Press, 1966, pp 99–112

26 Warren, R. L., *The Community in America*, Rand McNally, 1963, p 13

27 McIver, R. M. and Page, C. H., *Society: An Introductory Analysis*, Holt, Rinehart and Winston, 1949, p 10

28 Poplin, D. E., *Communities. A Survey of Theories and Methods of Research*, Macmillan, 1972, pp 25–7

29 Murdoch, S. and Sutton, W. A., *op. cit.*, 1974, pp 319–33

30 Stacey, Margaret, 'The Myth of Community Studies', *British Journal of Sociology*, 20, 1969, pp 134–47

31 The seven terms used to describe the rural–urban continuum are: Sacred–Secular; Status–Contract; Folk–Urban; Military–Industrial; Traditional–Rational; Mechanical Solidarity–Organic Solidarity; *Gemeinschaft—Gelleschaft*. See Reissman, L., *The Urban Process*, Free Press, 1964, p 123

32 Redfield, R., *The Folk Culture of Yucatan*, University of Chicago, 1941

33 Wirth, L., 'Urbanism as a Way of Life', *American Journal of Sociology*, 44, 1938, p 11

34 For an extended criticism, see Morris, R. N., *Urban Sociology*, Allen and Unwin, 1968

35 Gans, H. J., 'Urbanism and Suburbanism as Ways of Life' in Rose, A. M. (ed), *Human Behaviour and Social Processes*, Routledge and Kegan Paul, 1962, p 643

36 Pahl, R. E., *op. cit.*, 1966, pp 300–2

37 For a defence of the rural–urban continuum see Lupri, E., 'The Rural–Urban Variable Reconsidered: the Cross-cultural Perspective', *Sociologia Ruralis*, 7, 1967, pp 1–17; and, Oommen T. K., 'The Rural–Urban Continuum Re-examined in the Indian Context', *Sociologia Ruralis*, 7, 1967, pp 30–46

38 Poplin, D. E., *Communities: A Survey of Theories and Methods of Research*, Macmillan, 1972, pp 108–47

39 Hauser, P. M., 'Observations on the Urban-Folk and Urban-Rural Dichotomies as Forms of Western Ethnocentricism' in Hauser, P. M. and Schnore, L. F., *The Study of Urbanization*, Wiley, 1965, pp 516–17

40 *Gemeinschaft*-like relationships are characterised by 'mutual aid and helpfulness, mutual interdependence, reciprocal and binding sentiments, diffuse or blanket obligations, authority based upon age, wisdom and benevolent force. Furthermore, persons enmeshed in a *Gemeinschaft*-like relationship share sacred traditions and a spirit of brotherhood which grows out of bonds of blood, common locality, or mind.' Poplin, D. E., *op. cit.*, 1972, pp 116–17

41 *Gesellschaft*-like relationships are characterised by the participating individuals being separated rather than united, and individualism reaches its zenith. 'Because of this the relationships which emerge between members of the *Gesellschaft* are contractual and functionally specific and frequently involve the exchange of goods, money, or credit and obligations.' Poplin, D. E., *op. cit.*, 1972, p 117

42 Loomis, C. P., *Social Systems: Essays on their Persistence and Change*, Van Nostrand, 1960, p 60

43 Duncan, O. D., 'Community Size and the Rural-Urban Continuum' in Hatt, P. K. and Reiss, A. J. (eds), *Cities and Society*, Free Press, 1967, p 43

44 Frankenberg, R., *Communities in Britain*, Penguin, 1966, p 275

45 Burie, J. B., 'Prolegomena to a Theoretical Model of Intercommunity Variation', *Sociologia Ruralis*, 7, 1967, pp 347–62

46 Lockwood, D., 'Social Integration and System Integration' in Zollschan, C. K. and Hirsch, W. (eds), *Exploration in Social Change*, Routledge and Kegan Paul, 1964, pp 244–57

47 Schnore, L. F., 'Community' in Smelser, N. (ed), *Sociology*, Wiley, 1967, p 114

48 Schnore, L. F., 'The Rural-Urban Variable: An Urbanite's Perspective', *Rural Sociology*, 31, 1966, p 131

49 Hägerstrand, T., *Innovation Diffusion as a Spatial Process*, University of Chicago Press, 1969

50 Rogers, E. M. and Burdge, R. J., *Social Change in Rural Societies*, Prentice-Hall, 1972, p 1

51 Rogers, E. M. and Burdge, R. J., *ibid*, 1972, p 14

52 Rogers, E. M. and Burdge, R. J., *ibid*, 1972, p 14

53 Zelinsky, W., 'The Hypothesis of the Mobility Transition', *Geographical Review*, 61, 1971, pp 221–2

54 Zelinsky, W., *ibid*, 1971, p 231

55 Mitchell, G. D., 'The Relevance of Group Dynamics to Rural Planning Problems', *Sociological Review*, (O.S.) 43, 1951, pp 1–16

56 Thorns, D. C., 'The Changing System of Rural Stratification', *Sociologia Ruralis*, 8, 1968, pp 161–76

57 Rogers, E. M. and Burdge, R. J., *op. cit.*, 1972, pp 14–16

58 For a discussion of the usefulness of a systems perspective in geography see Langton, J., 'Potentialities and Problems of Adopting a Systems Approach to the Study of Change in Human Geography', *Progress in Geography*, 4, 1972, pp 125–79

59 Firth, R. E., *We, The Tikopia*, Allen and Unwin, 1936

60 Brookfield, H. C., 'The Money that Grows on Trees: The Consequences of an Innovation within a Man-Environment System', *Australian Geographical Studies*, 6, 1968, pp 97–119

61 Williams, W. M., *A West Country Village: Ashworthy*, Routledge and Kegan Paul, 1963

62 Hammond, H., 'Continuity and Conscious Models in County Clare and Ashworthy: A Reappraisal', *Sociology*, 2, 1968, pp 21–8

63 Lewis, G. J. and Maund, D. J., 'The Urbanization of the Countryside: A Framework for Analysis', *Geografiska Annaler*, 58B, 1976, pp 17–27

64 Pahl, R. E., *op. cit.*, 1966, pp 299–327

65 Burie, J. B., *op. cit.*, 1967, pp 347–62
66 Quoted in Williams, W. M., 'Changing Functions of the Community', *Sociologia Ruralis*, 4, 1964, p 299
67 The term *population* can be used in three ways: '1. An inhabited place; 2. the degree to which a place is populated or inhabited; hence, the total number of its inhabitants; 3. the action or process of peopling a place or region; increase of population'. *The Shorter Oxford English Dictionary*, vol. 2, Oxford University Press, 1968, p 1546. Population is defined here as 'the action or process of peopling a place or region'; see Lewis, G. J. and Maund, D. J., *op. cit.*, 1976, pp 17–27

Chapter Three

1 Ng, R. C. Y., 'Recent Internal Population Movement in Thailand', *Annals of the Association of American Geographers*, 59, 1969, pp 710–30
2 See, for example, Mangalam, J. J., *Human Migration*, University of Kentucky Press, 1968; and Lewis, G. J., *Human Migration*, D342.9, Open University Press, 1974
3 Roseman, C. C., 'Migration as a Spatial and Temporal Process', *Annals of the Association of American Geographers*, 61, 1971, pp 589–98
4 Cavalli-Sforza, H., 'The Distribution of Migration Distances: Models and Applications to Genetics' in Sutter, J. (ed), *Human Displacements*, Hachette, 1962, p 140
5 Petersen, W., 'General Typology of Migration', *American Sociological Review*, 1958, pp 256–66
6 Pryor, R. J., 'Migration and the Process of Modernization' in Kosinski, L. A. and Prothero, R. M. (eds), *People on the Move*, Methuen, 1975, pp 23–8
7 Mabogunje, A. L., 'Systems Approach to a Theory of Rural-Urban Migration', *Geographical Analysis*, 2, 1970, pp 1–18
8 Mabogune. A. L., *ibid*, 1970, p 16
9 Mabogunje, A. L., *ibid*, 1970, p 14
10 Mabogunje, A. L., *ibid*, 1970, p 16
11 Herberle, R., 'The Causes of Rural-Urban Migration: A Survey of German Theories', *American Journal of Sociology*, 43, 1938, pp 932–50
12 Eversley, Lord, 'The Decline in the Number of Agricultural Labourers in Great Britain', *Journal of the Royal Statistical Society*, 70, 1907, p 280
13 Eversley, Lord, *ibid*, 1907, p 280
14 Lowry, I. S. *Migration and Metropolitan Growth: Two Analytical Models*, Chandler, 1966
15 Rogers, A., *Matrix Analysis of Interregional Population Growth and Distribution*, University of California Press, 1968

16 For a summary see Willis, K. G., *Problems in Migration Analysis*, Saxon House, 1974, pp 16–28

17 Rodgers, A., 'Migration and Industrial Development: the Southern Italian Experience', *Economic Geography*, 46, 1970, pp 111–35

18 Hannan, D. F., 'Migration Motives and Migration Differentials Among Rural Youth', *Sociologia Ruralis*, 9, 1969, p 202

19 House, J. W. and Knight, E. M., *Migrants of North East England 1951–61: Character, Age and Sex*, University of Newcastle upon Tyne, Department of Geography, Papers on Migration and Mobility 2, 1965

20 Cowie, W. and Giles, A., 'An Enquiry into Reasons for the "Drift From the Land"', *Selected Papers in Agricultural Economics: University of Bristol*, 5, 1957, pp 70–113

21 Nalson, J. S., *Mobility of Farm Families*, Manchester University Press, 1968

22 Prothero, R. M., *Migrant Labour from Sokoto Province, Northern Nigeria*, Government Printer, Kaduna, 1959

23 Skinner, E. P., *The Mossi of the Upper Volta: the Political Development of a Sudanese People*, Stanford University Press, 1964

24 Imogene, S. O., 'Psycho-social Factors in Rural-Urban Migration', *Nigerian Journal of Economics and Social Studies*, 9, 1967, pp 375–85

25 Lewis, G. J., *A Study of Socio-geographic Change in the Welsh Borderland*, unpublished University of Leicester PhD thesis, 1969

26 For example, see Emerson, A. R. and Crompton, R., *Suffolk—Some Social Trends*, Suffolk Rural Community Council, 1969

27 Sternstein, L., 'Migration To and From Bangkok', *Annals of the Association of American Geographers*, 64, 1974, pp 138–47

28 Caldwell, J. C., 'Determinants of Rural-Urban Migration in Ghana', *Population Studies*, 22, 1968, pp 361–72

29 Lewis, G. J., *op. cit.*, 1969

30 Ravenstein, E. G., 'The Laws of Migration', *Journal of the Royal Statistical Society*, 48, 1895, pp 167–235; and 52, 1889, pp 241–305

31 Jones, H. R., 'A Study of Rural Migration in Central Wales', *Transactions of the Institute of British Geographers*, 37, 1965, pp 31–45

32 Zachariah, K. C., 'Bombay Migration Study: A Pilot Analysis of Migration in an Asian Metropolis', *Demography*, 37, 1966, pp 378–92; and Arunchalam, B., Phadke, V. S. and Deshpande, C. D., 'South Kolaba: A Study in Demographic Characteristics', paper presented at the Indo-British Seminar, Delhi, 1972

33 Harvey, M. E., 'Interregional Migration Studies in Tropical Africa', in Kosinski, L. and Prothero, R. M. (eds), *op. cit.*, 1975, p 155

34 Hunter, J. M., 'Cocoa Migration and Patterns of Land Ownership in the Densu Valley near Suhum, Ghana', *Transactions of the Institute of British Geographers*, 33, 1963, pp 61–88

35 Riddell, J. B. and Harvey, M. E., 'Development, Urbanization and Migration: A Test of a Hypothesis in the Third World' in Kosinski, L. and Prothero, R. M. (eds), *op. cit.*, 1975, pp 51–65
36 Stockel, J., Chowdhury, A. K. M. A. and Aziz, K. M. A., 'Out-migration from a Rural Area of Bangladesh', *Rural Sociology*, 37, 1972, pp 236–45
37 Kirk, W., 'The Frustration of the Indian Family Plan', *Geographical Magazine*, 47, 1975, pp 310–13
38 Prothero, R. M., *Migrants and Malaria*, Longman, 1965, p 43
39 Zipf, G. K., 'The $P_1 P_2/D$ Hypothesis in the Intercity Movement of Persons', *American Sociological Review*, 11, 1946, pp 677–86
40 For a summary see Willis, K. G., *op. cit.*, 1974, pp 86–9
41 Stouffer, S. A., 'Intervening Opportunities: A Theory Relating Mobility and Distance', *American Sociological Review*, 5, 1940, pp 846–67
42 Isbell, E. C., 'Internal Migration in Sweden and Intervening Opportunities', *American Sociological Review*, 9, 1944, pp 627–39
43 Stouffer, S. A., 'Intervening Opportunities and Competing Migrants', *Journal of Regional Science*, 2, 1960, pp 1–26
44 Lee, E. S., 'A Theory of Migration', *Demography*, 3, 1966, pp 47–57
45 Thomas, D. S., *Research Memorandum on Migration Differentials*, Social Science Research Council Bulletin, 43, 1938
46 Beshers, J. M. and Nishiura, E. N., 'A Theory of Internal Migration Differentials', *Social Forces*, 39, 1961, pp 214–18
47 For example, see Schwind, P. J., *Migration and Regional Development in the United States, 1950–1960*, University of Chicago, Department of Geography Research Paper, 133, 1971; Fielding, A. J., *Internal Migration in England and Wales*, Centre for Environmental Studies, UWP 14, 1971; and Fielding, A. J., 'Internal Migration and Regional Economic Growth: A Case Study of France', *Urban Studies*, 3, 1966, pp 200–14
48 Friedlander, D. and Roshier, R. J., 'A Study of Internal Migration in England and Wales', *Population Studies*, Part I, 19, 1966, pp 239–79; and Part II, 20, 1966, pp 45–59
49 Lewis, G. J., *op. cit.*, 1969
50 Gasson, R., 'Occupational Immobility of Small Farmers', *Journal of Agricultural Economics*, 20, 1969, pp 279–88
51 Nalson, J. S., *op. cit.*, 1968
52 Herrick, B., *Urban Migration and Economic Development in Chile*, MIT Monographs in Economics, 6, 1966
52 See, for example, Ng, R. C. Y., 'Internal Migration in Southeast Asian Countries' in Kosinski, L. and Prothero, R. M. (eds), *op. cit.*, 1975, pp 181–92
54 See, for example, Masser, I. and Gould, W. T. S., *Inter-regional Migration in Tropical Africa*, Institute of British Geographers Special Publication 8, 1975

55 Caldwell, J. C., *op. cit.*, 1968, pp 361–72

56 Gosal, G. S. and Krishan, G., 'Patterns of Internal Migration in India' in Kosinski, L. and Prothero, R. M. (eds), *op. cit.*, 1975, pp 199–202

57 Stockel, J., Chowdhury, A. K. M. A. and Aziz, K. M. A., *op. cit.*, 1972, pp 236–45

58 Caldwell, J. C., *op. cit.*, 1968, pp 361–72

59 Bogue, D. J., *The Principles of Demography*, Wiley, 1969, p 797

60 Wolpert, J., 'Behavioural Aspects of the Decision to Migrate', *Papers and Proceedings, Regional Science Association*, 15, 1965, pp 159–69

61 Gould, P. R. and White, R. R., *Mental Maps*, Penguin, 1974

62 Hannan, D. F., *Rural Exodus*, Chapman, 1970

63 Lewis, G. J., *op. cit.*, 1969

64 Rambaud, P., *Société Rurale et Urbanisation*, Seuil, 1969, pp 21–2

65 Hillery, G. A. and Brown, J. S., 'Migrational Systems of the Southern Appalachians: Some Demographic Observations', *Rural Sociology*, 30, 1965, p 47

66 Brown, J. S., Schwarzweller, H. K. and Mangalam, J. J., 'Kentucky Mountain Migration and the Stem-family: An American Variation on the Theme of Le Play', *Rural Sociology*, 28, 1963, pp 53–4

67 Caldwell, J. C., *African Rural-Urban Migration*, Australian National University Press, 1969, pp 120–39

68 Lewis, G. J., *op. cit.*, 1969

69 For a summary see Moore, E. G., *Residential Mobility in the City*, Commission on College Geography Research Paper 13, Association of American Geographers, 1972

Chapter Four

1 Barnet, H. G., *Innovation: The Basis of Cultural Change*, McGraw-Hill, 1951, p 7

2 Gould, P., *Spatial Diffusion*, Association of American Geographers, Commission on College Geography, Resource Paper Series, 1969, p 50

3 For example, Lionberger, H. F., *Adoption of New Ideas and Practices*, Iowa State University, 1960; Rogers, E. M., *Diffusion of Innovation*, Free Press, 1962; Jones, G. E., 'The Diffusion of Agricultural Innovation', *Journal of Agricultural Economics*, 15, 1963, pp 387–405; Jones, G. E., 'The Adoption and Diffusion of Agricultural Practices', *World Agricultural Economics and Rural Sociology Abstracts*, 9, 1967, pp 1–34

4 For a review of geographical research on innovation diffusion see Brown, L. A., *Diffusion Process and Location. A Conceptual Framework and Bibliography*, Regional Science Research Institute Bibliography No. 4, 1968; Brown, L. A., *Diffusion Dynamics. A Review of the Quantitative Theory of the Spatial Diffusion of Innovation*, Lund Studies in Geo-

graphy, Series B, No. 29, 1968; Brown, L. A. and Moore E. G., 'Diffusion Research in Geography. A Perspective', *Progress in Geography*, 1,
1969, pp 119–57; Hudson, J. C., *Geographical Diffusion Theory*, Northwestern University Studies in Geography, 19, 1972

5 Sauer, C. O., *Agricultural Origins and Dispersals*, American Geographical Society, Bowman Memorial Lectures No. 2, 1952

6 Turner, F. J., *The Frontier in American History*, Holt, Rinehart and Winston, 1920

7 Hägerstrand, T., *The Propagation of Innovation Waves*, Lund Studies in
Geography, Series B, No. 4, 1952; Hägerstrand, T., *Innovation Diffusion
as a Spatial Process*, University of Chicago Press, 1968

8 'Studies in Spatial Diffusion Processes I and II', *Economic Geography*,
50, No 1, 1974 and 51, No. 3, 1975

9 Riddell, J. B., *The Spatial Dynamics of Modernization in Sie, 1970*

10 Gould, P., *op. cit.*, 1969, pp 47–50

11 Loboda, J., 'The Diffusion of Television in Poland', *Economic Geography*, 50, 1974, pp 70–82

12 Coleman, J. S., *Introduction to Mathematical Sociology*, Free Press, 1964

13 Hägerstrand T., 'Quantitative Techniques for Analysis of the Spread of
Information and Technology' in Anderson, C. A. and Bowman, M. J.
(eds), *Education and Economic Development*, Aldine, 1965, pp 244–80

14 Rogers, E. M., 'Categorizing the Adopters of Agricultural Practices',
Rural Sociology, 23, 1958, pp 345–54

15 Brown, L. A., Malecki, E. J. and Spector, A. N., 'Adopter Categories in a
Spatial Context: Alternative Explanations for an Empirical Regularity',
Rural Sociology, 41, 1976, pp 99–118

16 Hägerstrand, T., *op. cit.*, 1965, pp 261–2

17 Chapin, F. S., *Cultural Change*, Century, 1928, pp 203–14

18 Pemberton, H. E., 'The Curve of Cultural Diffusion Rate', *American Sociological Review*, 1, 1936, pp 547–6

19 Bose, S. P., 'The Diffusion of Farm Practice in India', *Rural Sociology*,
29, 1954, pp 53–66

20 Rogers, E. M. with Svenning, L., *Modernization Among Peasants. The
Impact of Communication*, Holt, Rinehart and Winston, 1969, pp 292–4

21 For example, Mansfield, E., 'Technical Change and the Rate of Imita-
tion', *Econometrica*, 29, 1961, pp 741–66; Casetti, E., 'Why Do Diffusion
Processes Conform to Logistic Trends', *Geographical Analysis*, 1, 1969,
pp 101–5; Casetti, E. and Semple, R. K., 'Concerning the Testing of Spatial Diffusion Hypotheses', *Geographical Analysis*, 1, 1969, pp 254–9

22 Brown, L. A. and Cox, K., 'Empirical Regularities in the Diffusion of
Innovation', *Annals of the Association of American Geographers*, 61,
1971, pp 551–60

23 This was based on the work of Ryan, B. and Goss, N. C., 'The Diffusion
of Hybrid Seed Corn in Two Iowa Communities', *Rural Sociology*, 8,

1943, pp 15–24; and Wilkening, E. A., 'The Process of Acceptance of Technological Innovations in Rural Society' in Bertrand, A. E. (ed), *Rural Sociology: An Analysis of Contemporary Rural Life*, McGraw-Hill, 1958, pp 386–99

24 Beal, G. M. and Rogers, E. M., *The Adoption of Two Farm Practices in a Central Iowa Community*, Iowa Agricultural and Home Economics Experiment Station Special Report 26, 1960

25 Dasgupta, S., 'Relative Predictability of the Five Indices of Adoption of Recommended Farm Practices', *Sociologia Ruralis*, 8, 1968, pp 1–20

26 Campbell, R. R., 'A Suggested Paradigm on the Individual Adoption Process', *Rural Sociology*, 31, 1966, pp 458–66

27 Coughenor, C. M., 'Some Present Problems in Diffusion from the Perspective of the Theory of Social Action' in *Diffusion Research Needs*, Missouri Agricultural Experiment Station, North Central Region Bulletin, No 186, 1968, p 10

28 Klonglan, G. E., Beal, G. M. Bohlen, J. M. and Coward, E. W., 'Conceptualizing and Measuring the Diffusion of Innovations', *Sociologia Ruralis*, 11, 1971, pp 36–72

29 Sawhney, M. M., 'Farm Practice Adoption and the Use of Information Sources and Media in a Rural Community in India', *Rural Sociology*, 32, 1967, pp 310–23

30 Katz, B., Levin, M. L. and Hamilton, H., 'Tradition of Research on the Diffusion of Innovations', *American Sociological Review*, 28, 1963, p 252

31 Hägerstrand, T., *Innovation Diffusion as a Spatial Process*, University of Chicago Press, 1968

32 The areal extent of 'neighbourhood' with reference to information transmission and reception has been extensively researched by geographers, for example, Marble, D. and Nystuen, J. D., 'An Approach to the Direct Measurement of Community Mean Information Fields', *Papers of the Regional Science Association*, 11, 1962, pp 99–110; Bowden, L. W., *Diffusion of the Decision to Irrigate*, University of Chicago, Department of Geography Research Paper, No. 97, 1965; Hägerstrand, T., 'Aspects of the Spatial Structure of Social Communication and the Diffusion of Information', *Papers of the Regional Science Association*, 16, 1966, pp 27–42; Morrill, R. L. and Pitts, F. R., 'Marriage, Migration and the Mean Information Field: A Study in Uniqueness and Generality', *Annals of the Association of American Geographers*, 57, 1967, pp 401–22; Cox, K. R. 'The Genesis of Acquaintanceship Field Spatial Structures', in Cox, K. R. and Golledge, R. G. (eds), *Behavioural Problems in Geography: A Symposium*, Northwestern University, Studies in Geography, 1969; Spector, A. N., Brown, L. A. and Malecki, E. J., 'Acquaintance Circles and Communication: An Exploration of Hypotheses Relating to Innovation Adoption', *Professional Geographer*, 28, 1970, pp 267–76

228   NOTES

33 Hudson, J. C., *op. cit.*, 1972
34 Hannemann, G. J. and Carroll, T. W., *Simulation of Information Diffusion in a Peasant Community*, Michigan State University, Technical Report No 7, 1970
35 Cliff, A. D., 'The Neighbourhood Effect in the Diffusion of Innovations', *Transactions of the Institute of British Geographers*, 44, 1968, pp 75–84
36 Törnqvist, G., *Contact Systems and Regional Development*, Lund Studies in Geography, Series B, No 35, 1970
37 Wilkening, E. A., *Adoption of Improved Farm Practices as Related to the Family Factors*, Research Bulletin Wisconsin Agricultural Experimental Station No 183, 1953
38 Rogers, E. M. with Svenning, L., *op. cit.*, 1969, pp 124–45
39 Blaikie, P. M. *Diffusion Theory and the Family Planning Programme of India*, University of Reading, Geographical Papers, No 1, 1972
40 Myren, D. T., 'The Rural Communications Media as a Determinant of the Diffusion of Information about Improved Farm Practices in Mexico'. Paper presented at Rural Sociology Society, Washington D.C. (1962), quoted in Rogers, E. M. with Shoemaker, F. F., *Communication of Innovations*, Free Press, 1971, p 258
41 Wilkening, E. A., *Acceptance of Improved Farm Practices as Related to Family Factors*, Wisconsin Agricultural Extension Service Bulletin 183, 1953
42 Beal, G. M. and Rogers, E. M. *op. cit.*, 1960, p 19
43 Wilkening, E. A., *op. cit.*, 1953
44 Blaikie, P. M., 'The Spatial Structure of Information Networks and Innovative Behaviour in the Ziz Valley, Southern Morocco', *Geografiska Annaler*, 55B, 1973, pp 83–105
45 Hudson, J. C., *op. cit.*, 1972
46 Lionberger, H. F., 'Some Characteristics of Farm Operators Sought as Sources of Farm Information in a Missouri Community', Rural Sociology, 18, 1953
47 Rapoport, A., 'Spread of Information Through a Population with a Sociostructural Bias', *Bulletin of Mathematical Biophysics*, 15, 1953, pp 523–47
48 Mayfield, R. C. and Yapa, L. S., 'Information Fields in Rural Mysore', *Economic Geography*, 50, 1974, pp 313–23
49 Hudson, J. C., 'Diffusion in a Central Place System', *Geographical Analysis*, 1, 1969, pp 45–58
50 For studies of information flows between national urban systems see Pederson, P. O., 'Innovation Diffusion Within and Between National Urban Systems', *Geographical Analysis*, 2, 1970, pp 203–54; and, Pred, A. R. and Törnqvist, G., *Systems of Cities and Information Flows*, Lund Studies in Geography, Series B, 38, 1973

51 Feaster, J. G., 'Measurement and Determinants of Innovativeness Among Primitive Agriculturalists', *Rural Sociology*, 33, 1968, pp 339–48

52 For a summary of the evidence see Rogers, E. M. with Shoemaker, F. F., *op. cit.*, 1971, pp 185–90; and, for an interesting micro-study, see Balderson, J., *The Diffusion of an Agricultural Innovation in Kesteven, Lincolnshire*, unpublished BA dissertation, University of Leicester, 1975

53 For an introduction to factor analysis, see Harman, H., *Modern Factor Analysis*, University of Chicago Press, 1967

54 Rogers, E. M. with Svenning, L., *Modernization Among Peasants*, Holt, Rinehart and Winston, 1969, pp 316–42

55 Fuller, G., 'On the Spatial Diffusion of Fertility Decline: The Distance-to-Clinic Variable in a Chilean Community', *Economic Geography*, 50, 1974, pp 324–32

56 Blaikie, P. M., *Family Planning in India: Diffusion and Policy*, Arnold, 1975

57 Kivlin, J. E. and Fliegel, F. C., 'Attributes of Innovations as Factors in Diffusion', *American Journal of Sociology*, 72, 1966, pp 235–48

58 Fliegel, F. C., 'Traditionalism in the Farm Family and Technological Change', *Rural Sociology*, 27, 1962, p 74

59 Brookfield, H. C., 'The Money that Grows on Trees: The Consequences of an Innovation within a Man-Environment System', *Australian Geographical Studies*, 6, 1968, pp 97–119

60 Rogers, E. M., *Diffusion of Innovations*, Free Press, 1962

61 Apodoca, A., 'Corn and Custom: Introduction of Hybrid Corn to Spanish American Farmers in New Mexico' in Spicer, E. H. (ed), *Human Problems in Technical Change*, Sage, 1952, p 35

62 Fliegel, F. C. and Kivlin, J. E., 'Farm Practice Attributes and Adoption Rates', *Social Forces*, 40, 1962, pp 364–70

63 Fliegel, F. C. and Kivlin, J. E., *ibid*, 1962, pp 364–70

64 See, for example, Gross, N. C., 'The Differential Characteristics of Acceptors and Non-acceptors of an Approved Agricultural Practice', *Rural Sociology*, 14, 1949, pp 148–56; and Ryan, B., 'A Study in Technological Diffusion', *Rural Sociology*, 13, 1948, pp 273–85

65 Erasmus, C. J., *Man Takes Control: Cultural Development and American Aid*, University of Minnesota Press, 1961, p 23

66 Hrushka, E., quoted in Rogers, E. M., *op. cit.*, 1962, p 132

67 Kivlin, J. E., *Characteristics of Farm Practices Associated with Rates of Adoption*, unpublished Pennsylvanian State University PhD thesis, 1960, quoted in Rogers, E. M., *op. cit.*, 1962, p 135

68 Griliches, Z., 'Hybrid Corn and the Economics of Innovation', *Science*, 132, 1960, pp 275–80

69 Powell, L. C. and Roseman, C. C., 'An Investigation of the Subprocesses of Diffusion', *Rural Sociology*, 37, 1972, pp 221–8

70 See, for example, Meyer, J. W., 'Diffusers and Social Innovations: Increasing the Scope of Diffusion Models', *Professional Geographer*, 28, 1976, pp 17–22

Chapter Five

1 Jordan, T. G., 'On the Nature of Settlement Geography', *Professional Geographer*, 18, 1966, pp 26–8
2 Stone, K. H., 'The Development of a Focus for the Geography of Settlement', *Economic Geography*, 41, 1965, p 347
3 Pióro, Z., 'Ecological Interpretation of Settlement Systems', *International Social Science Journal*, 18, 1966, pp 527–38
4 *Reports of the Commission on Types of Rural Settlement*, International Geographical Union, 1928, 1930 and 1931
5 Houston, J. M., *A Social Geography of Europe*, Duckworth, 1953, p 80
6 An important contribution in this field is Roberts, B. K., *Rural Settlement in Britain*, Dawson, 1977
7 Hoskins, W. G., *The Making of the English Landscape*, Hodder and Stoughton, 1957
8 Aurousseau, M., 'The Arrangement of Rural Populations', *Geographical Review*, 10, 1920, pp 223–40
9 Demangeon, A., 'Types de Villages en France', *Annales de Geographie*, 48, 1939, pp 1–21
10 Thorpe, H., 'Rural Settlement' in J. W. Watson and J. B. Sissons (eds), *British Isles*, Nelson, 1964, pp 358–79
11 Sylvester, D., *The Rural Landscape of the Welsh Borderland*, Macmillan, 1969, p 190
12 Stone, K. H. 'Regionalization of Spanish Units of Settlements', *Tijdschrift voor Economische en Sociale Geografie*, 61, 1970, pp 232–41
13 Stone, K. H., 'Multiple Classifications for Rural Settlement Geography', *Acta Geographica*, 20, 1968, p 318
14 For a detailed summary see Jordan, T. G., *European Culture Area: A Systematic Geography*, Harper and Row, 1973
15 Meitzen, A., *Siedelung und Agrarwesen der Westgermanen und Ostgermanen, der Kelten, Römer, Finnen und Slawen*, Wilhelm Hertz, 1895
16 Dickinson, R. E., 'Rural Settlement in German Lands', *Annals of the Association of American Geographers*, 39, 1949, pp 239–63
17 Evans, E. E., 'Some Survivals of the Irish Open Field System', *Geography*, 24, 1939, pp 24–36
18 Evans, E. E., *ibid*, 1939, pp 27–8
19 Evans, E. E., *ibid*, 1939, p 28
20 For example, in North Wales a number of detailed studies have been carried out: see Jones-Pierce, T., 'Medieval Settlements in Anglesey', *Anglesey Antiquarian Society Transactions*, 1951, pp 1–33; Jones, G. R. J.,

'Some Medieval Rural Settlements in North Wales', *Transactions of the Institute of British Geographers*, 19, 1953, pp 51–72; Thomas, C., 'Enclosure and the Rural Landscape of Merioneth in the Sixteenth Century', *Transactions of the Institute of British Geographers*, 42, 1975, pp 153–62

21 Bowen, E. G., 'The Dispersed Habitat of Wales' in Buchanan, R. H., Jones, E. and McCourt, D., *Man and His Habitat*, Routledge and Kegan Paul, 1971, p 200

22 Bowen, E. G., *ibid*, 1971, p 200

23 Whittlesey, D., 'Sequent Occupance', *Annals of the Association of American Geographers*, 19, 1929, pp 162–5

24 Jefferson, M., 'Some Consideration on the Geographical Provinces of the United States', *Annals of the Association of American Geographers*, 7, 1917, p 3

25 Brown, R. H., 'Some Sequential Time-Lines in Minnesota', *Annals of the Association of American Geographers*, 50, 1960, pp 306–7

26 Brown, R. H., 'The Upsala, Minnesota, Community: A Case Study in Rural Dynamics', *Annals of the Association of American Geographers*, 57, 1967, pp 267–300

27 Bylund, E., 'Theoretical Consideration Regarding the Distribution of Settlement in Inner North Sweden', *Geografiska Annaler*, 42, 1960, p 225

28 For another example of the simulation of settlement evolution see Morrill, R. L., *Migration and the Spread and Growth of Urban Settlement*, Lund Studies in Geography No 26, 1965

29 Bylund, E., *op. cit.*, 1960, p 230

30 Norton, W., 'Constructing Abstract Worlds of the Past', *Geographical Analysis*, 8, 1976, pp 269–88

31 Hudson, J. C., 'A Location Theory for Rural Settlement', *Annals of the Association of American Geographers*, 59, 1969, pp 365–81

32 Hudson, J. C., *ibid*, 1969, pp 375–81

33 Olsson, G., 'Complementary Models: A Study of Colonization Maps', *Geografiska Annaler*, 50 B, 1968, pp 115–32

34 Siddle, D. J., 'Location Theory and the Subsistence Economy: The Spacing of Rural Settlement in Sierra Leone', *Journal of Tropical Geography*, 31, 1970, pp 79–90

35 Grossman, D., 'Do We Have a Theory for Settlement Geography?—The Case of Iboland', *Professional Geographer*, 23, 1971, p 197

36 Hunter, J. M., 'The Social Roots of Dispersed Settlement in Northern Ghana', *Annals of the Association of American Geographers*, 57, 1967, pp 338–49

37 Grossman, D., 'The Process of Frontier Settlement: The Case of Nikeland (Nigeria)', *Geografiska Annaler*, 53 B, 1971, pp 107–28

38 Houston, J. M., *op. cit.*, 1953, pp 80–108

39 Chisholm, M., *Rural Settlement and Land Use*, Hutchinson, 1962, pp 126–38

40 Clark, P. J. and Evans, F. C., 'Distance to Nearest Neighbour as a Measure of Spatial Relationships in Populations', *Ecology*, 35, 1954, pp 445–53

41 Dacey, M. F., 'The Analysis of Central Place and Point Patterns by a Nearest Neighbour Method' in Norburg, K. (ed), *Symposium on Urban Geography, Lund, 1960*, International Geographical Union, 1962, p 55

42 Haynes, K. E. and Enders, W. T., 'Distance, Direction and Entropy in the Evolution of a Settlement Pattern', *Economic Geography*, 51, 1975, p 357

43 For a more general discussion see Curry, L., 'The Random Spatial Economy: An Exploration in Settlement Theory', *Annals of the Association of American Geographers*, 54, 1964, pp 138–46

44 Birch, B. P., 'The Measurement of Dispersed Patterns of Settlement', *Tijdschrift voor Economische en Sociale Geografie*, 58, 1967, pp 68–75

45 Hudson, J. C., 'Pattern Recognition in Empirical Map Analysis', *Journal of Regional Science*, 9, 1969, pp 189–99

46 Kariel, H. G., 'Analysis of the Alberta Settlement Pattern for 1961 and 1966 by Nearest Neighbour Methods', *Geografiska Annaler*, 52B, 1970, p 128

47 Kariel, H. G., *ibid*, 1970, pp 127–8

48 Kariel, H. G., *ibid*, 1970, p 128

49 Clark, P. J. and Evans, E. C., *op. cit.*, 1954, p 451

50 Medvedkhov, Y. V., 'The Concept of Entropy in Settlement Pattern Analysis', *Papers of the Regional Science Association*, 18, 1967, pp 165–8

51 Semple, R. K. and Golledge, R. G., 'An Analysis of Entropy Changes in a Settlement Pattern over Time', *Economic Geography*, 46, 1970, pp 157–60

52 Haynes, K. E. and Enders, W. T., *op. cit.*, 1975, pp 445–53

53 Clawson, M., 'Factors and Forces Affecting the Optimum Future Rural Settlement Pattern in the United States', *Economic Geography*, 42, 1966, p 383

54 See, for example, Whitby, M. C., Robins, D. L. J., Tansey, A. W. and Willis, K. G., *Rural Resource Development*, Methuen, 1974; and Woodruffe, B. J., *Rural Settlement Policies and Plans*, Oxford University Press, 1976

55 Clawson, M., *op. cit.*, 1966, p 287

56 For a more detailed discussion of this theme see Chapter 7

57 Woodruffe, B. J., *op. cit.*, 1976, pp 28–45

58 Edwards, J. A., 'The Viability of Lower Size-order Settlements in Rural Areas: The Case of North-east England', *Sociologia Ruralis*, 3, 1971, pp 247–74

59 Warford, J. J., *The South Atcham Scheme: An Economic Appraisal*, H.M.S.O., 1969

60 McEntire, D. and Agostini, D. (ed), *Towards Modern Land Policies*, University of Padua Press, 1970, p 198

61 Lambert, A. M., 'Farm Consolidation in Western Europe', *Geography*, 48, 1963, pp 31–48

62 Mayhew, A., 'Agrarian Reform in West Germany: An Assessment of the Integrated Development Project Mooriem', *Transactions of the Institute of British Geographers*, 52, 1971, pp 61–76

63 Mayhew, A., *ibid*, 1971, p 68

64 Farmer, B. H., *The Agricultural Colonization in India Since Independence*, Oxford University Press, 1974

65 Quoted in Farmer, B. H., 'Urban-Rural Relations in India Colonization Schemes', paper presented at the Indo-British Seminar, Delhi, 1972, p 4

66 Farmer, B. H., *Pioneer Peasant Colonization in Ceylon*, Oxford University Press, 1957, p 255

Chapter Six

1 Galpin, C. J., 'The Social Anatomy of an Agricultural Community', *University of Wisconsin Agricultural Experimental Station Research Bulletin*, 34, 1915; Kolb, H. J., 'Service Relations of Town and Country', *University of Wisconsin Agricultural Experimental Station Research Bulletin*, 58, 1923

2 For a succinct review see Carter, H., *The Study of Urban Geography*, Arnold, 1972, pp 18–132

3 Von Bertalanffy, L., 'General System Theory', *General Systems*, 1, 1956, pp 1–10

4 Belshaw, C. S., *Traditional Exchange and Modern Markets*, Prentice-Hall, 1965

5 Jones, G., *Patterns of Rural Life*, Longman, 1973, pp 56–78

6 Frankenberg, R., *Communities in Britain*, Penguin, 1966

7 Christaller, W. (translated by C. W. Baskin), *Central Places in Southern Germany*, Prentice-Hall, 1966

8 See Murphy, R. E., *The American City*, McGraw-Hill, 1966; and Berry, B. J. L., *Geography of Market Centres and Retail Distribution*, Prentice-Hall, 1967

9 See Marshall, J. U., *Location of Service Centres: An Approach to the Analysis of Central Place Systems*, University of Toronto, Department of Geography Research Publication, 1969; Scott, P., *Geography of Retailing*, Hutchinson, 1970; and Davies, R. L., *Marketing Geography*, RPA, 1976

10 Harvey, D., *Explanation in Geography*, Arnold, 1969, p 138

11 Berry, B. J. L. and Garrison, W. L., 'A Note on Central Place Theory and the Range of a Good', *Economic Geography*, 34, 1958, pp 304–11

12 Berry, B. J. L. and Garrison, W. L., *ibid*, 1958, pp 304–11
13 Lösch, A. (translated by Woglom, W. H. and Stolper, W. F.), *The Economics of Location*, Yale University, 1954
14 Berry, B. J. L. and Garrison, W. L., 'The Functional Bases of Central Place Theory', *Economic Geography*, 34, 1958, pp 145–54
15 Davies, W. K. D., 'Centrality and Central Place Hierarchy', *Urban Studies*, 4, 1967, pp 61–79
16 Davies, W. K. D., *ibid*, 1967, p 63
17 O'Farrell, P. N., 'Continuous Regularities and Discontinuities in the Central Place System', *Geografiska Annaler*, 52 B, 1969, pp 104–14
18 Rowley, G., 'Central Places in Rural Wales: A Case Study', *Tijdschrift Voor Economische en Sociale Geografie*, 61, 1970, pp 32–40
19 Wanmali, S., 'Ranking of Settlements: A Suggestion', *Behavioural Sciences and Community Development*, 5, 1971, pp 97–111
20 Haggett, P. and Gunawardena, K. A., 'Determination of Population Thresholds for Settlements Function by Reed-Muench Method', *Professional Geographer*, 16, 1964, pp 6–9
21 Abiodun, J. C., 'Urban Hierarchy in a Developing Country', *Economic Geography*, 43, 1967, pp 343–67
22 Bell, T. L., Lieber, S. R. and Rushton, G., 'Clustering of Services in Central Places', *Annals of the Association of American Geographers*, 64, 1974, pp 214–25
23 Hassinger, E., 'The Relationship of Retail-Service Patterns to Trade-Center Population Change', *Rural Sociology*, 22, 1957, pp 235–40
24 For an elementary introduction see Coombs, C. H., Davies, R. M. and Tversky, A., *Mathematical Psychology: An Elementary Introduction*, Prentice-Hall, 1970, pp 38–41
25 Berry, B. J. L., Barnum, H. G. and Tennant, R. J., 'Retail Location and Consumer Behaviour', *Papers and Proceedings of the Regional Science Association*, 9, 1962, pp 65–106
26 Abiodun, J. C., *op. cit.*, 1967, pp 343–67
27 Davies, M. L., *Town, Village and Hamlet in Mid-Wales*, unpublished PhD thesis, University of Wales, 1965
28 Hawley, A. H., *Human Ecology: A Theory of Community Structure*, Ronald Press, 1955, pp 255–8
29 Dickinson, R. E., 'The Distribution of Functions of the Smaller Urban Settlements of East Anglia', *Geography*, 17, 1932, pp 19–31; and 'The Markets and Market Areas of East Anglia', *Economic Geography*, 10, 1934, pp 172–82
30 Bracey, H. E., *Social Provision in Rural Wiltshire*, Methuen, 1952
31 For example, Rowley, G., 'Central Places in Rural Wales', *Annals of the Association of American Geographers*, 61, 1971, pp 537–50
32 O'Farrell, P. N., *op. cit.*, 1969, pp 104–14

33 For example, Davies, W. K. D. and Robinson, G. W. S., 'The Nodal Structure of the Solent Area', *Journal of the Town Planning Institute*, 54, 1968, pp 18–23; and Davies, W. K. D. and Lewis, C. R., 'Regional Studies in Wales: Two Studies of Connectivity' in Davies, W. K. D. and Carter, H. (eds), *Urban Essays: Studies in the Geography of Wales*, Longman, 1970, pp 31–45

34 Nystuen, J. D. and Dacey, M. F., 'A Graph Theory Interpretation of Nodal Regions', *Papers of the Regional Science Association*, 7, 1961, p 41

35 Carter, H., *op. cit.*, 1972, p 121

36 Golledge, R. G., Rushton, G. and Clark, W. A. V., 'Some Spatial Characteristics of Iowa's Dispersed Farm Population and their Implications for the Grouping of Central Place Functions', *Economic Geography*, 42, 1966, pp 261–72

37 Golledge, R. G., Rushton, G. and Clark, W. A. V., *ibid*, 1966, p 271

38 Swedner, H., *Ecological Differentiation of Habits and Attitudes*, Gleerup, 1960

39 Maund, D. J., *Shopping Centres in Herefordshire*, unpublished BA dissertation, University of Leicester, 1968

40 Ray, D. M., 'Cultural Differences in Consumer Travel Behaviour in Eastern Ontario', *Canadian Geographer*, 11, 1967, pp 143–56

41 Murdie, R. A., 'Cultural Differences in Consumer Travel', *Economic Geography*, 41, 1965, pp 211–33

42 Abiodun, J. C., 'Service Centres and Consumer Behaviour within the Nigerian Cocoa Area', *Geografiska Annaler*, 53B, 1971, pp 78–93

43 Prakasa Rao, V. L. S. and Ramachandran, R., 'Mobility and Choice of Central Places', *Analytical Geography*, 1, 1971, pp 17–32

44 Cadwallader, M., 'A Behavioural Model of Consumer Spatial Decision Making', *Economic Geography*, 51, 1975, pp 339–49

45 Balderson, W. A., *Central Places in a Part of Lincolnshire*, unpublished BA dissertation, University of Leicester, 1975

46 See, for example, Carter, H. and Lewis, C. R., *Dulas Valley Enquiry: A Survey of Demographic and Community Characteristics*, University College of Wales, Aberystwyth, Department of Geography Publication, 1970, p 9; and Weekley, I. G., 'Lateral Interdependence as an Aspect of Rural Service Provision: a Northamptonshire Case Study', *East Midland Geographer*, 6, 1977, pp 361–74

47 Wanmali, S., 'Central Places and their Tributary Population: Some Observations', *Behavioural Sciences and Community Development*, 6, 1972, pp 11–39

48 Hodder, B. W., 'The Distribution of Markets in Yorubaland', *Scottish Geographical Magazine*, 81, 1965, pp 48–58

49 See Bromley, R. J., Markets in Developing Countries: A Review', *Geography*, 56, 1971, pp 124–32; Smith, R. H. T. (ed), 'Spatial Structure and Process in Tropical Africa', *Economic Geography*, 50, 1972, pp 228–355;

Bromley, R. J., Synanski, R. and Good, C. M., 'The Rationale of Periodic Markets', *Annals of the Association of American Geographers*, 65, 1975, pp 530–7; and Smith, C. A. (ed), *Regional Analysis. Vol. 1. Economic Systems*, Academic Press, 1976

50 Skinner, G. W., 'Marketing and Social Structure in Rural China', *Journal of Asian Studies*, 24, 1964, p 4

51 Stine, W., 'Temporal Aspects of Tertiary Production Elements in Korea' in Pitts, F. R., *Urban Systems and Economic Development*, University of Oregon, 1962, pp 66–88

52 Skinner, G. W., *ibid*, 1964, pp 3–44

53 Hodder, B. W., 'The Yoruba Rural Market' in Bohannan, P. and Dalton, G., *Markets in Africa*, Northwestern University Press, 1962, p 104

54 Hodder, B. W., 'Some Comments on the Origin of Traditional Markets in Africa South of the Sahara', *Transactions of the Institute of British Geographers*, 36, 1965, p 97

55 Bromley, R. J. and Symanski, R., 'Marketplace Trade in Latin America', *Latin American Research Review*, 9, 1974, pp 3–38

56 Smith, R. H. T., 'West African Market Places: Temporal Periodicity and Locational Spacing' in Meillasoux, C. (ed), *The Development of Indigenous Trade and Markets in West Africa*, Oxford University Press, 1971, pp 319–46

57 Harriss, B., 'Poverty, Caste and the Rurality of Transactions: A Speculative Explanation for Periodic Marketing in Northern Tamil Nadu', paper presented at Indo-British Seminar, Cambridge, 1975

58 Harriss, B., *ibid*, 1975

59 Smith, R. H. T., *op. cit.*, 1971, pp 319–46

60 Smith, C. A., 'Stratification Systems Through Peasant Marketing Arrangements: An Appreciation of Some Models from Economic Geography', *Man*, 10, 1975, pp 95–122

61 Jackson, R. T., 'Periodic Markets in Southern Ethiopia', *Transactions of the Institute of British Geographers*, 53, 1971, pp 31–42

62 Janelle, D. G., 'Central Place Development in a Time-Space Framework', *Professional Geographer*, 20, 1968, pp 5–10

63 Berry, B. J. L., *Geography of Market Centres and Retail Distribution*, Prentice-Hall, 1967, p 106

64 Polanyi, K., *Trade and Markets in the Early Empires*, Free Press, 1957

65 Forde, C. D., *Habitat, Economy and Society*, Methuen, 1934

66 Firth, R., *We, The Tikopia*, Allen and Unwin, 1936

67 Forde, C. D., *op. cit.*, 1934, pp 287–307

68 Malinowski, B., *Argonauts of the Western Pacific*, Routledge and Kegan Paul, 1922; and, more recently, Nisbett, A., 'Kula Custom: Giving Till it Hurts', *The Listener*, 94, 1975–76, pp 859–60

69 Stine, J. H., *op. cit.*, 1962 pp 68–9

70 Brookfield. H. C., 'The Money that Grows on Trees: The Consequences of an Innovation within a Man-Environment System', *Australian Geographical Studies*, 6, 1968, pp 97–119

71 Clark, R. J., 'Land Reform and Peasant Market Participation on the Northern Highlands of Bolivia', *Land Economics*, 44, 1968, pp 153–72

72 Preston, D. A., 'New Towns—A Major Change in the Rural Settlement Pattern in Highland Bolivia', *Journal of Latin American Studies*, 2, 1970, pp 2–27

73 Hodge, G., 'The Prediction of Trade Centre Variability in the Great Plains', *Papers and Proceedings of the Regional Science Association*, 16, 1965, pp 87–115

74 Chittick, D., *Growth and Decline of South Dakota Trade Centers: 1901–1951*, South Dakota Agricultural Experiment Station, Bulletin 448, 1955

75 Johanssen, H. E. and Fuguitt, G. V., 'Changing Retail Activity in Wisconsin Villages: 1939, 1954 and 1970', *Rural Sociology*, 38, 1973, pp 207–18

76 Pahl, R. E., *Urbs in Rure: The Metropolitan Fringe in Hertfordshire*, London School of Economics Geographical Papers No. 2, 1964, p 72

77 Wanmali, S., 'Rural Service Centres in India: Present Identification and the Acceptance of Extension', *Area*, 7, 1975, p 169

78 Wanmali, S., *ibid*, 1975, p 169

Chapter Seven

1 See, for example, Herbert, D. T. and Johnston, R. J. (eds), *Social Areas in Cities*, vols I and II, Wiley, 1976

2 Wirth, L., 'Urbanism as a Way of Life', *American Journal of Sociology*, 44, 1938, pp 46–63

3 For a controversial discussion see Pahl, R. E., 'The Rural-Urban Continuum', *Sociologia Ruralis*, 6, 1966, pp 299–327

4 Brooke, M. Z., *Le Play, Engineer and Social Scientist*, Longman, 1970

5 Gans, H. J., 'Urbanism and Suburbanism as Ways of Life' in Rose, A. M. (ed), *Human Behaviour and Social Processes*, Routledge and Kegan Paul, 1962, p 643

6 Pahl, R. E., *op. cit.*, 1966, pp 299–327

7 Pahl, R. E., *ibid*, 1966, p 322

8 Lewis, G. J. and Maund, D. J., 'The Urbanization of the Countryside: A Framework for Analysis', *Geografiska Annaler*, 58 B, 1976, pp 17–27

9 Martin, W. T., 'Ecological Change in Satellite Rural Areas', *American Sociological Review*, 22, 1957, pp 173–83

10 Martin, W. T., *ibid*, 1957, pp 76

11 Hawley, A. H., *Human Ecology*, Ronald Press, 1950, p 420

238 NOTES

12 Martin, W. T., *op. cit.*, 1957, pp 76–7
13 Wheeler, J. O., 'Commuting and the Rural Nonfarm Population', *Professional Geographer*, 23, 1971, pp 118–22
14 Lewis, G. J. and Maund, D. J., *op. cit.*, 1976, pp 17–27
15 Wheeler, J. O., *op. cit.*, 1971, pp 118–22
16 Lawton, R., 'The Journey to Work in England and Wales: Forty Years of Change', *Tijdschrift voor Economische en Sociale Geografie*, 54, 1963, pp 61–9; and 'The Journey to Work in Britain: Some Trends and Problems', *Regional Studies*, 2, 1968, pp 27–40
17 Berry, B. J. L., 'The Geography of the United States in the Year 2000', *Transactions of the Institute of British Geographers*, 51, 1970, pp 21–54
18 Lewis, G. J., 'Commuting and the Village in Mid-Wales', *Geography*, 52, 1967, pp 294–304
19 Holmes, J. H., 'The Suburbanization of Cessnock Coalfield Towns: 1954–61', *Australian Geographical Studies*, 3, 1965, pp 105–28
20 Maund, D. J., *The Urbanization of the Countryside: A Case-Study in Herefordshire*, unpublished University of Leicester MA thesis, 1976
21 Bogue, D. J., *The Structure of the Metropolitan Community: A Study of Dominance and Subdominance*, University of Michigan, 1949, p 47
22 Anderson, T. R. and Collier, J., 'Metropolitan Dominance and the Rural Hinterland', *Rural Sociology*, 21, 1956, pp 152–7
23 For an aggregate analysis of the impact of metropolitan centres upon rural society see Lamb, R., *Metropolitan Impacts on Rural America*, University of Chicago, Department of Geography Research Paper 162, 1975
24 For the only comparable study outside North America see Scott, P., 'Trade Center Population Change, Centralization and Trade Area Farming Type', *Rural Sociology*, 33, 1968, pp 424–36
25 Doerflinger, J., *Geographic and Residential Distribution of Iowa's Population and Distance from Larger Towns*, Iowa State University, Department of Economics and Sociology, 1962
26 Fanelli, A. A. and Pederson, H. A., *Growth Trends of Mississippi Population Centers 1900–50*, State College, Mississippi: Community Series 10, 1956
27 Fuguitt, G. V., 'The Growth and Decline of Small Towns as a Probability Process', *American Sociological Review*, 30, 1965, pp 403–11
28 Rikkinen, K., 'Change in Village and Rural Population with Distance from Duluth', *Economic Geography*, 44, 1968, pp 312–25
29 Borchert, J. R., 'The Urbanization of the Upper Midwest: 1930–60', *Upper Midwest Economic Study*, University of Minneapolis, 1963, pp 13–19
30 Fuguitt, G. V., 'Some Demographic Aspects of the Small Towns in the United States', *Sociologia Ruralis*, 12, 1972, pp 146–59
31 Hassinger, E., 'The Relationship of Trade-Center Population Change to Distance from Larger Centers in an Agricultural Area', *Rural Sociology*,

22 (1957), 131–6; and 'The Relationship of Retail-Service Patterns to Trade-Center Population Change', *Rural Sociology*, 22, 1957, pp 235–40

32 Butler, J. E. and Fuguitt, G. V., 'Small Town Population Change and Distance from Larger Towns: A Replication of Hassinger's Study', *Rural Sociology*, 35, 1970, pp 396–409

33 Hart, J. F. and Salisbury, N. E., 'Population Change in Middle Western Villages: A Statistical Approach', *Annals of the Association of American Geographers*, 55, 1965, pp 140–60

34 Fuguitt, G. V. and Thomas, D. W., 'Small Town Growth in the United States: An Analysis by Size Class and Place', *Demography*, 9, 1972, pp 295–308

35 Fuguitt, G. V., *op. cit.*, 1972, p 154

36 For a discussion of village growth in rural America see Hart, J. F., Salisbury, N. E. and Smith, E. G., 'The Dying Village and Some Notions about Urban Growth', *Economic Geography*, 44, 1968, pp 344–9

37 Fuguitt, G. V. and Field, D. R., 'Some Population Characteristics of Villages Differentiated by Size, Location and Growth', *Demography*, 9, 1972, pp 295–308

38 For a general survey see Richardson, J. L. and Larson, C. F., 'Small Community Trends: A 50-year Perspective on Socio-Economic Change in Thirteen New York Communities', *Rural Sociology*, 41, 1970, pp 45–59

39 Rikkinen, K. and Alanen, A., 'Changing Age Structure in a Rural-Urban Continuum', *Geografiska Annaler*, 52 B, 1969, pp 57–71

40 Another interesting example is Stoeckel, J. and Beegle, J. A., 'The Relationship Between the Rural-Farm Age Structure and Distance from a Metropolitan Area', *Rural Sociology*, 31, 1966, pp 346–54

41 For example, Odum, H. W., *Southern Regions of the United States*, University of Northern Carolina Press, 1936; and Lively, C. E. and Gregory, C. L., *Rural Social Areas in Missouri*, Missouri Agricultural Experiment Station 305, 1939

42 Maund, D. J., *op. cit.*, 1976

43 Lively, C. E. and Almack, R. B., *A Method of Determining Rural Social Sub-Areas with Application to Ohio*, Ohio State University and Ohio Agricultural Experiment Station Mimeograph Bulletin 106, 1938

44 Hagood, M. J., Danilevsky, N. and Beum, C. O., 'An Examination of the Use of Factor Analysis in the Problem of Subregional Delineation', *Rural Sociology*, September 1941, pp 216–33

45 Bertrand, A. L., *The Many Louisianas, Rural Social Areas and Cultural Islands*, Louisiana Sate University Experiment Station Bulletin 496, 1955

46 Gregory, C. L., *Rural Social Areas in Missouri*, University of Missouri Agricultural Experiment Station Bulletin 665, 1958

47 Giggs, J. A. and Mather, P. M., 'Factor Ecology and Factor Invariance: An Investigation', *Economic Geography*, 51, 1975, pp 366–82

48 Harvey, M. E. and Bhardwaj, S. M., 'Spatial Dimensions of Moderniza-
    tion in a Rural Environment: Rajasthan, India', *Tijdschrift voor Econom-
    ische en Sociale Geografie*, 64, 1973, pp 145–59
49 For a preliminary factor analysis of a Third World rural community see
    Naidu, N., *Spatial Aspects of Social Change*, Lund Studies in Geo-
    graphy, Series B, 41, 1975
50 Sommers, L. M. and Gade, O., 'The Spatial Impact of Government
    Decisions on Postwar Economic Change in North Norway', *Annals of
    the Association of American Geographers*, 61, 1971, pp 522–36
51 Pryor, R. J., 'Urbanisation in Peninsular Malaysia: A Factor Analytical
    Approach', *Australian Geographical Studies*, 13, 1975, pp 13–52
52 Horton, F. E., McConnell, H. and Tirtha, C., 'Spatial Patterns of Socio-
    Economic Structure in India', *Tijdschrift voor Economische en Sociale
    Geografie*, 61, 1970, pp 101–13

Chapter Eight

1 Lewis, G. J. and Maund, D. J., 'The Urbanization of the Countryside: A
   Framework for Analysis', *Gegrafiska Annaler*, 58 B, 1976, pp 17–27
2 Webber, M. M., 'Order in Diversity: Community without Propinquity'
   in Wingo, L. (ed), *Cities and Space*, Johns Hopkins Press, 1963, p 29
3 See, for example, Chapin, F. S., *Human Activity Patterns in the City*,
   Wiley, 1974
4 Stacey, M., 'The Myth of Community Studies', *British Journal of Sociology*, 20, 1969, pp 134–47
5 Stacey, M., *ibid*, 1969, p 140
6 The numbers used within text accord with those used by Stacey in her
   paper
7 Stacey, M., *op. cit.*, 1969, p 142
8 Stacey, M., *ibid*, 1969, p 145
9 Stacey, M., *ibid*, 1969, p 144
10 Stacey, M., *ibid*, 1969, p 144
11 Stacey, M., *ibid*, 1969, p 144
12 Banton, M. (ed), *The Social Anthropology of Complex Societies*, Tavis-
    tock, 1966
13 Evans-Pritchard, E. C., *Essays in Social Anthropology*, Faber and Faber,
    1962
14 The pioneering modern community study in the United States was Lynd,
    R. S. and Middletown, H. M., *A Study in Contemporary American Cul-
    ture*, Harcourt Brace, 1929
15 Arensberg, C. M., *The Irish Countryman. An Anthropological Study*,
    Macmillan, 1939; and Arensberg, C. M. and Kimball, S. T., *Family and
    Community in Ireland*, Peter Smith, 1940

16 For a set of readings see Bell, C. and Newby, H., *The Sociology of Community*, Cass, 1974; and for two useful reviews see Frankenberg, R., *Communities in Britain*, Penguin, 1966; and Bell, C. and Newby, H., *Community Studies*, Allen and Unwin, 1971

17 For a set of recent review see Shanin, T. (ed), *Peasants and Peasant Scoiety*, Penguin, 1971; and Beteille, A. (ed), *Social Inequality*, Penguin, 1969; for a series of original essays see Brookfield, H. C. (ed), *The Pacific in Transition*, Arnold, 1973

18 For details of these studies see Lewis, G. J., 'A Welsh Rural Community in Transition: A Case-Study in Mid-Wales', *Sociologia Ruralis*, 10, 1970, 143–61; and Lloyd, M. G. and Thomason, G. F., *Welsh Society in Transition*, Council of Social Services for Wales and Monmouthshire, 1963

19 For a discussion of this method see Frankenberg, R., 'Participant Observer', *New Society*, 23, March 1963, pp 22–3; and Swantz, M. L., 'The Role of Participant Research in Development', *Geografiska Annaler*, 57 B, 1975, pp 109–18

20 This is based on the evidence contained in Rees, A. D., *Life in a Welsh Countryside*, University of Wales Press, 1950; and Davies, E. and Rees, A. D. (eds), *Welsh Rural Communities*, University of Wales Press, 1960

21 This is based on the evidence contained in two studies: Frankenberg, R., *Village on the Border*, Cohen and West, 1957; and Emmett, I., *A North Wales Village*, Routledge and Kegan Paul, 1964

22 For a discussion see Frankenberg, R., 'British Community Studies: Problems of Synthesis' in Banton, M. (ed), *op. cit.*, 1966, pp 123–54

23 Glass, Ruth, 'Conflict in Cities' in *Conflict in Society*, Churchill, 1968, p 148

24 See Simpson, R. L., 'Sociology of the Community: Current Status and Prospects', *Rural Sociology*, 30, 1965, pp 127–49

25 Shanin, T. (ed), 'Introduction', *op. cit.*, 1971, pp 14–15

26 Franklin, S. H., *The European Peasantry: The Final Phase*, Methuen, 1969; and *Rural Societies,* Macmillan, 1971

27 Emerson, G., *Voiceless India*, John Day, 1931

28 Wiser, C. and W. H., *Behind Mud Walls in India*, University of California Press, 1930

29 Duke, S. C., *Indian Village*, Routledge and Kegan Paul, 1958

30 Srinivas, M. N., *Religion and Society Among the Coorgs of South India,* Oxford University Press, 1952

31 Mayer, A. C., *Land and Society in Malabar*, Oxford University Press, 1952

32 Dumont, R., 'Indian Village Studies', *Contributions to Indian Sociology*, 1, 1957, p 23

33 For a detailed discussion of caste see Srinivas, M. N., *op. cit.*, 1952

34 Redfield, R., *Peasant, Society and Culture*, University Chicago Press, 1956, p 34

35 Srinivas, M. N., Darule, Y. B., Shahani, S. and Beteille, A., 'Caste: A Trend Report and Bibliography', *Current Sociology*, 8, 1959, p 141

36 Lambert, R. D., 'The Impact of Urban Society upon Village Life' in Turner, R. (ed), *India's Urban Future*, University of Calfornia Press, 1962

37 Majumder, D. N., *Caste and Communication in an Indian Village*, Asian Publishing House, 1958

38 Pareek, V. and Trivedi, G., 'Factor Analysis of Socio-Economic Status of Farmers in India', *Rural Sociology*, 30, 1965, pp 311–21

39 Bopegamage, A. and Kulahali, R. N., 'Caste and Occupation in Rural India: A Regional Study in Urbanization and Social Change', *Rural Sociology*, 37, 1972, pp 352–88

40 Sinha, D., *Indian Villages in Transition*, Asian Publishing House, 1969

41 Beteille, A., *Caste, Class and Power: Changing Patterns of Stratification in a Tanjore Village*, University of Cambridge Press, 1966

42 Epstein, T. S., *Economic Development and Social Change in South India*, Manchester University Press, 1962

43 For a study of a village at the urban fringe see Rao, M. S. A., *Urbanization and Social Change of a Rural Community on a Metropolitan Fringe*, Orient Longman, 1970·

44 Epstein, T. S., *op. cit.*, 1962, p 204

45 Epstein, T. S., *ibid*, 1962, p 10

46 Epstein, T. S., *South India: Yesterday, Today and Tomorrow*, Macmillan, 1973, p 86

47 Epstein, T. S., *ibid*, 1973, p 238

48 Epstein, T. S., *ibid*, 1973, p 242. A. K. is an abbreviation for Adikarnataka, the village scheduled castes in the Mandya region

49 Beteille, A., *op. cit.*, 1966

50 Sinha, D., *op. cit.*, 1969

51 Bailey, F. G., *Caste and Economic Frontier*, Manchester University Press, 1957

52 Lerner, D., *The Passing of Traditional Society*, Free Press, 1958

53 Ambrose, P., *The Quiet Revolution*, Chatto and Windus, 1974

54 Arensberg, C. M., *op. cit.*, 1939; and Arensberg, C. M. and Kimball, S. T., *op. cit.*, 1940

55 Rees, A. D., *op. cit.*, 1950

56 Williams, W. M., *The Sociology of an English Village: Gosforth*, Routledge and Kegan Paul, 1956, p 76

57 Rees, A. D., *op. cit.*, 1950, p 31

58 Rees, A. D., *ibid*, 1950, p 143

59 Arensberg, C. M. and Kimball, S. T., *op. cit.*, 1940, p 301

60 Williams, W. M., *op cit.*, 1956

61 Williams, W. M., *A West Country Village: Ashworthy*, Routledge and Kegan Paul, 1963, p xviii

62 Jenkins, D., *The Agricultural Community in South West Wales at the Turn of the Twentieth Century*, University of Wales Press, 1971

63 Williams, W. M., *The Sociology of an English Village: Gosforth*, Routledge and Kegan Paul, 1956, pp 202–3

64 Jackson, V., *Population in the Countryside: Growth and Stagnation in the Cotswolds*, Cass, 1968

65 Mitchell, G. D., 'Social Disintegration in a Rural Community', *Human Relations*, 3, 1950, pp 279–306

66 Littlejohn, J., *Westrigg: The Sociology of a Cheviot Parish*, Routledge and Kegan Paul, 1963

67 For a general discussion within an Irish context see Hannan, D., 'Kinship, Neighbourhood and Social Change in Irish Rural Communities', *The Economic and Social Review*, 3, 1972, pp 163–213

68 For a useful summary of the 'second-home' phenomenon see Coppock, J. T., *Second Homes: Curse or Blessing*, Pergamon, 1977; for its effects see Rothman, R. A., Bates, R. A. and Eckhardt, K. W., 'The Undulating Community: Typology of Recurrent Migrations', *Rural Sociology*, 42, 1977, pp 93–100

69 Lewis, G. J., *Consequences of Labour Migration*, D342.10, Open University Press, 1974

70 These studies include several by county planning authorities: *Kent Development Plan*, Quinquennial Review, Kent C.C., 1963; *Village Life in Hampshire*, Hampshire C. C., 1966; *Development Plan Review, Report of Survey*, Cambridgeshire C. C., 1968; and a number by individual researchers: Pahl, R. E., *Urbs in Rure: The Metropolitan Fringe in Hertfordshire*, L.S.E. Geographical Papers 2, 1965 and *Whose City*, Longman, 1970; Masser, F. I. and Stroud, D. C., 'The Metropolitan Village', *Town Planning Review*, 36, 1965, pp 111–24; Green, P., 'Drymen: Village Growth and Community Problems', *Sociological Review*, 4, 1964, pp 52–62; Thorns, D. C., 'The Changing System of Rural Stratification', *Sociological Review*, 8, 1968, pp 161–78; Emerson, A. R. and Crompton, R., *Suffolk—Some Social Trends*, Suffolk Rural Community Council, 1969; Lewis, G. J., 'Commuting and the Village in Mid-Wales', *Geography*, 52, 1967, pp 294–304; Radford, E., *The New Villages*, Cass, 1970; Ambrose, P., *op. cit.*, 1970. For a brief review see Connell, J., 'The Metropolitan Village: Spatial and Social Processes in Discontinuous Suburbs' in Johnson, J. H., *op. cit.*, 1974, pp 77–100

71 Elias, N. and Scotson, J. L., *The Established and the Outsiders*, Cass, 1965

72 Pahl, R. E., 'The Rural-Urban Continuum', *Sociologia Ruralis*, 3–4, 1966, pp 305–6

73 See, for Hertfordshire and Kent, Pahl, R. E., *Urbs in Rure: The Metropolitan Fringe in Hertforshire*, L.S.E. Geographical Papers 2, 1965 and *Whose City*, Longman, 1970; and, for Sussex, Ambrose, P., *op. cit.*, 1974

74 Lewis, G. J., 'Suburbanisation in Rural Wales: A Case Study' in Carter, H. and Davies, W. K. D. (Eds), *Urban Essays: Studies in the Geography of Wales*, Longman, 1970, pp 144–76

Chapter Nine

1 Thomas, W. I. and Znaniecki, F., *The Polish Peasant in Europe and America*, Owen, 1958
2 Germani, G., 'Migration and Acculturation' in *Handbook for Social Research in Urban Areas*, UNESCO, 1966, p 164
3 Germani, G., *ibid*, 1966, p 164
4 Germani, G., *ibid*, 1966, p 163
5 For a summary see Price, C., 'The Study of Assimilation' in Jackson, J. A. (ed), *Migration*, Cambridge University Press, 1969, pp 181–238
6 Drabick, L. W. and Buck, R. C., 'Measuring Locality Group Consensus', *Rural Sociology*, 24, 1959, p 110
7 Chapin, F. S., *Experimental Designs in Sociological Research*, Harper and Row, 1947
8 Kaufman, H. F., *Participation in Organized Activities in Selected Kentucky Localities*, Kentucky Agricultural Experimental Station, Bulletin 528, 1949, p 42
9 Emerson, A. R. and Crompton, R., *Suffolk—Some Social Trends*, Suffolk Rural Community Council, 1969
10 Ambrose, P., *The Quiet Revolution*, Chatto and Windus, 1974
11 Lewis, G. J. and Strachan, A. J., *The Corby Village Survey*, University of Leicester, Department of Geography publication, 1974
12 Lewis, G. J., *Village Communities in Pembrokeshire*, University of Leicester, Department of Geography mimeograph, 1972
13 See *Research Study 9, Royal Commission on Local Government in England*, H.M.S.O., 1969
14 Wilkinson, K. P., 'A Behavioural Approach to Measurement and Analysis of Community Field Structure', *Rural Sociology*, 39, 1974, pp 248–56
15 Ambrose, P., *op. cit.*, 1974, p 137
16 Mitchell, J. C., 'The Concept and Use of Social Networks' in Mitchell, J. C. (ed), *Social Networks in Urban Situations*, Manchester University Press, 1969, p 1
17 Barnes, J. C., 'Class and Committees in a Norwegian Island Parish', *Human Relations*, 7, 1954, pp 39–58
18 Barnes, J. C., *ibid*, 1954, p 43
19 Barnes, J. C., *ibid*, 1954, p 43
20 See, for example, the essays contained in Mitchell J. C., *op. cit.*, 1969
21 For a detailed review see Haggett, P. and Chorley, R. J., *Network Analysis in Geography*, Arnold, 1969

22 Mitchell, J. C., *op. cit.*, 1969, pp 20–9
23 Barnes, J C., 'Networks and Political Process' in Mitchell, J. C. (ed), *ibid*, 1969, p 57
24 For a more technical paper see Barnes, J. C., 'Graph Theory and Social Networks: A Technical Comment on Connectedness and Connectivity', *Sociology*, 3, 1969, pp 215–32
25 Bott, E., *Family and Social Networks*, Tavistock, 1957
26 Srinivas, M. M. and Beteille, A., 'Networks in Indian Social Structure', *Man*, 64, 1964, pp 165–8
27 Barnes, J. C., 'Networks and Political Process' in Mitchell, J. C. (ed), *op. cit.*, 1969, p 75
28 Lewis, G. J., *op. cit.*, 1972
29 Fessler, D. R., 'The Development of a Scale for Measuring Community Solidarity', *Rural Sociology*, 17, 1952, p 145
30 Osgood, C. E., Suci, G. J. and Tannenbaum, P. H., *The Measurement of Meaning*, University of Illinois Press, 1957
31 Maund, D. J., *The Urbanization of the Countryside: A Case-Study in Herefordshire*, unpublished University of Leicester MA thesis, 1976
32 Davis, V., 'Development of a Scale to Rate Attitude of Community Satisfaction', *Rural Sociology*, 10, 1945, p 74–85
33 Jesser, C. J., 'Community Satisfaction Patterns of Professionals in Rural Areas', *Rural Sociology*, 32, 1967, pp 56–69
34 Lewis, G. J. and Strachan, A. J., *op. cit.*, 1974
35 *Kent Development Plan, Quinquennial Review*, Kent C. C., 1963
36 *Village Life in Hampshire*, Hampshire C. C., 1966
37 *Development Plan Review, Report of Survey*, Cambridgeshire C. C., 1968
38 Emerson, A. R. and Crompton, R., *op. cit.*, 1969
39 Johnson, R. L. and Knop, E., 'Rural-Urban Differentials in Community Satisfaction', *Rural Sociology*, 35, 1970, pp 544–8
40 Campbell, A. and Converse, P. E., *The Human Meaning of Social Change*, Sage, 1972
41 See, for example, Suttles, G., *The Social Order of the Slums*, University of Chicago Press, 1968
42 Marans, R. W. and Rodgers, W., 'Towards an Understanding of Community Satisfaction' in Hawley, A. and Rock, V. (eds), *Metropolitan America: Papers on the State of Knowledge*, National Academy of Sciences, Washington, D.C., 1974, pp 311–75
43 Rojek, D. G., Clemente, F. and Summers, G. F., 'Community Satisfaction: A Study of Contentment with Local Services', *Rural Sociology*, 40, 1975, pp 177–92
44 Drabick, L. W. and Buck, R. C., 'Measuring Locality Group Consensus', *Rural Sociology*, 24, 1959, pp 107–17
45 Drabick, L. W. and Buck, R. C., *ibid*, 1959, p 113
46 Drabick, L. W. and Buck, R. C., *ibid*, 1959, p 113

47 Young, R. C. and Larson, O. F., 'Social Ecology of a Rural Community', *Rural Sociology*, 3, 1970, pp 337–53
48 Drabick, L. W. and Buck, R. C., *op. cit.*, 1959, p 110

Conclusion

1 *Report of the Committee on Depopulation in Mid-Wales*, H.M.S.O., 1964, pp 1–2
2 Rogers, E. M. and Burdge, R. J., *Social Change in Rural Societies*, Prentice-Hall, 1972, pp 402–3

Acknowledgements

The author and publisher gratefully acknowledge permission received from the following to modify and make use of copyright material in diagrams and tables: American Geographical Society, Fig. 4; American Sociological Association, Fig. 13; Association of American Geographers, Figs. 7, 8, 15, 18, 31, 33, 34, 55, 56 and 62; A. L. Bertrand and Louisiana State University, Fig. 59; H. Carter and C. R. Lewis, Fig 67; M. L. Davies, Fig. 40; Economic Geography, Figs. 11a, 11b, 19, 26a, 26b and 54; European Society for Rural Sociology, Figs. 3 and 5; D. Friedlander and Population Studies, Fig. 13; Geografiska Annaler, Figs. 6, 25, 32, 37, 39, 43, 48, 49, 50 and 51. Geographical Association, Fig. 52; Geographische Zeitschrift, Fig. 35; Holt, Rinehart and Winston, Fig. 21b; Hutchinson, Fig. 38; Institute of Australian Geographers, Figs. 27, 45 and 63; Macmillan (London and Basingstoke), Figs. 66a and 66b; D. J. Maund, Figs. 42 and 57; Methuen (ABP), Figs. 9 and 12; Thomas Nelson, Fig. 28; North Western University Press, Fig. 17; Ohio State University Press, Fig. 10; D. A. Preston and Journal of Latin American Studies, Fig. 46; Prentice-Hall, Fig. 16 (right) and Table 1; Regional Studies, Fig. 16 (left); Royal Dutch Geographic Society, Figs. 29, 64 and Table 5; Rural Sociology, Figs. 21a, 23, 58 and 72; Russell and Russell, Fig. 53; Strecker and Schroeder, Fig. 30; G. Tornqvist and C. W. K. Gleerup, Lund, Fig. 24; University of Missouri-Columbia, Fig. 60; S. Wanmali, Fig. 44.

Index

Page numbers in italics indicate illustrations

social relationships, 30, 40, 141, 174, 198
sociology, 18, 36, 138, 141, 158, 177, 198
Sommers, L.M., *168,* 169
spatial milieu, 18
space-time, 37, 135
Spain, 97, *98*
sphere of influence, 118
Srinivas, M.N., 178, 200
Stacey, M., 32
Sternstein, L., 54
Stine, W., 133
Stone, K.H., *96,* 97, *98*
Stouffer, S., 57, 58
Strachan, A.J., *187*
succession, 35
Suffolk, 27
Summers, G.F., 206
Svenning, L., 74, 75, *86*
Sweden, 58, *58, 80,* 102, *103*
Swedner, H., 128
system: closed, 118;
    cultural, 32;
    ecological, 19, 29, 31, 211;
    local, 173-4, 178, 179, 180, 183, 184, 186, 188, 191, 211;
    marketing, 136-7;
    open, 118;
    social, 19, 31, 32, 36, 172, 173, 174, 189, 198;
    structure, 39

Tanzania, *71,* 71
territory, 29, 32
Thailand, *46,* 47
Thomas, D.S., 59
Thomas, D.W., 156
Thomas, W.I., 193
Thorns, D.C., *38,* 39
Thorpe, H., *94,* 95
threshold population, 120, 122
Tikopia, 39
time-space framework, 143-8
Tirtha, R., 170, 171
Tornquist, G., *80,* 81
town-country interdependence, 23, 26

trend surface analysis, 71-2, 105
Trivedi, G., 179
Turner, F.J., 69
typology of villages, 38

United Nations, 22
United States, 26, 59, 81, 89, 91, 100-1, *102,* 109, *155, 157*
urban ecology, 17, 141
urban geography, 15, 21, 27, 95
urban growth, 17, 23, 24
urban hierarchy, 22
urbanisation, 15, 21, 23, 24, 26, 142, 169, 191
urbanism, 32
urban land, 22
urban planners, 22

values: local, 42, 190, 196; national, 43, 190
value system, 43, 44
vertical mobility, 33
voluntary organisations, 196

Wanmali, S., 122, *132,* 132-3
Wales, 23, 45, 51, 55, 59, 64, 67, 109, *150,* 175, *176, 185*
Warford, J.J., 115
Warren, R.L., 31
Watson, J.W., *94*
Webber, M.H., 30
West Africa, 57, 61, 105
Western Europe, 21, 25, 27
White, R.R., 64
Whiting, G.C., *86*
Whittlesey, D., 100
Wibberley, G.P., 22
Wilhelmy, H., *108*
Wilkening, E.A., 81, 82
Wilkinson, K.P., 197
Williams, W.M., 40, 186
Wirth, L., 32, 141
Wisers, C., 178

Yapa, L.S., 84, *84*
Young, R.C.,

Zaire, 173
Zaniecki, F., 193
Zelinsky, W., 36, *37*